LOSING THE THREAD

Cotton, Liverpool and the American Civil War

LOSING THE THREAD

Cotton, Liverpool and the
American Civil War

JIM POWELL

LIVERPOOL UNIVERSITY PRESS

First published 2021 by
Liverpool University Press
4 Cambridge Street
Liverpool
L69 7ZU

Copyright © 2021 Jim Powell

The right of Jim Powell to be identified as the author of this book has been
asserted by him in accordance with
the Copyright, Designs and Patents Act 1988.

All rights reserved. No part of this book may be reproduced, stored in a
retrieval system, or transmitted, in any form or by any means, electronic,
mechanical, photocopying, recording, or otherwise, without the prior written
permission of the publisher.

British Library Cataloguing-in-Publication data
A British Library CIP record is available

ISBN 978-1-78962-249-2 cased

Typeset by Carnegie Book Production, Lancaster
Printed and bound by CPI Group (UK) Ltd, Croydon CR0 4YY

In memory of my great-great grandfather
William Mayne Neill
and of his brother
Henry Montgomery Neill

Acknowledgments

This book has developed from a doctoral thesis submitted to the University of Liverpool in 2018. The thesis developed in turn from family history research, in which I discovered for the first time the exploits of my great-great grandfather, William Mayne Neill, and his brother, Henry Montgomery Neill – the Neill brothers of this book. William and Henry were prominent cotton commentators over an extended period, but especially during the American Civil War. They were also cotton merchants, in both Britain and America, who were bankrupted by the war. They had been involved in, and had commented upon, tempestuous times, and I wanted to discover more. In acknowledging their part in inspiring my research, I am also declaring a family interest.

The writing of the thesis, and now the book, has been immensely stimulating and enjoyable, but it would not have been possible without the help and encouragement of others. My greatest debt is to Dr Richard Huzzey, now Associate Professor at Durham University, who was brave enough to take me on as a postgraduate student at the University of Liverpool and who gently re-educated me in the ways of academia after a lapse of more than 40 years. Richard was my primary supervisor in the early years of the thesis and has continued to be an invaluable mentor from the banks of the Wear. Early in our acquaintance, he informed me that his greatest task was to get me to write badly, which is not the sort of thing you should say to a novelist. I think he was seeking to discourage stylistic flourishes and conceits which he felt would detract from the gravitas of the work. Since then, we have arm-wrestled constantly on the subject, with a result that can tactfully be described as a draw.

I am also grateful to Dr William Ashworth of Liverpool, who took on the role of primary supervisor after Richard had moved to Durham, and who guided the thesis enthusiastically through to its completion. Dr Graeme Milne of Liverpool was my secondary supervisor throughout, as well as the source of much essential material on the commercial history of the port. I thank him particularly for allowing me to use his analysis of Liverpool dock tonnage and revenues from the Merseyside Docks and Harbour Board collection. My three supervisors could not have offered a more complete balance of historical interests and experience, as reflected in their published works quoted here. This book would not have been possible without them. I would also like to thank Lucy Kilfoyle for sharing her work on the Liverpool satirical paper, the *Porcupine*.

My thesis was examined by Anthony Howe, Professor of Modern History at the University of East Anglia and the author of *The Cotton Masters*, amongst many other works, and by Professor Elaine Chalus, head of the History Department at the University of Liverpool. I am grateful to both for their positive reactions, and for their kindness and help.

Many libraries and their staff have offered essential assistance to my research. I would like to thank in particular Helena Smart and her team in the Liverpool Record Office at the Central Library, Sarah Starkey and her colleagues in the Archive Room at the Merseyside Maritime Museum, the Library of the Athenaeum Club in Liverpool, the Sydney Jones Library at the University of Liverpool, the John Rylands Library in Manchester, the Cambridge University Library, the British Library, the Bodleian Library in Oxford, and the Joule Library in Manchester.

I am extremely grateful to Alison Welsby, Patrick Brereton and all at Liverpool University Press for their friendly assistance, and for making this book possible.

Finally, I would like to thank my wife Kay, who now probably knows a lot more about the cotton trade than she would have liked, but who has been an indispensable sounding board throughout, as well as encouraging me to undertake the thesis in the first place. Her long experience as an editor has been as invaluable to this book as it has been to my novels.

Contents

List of Illustrations xi

List of Figures xiii

List of Tables xv

List of Abbreviations xvii

Introduction 1

1 Feast and Famine 15
   Britain's cotton trade on the eve of the American Civil War

2 The Saturday Afternoon Syndrome 31
   Why nothing was able to replace American cotton

3 A Three-Phase Supply 51
   How the cotton trade reacted to the civil war

4 Unfathomed Depths; Uncharted Mountains 71
   Why the cotton famine was not caused by pre-war over-production

5 Liverpool, Louisiana? 101
   The town's contradictory response to the civil war

6 A Toll Booth on the Mersey 121
How Liverpool enriched itself at Manchester's expense

7 The Brokers and the Broken 143
The nearest truth about Liverpool's cotton brokers

8 When Johnny Went Marching Home 167
Aftermath and conclusions

Appendix: Notes on Statistical Sources 187

Notes to Chapters 191

Bibliography 209

Index 221

Illustrations

Punch magazine, London, 16 November 1861	xviii
William Neill (held by the author)	5
Henry Neill (reproduced by permission of the Wisconsin Historical Society, WHS-144668)	5
Samuel Smith (LRO 380 COT/1/14/1, reproduced by permission of the International Cotton Association)	41
Thomas Ellison (LRO 380 COT/1/14/1, reproduced by permission of the International Cotton Association)	73
Engraving of the Princes' Dock, Liverpool, 1830 (reproduced by permission of the International Cotton Association)	108
Hugh Mason (from Wikipedia; in the public domain)	139
Liverpool, The Exchange, 1887 (copyright: The Francis Frith Collection)	146
Liverpool Cotton Brokers' Association Membership List, 1866 (LRO 380 COT/1/7/1, reproduced by permission of the International Cotton Association)	164

Figures

1	British raw cotton consumption and prices, 1800–1900	21
2	British imports of Indian cotton and its Liverpool price, 1859–1867	43
3	Weekly raw cotton prices in Liverpool, 1861–1865	52
4	Collapse of cotton imports from America, 1861	56
5	Calculated spinning volume, 1861–1866	82
6	British production of cotton yarn and cloth, 1853–1861	92
7	British exports of cotton yarn and cloth, 1853–1861	92
8	Rough value of British raw cotton imports, 1800–1900	126
9	Sales of raw cotton to British spinners, 1858–1867	137
10	Recorded Liverpool cotton broking firms, 1864	149
11	American cotton earnings per acre, 1869–1899	177

Tables

1	British raw cotton imports, 1853–1867	26
2	Source of British raw cotton imports, 1857–1868	47
3	Long-term share of British raw cotton imports, 1840–1900	50
4	Yarn produced by British spinners, 1856–1867	79
5	Manufacturing costs and margins, 1856–1866	83
6	Stocks of cotton goods, 1856–1866	94
7	Estimated consumption deficit of British cotton, 1861–1867	99
8	Value of British raw cotton imports, 1858–1867	126
9	Non-broker recipients of cotton consignments, 1860 and 1864	153
10	Cotton received by members of the Liverpool Cotton Brokers' Association, 1860 and 1864	156

Abbreviations

ABHS	B. Mitchell with P. Deane, *Abstract of British Historical Statistics* (Cambridge: Cambridge University Press, 1962)
BNA	British Newspaper Archive
CC	cotton circular
CSA*	Cotton Supply Association
EIC	East India Company
JRL, OTEA	John Rylands Library, Archive of the Oldham Textile Employers' Association
LCBA	Liverpool Cotton Brokers' Association
LRO	Liverpool Record Office
MP	Member of [the British] Parliament
NA	National Archives
ODNB	*Oxford Dictionary of National Biography*
USBC	US Bureau of the Census

* It is unhelpful that three relevant organisations have the initials CSA. In this book, the Cotton Supply Association alone is shortened to the CSA. The Cotton Spinners' Association is referred to as the Spinners' Association and the Confederate States of America as the Confederacy.

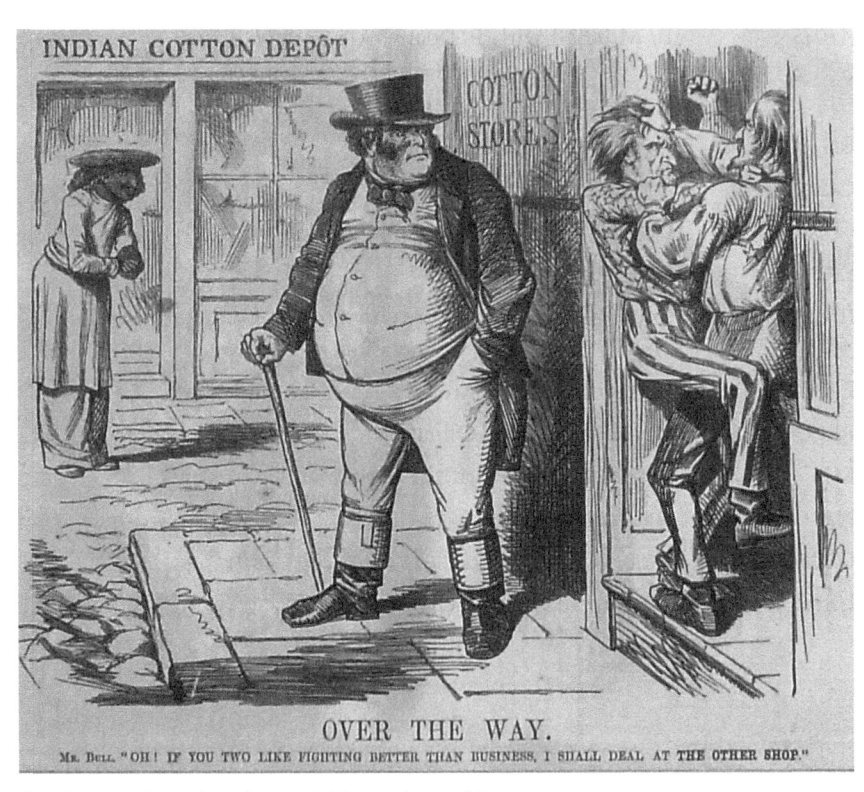

Punch magazine, London, 16 November 1861

Introduction

The cotton trade was the biggest single contributor to the industry of Victorian Britain. The manufacturing and merchanting of cotton dominated Manchester and its surrounding areas, while the trade in raw cotton dominated Liverpool. Cotton, almost single-handedly, was responsible for the phenomenal growth and prosperity of both metropolises in the nineteenth century. Eighty per cent of the raw material for this trade came from the USA. During the American Civil War (1861–65), this fell to little more than zero, making the war by far the most significant outside event in the history of the British cotton trade. Yet, apart from studies of the Lancashire cotton famine, there has been no full-length work on the crisis in the cotton trade itself during the civil war, and only the cotton broker and historian Thomas Ellison has made a substantial study of the raw cotton market in Liverpool, and that was more than 130 years ago. Both omissions are startling.

This book attempts to remedy these omissions. It has two main objectives. The first is to establish the factual record of Britain's raw cotton supply during the civil war: how much there was of it, in absolute terms and in relation to the demand, where it came from, how much it cost, and what effect the reduced supply had on Britain's cotton manufacture. The emphasis of the study is on raw cotton and on Liverpool because they are the most neglected fields of research; however, the narrative also needs to involve the manufacturing arm, especially the spinners. The second objective is to examine the impact of the civil war on Liverpool, and on the operation of the raw cotton trade there, with specific reference to the role of the cotton brokers.

Historians have tended to regard the British cotton trade as starting with the spinning process, and to regard the story of raw cotton as ending when it left the ports of the producing countries. Liverpool fits into neither narrative. The port was simultaneously the final link in the producing chain and the first link in the manufacturing chain: the moment a Liverpool buying broker bought cotton from a Liverpool selling broker was the moment of the shift from one chain to the other. But Liverpool's crucial role as the link between the two chains has remained largely unexamined. A 1996 anthology of writings on the Lancashire cotton industry contains no section on Liverpool. Neither do two American works that describe the transatlantic marketing of the American cotton crop. In the absence of substantial subsequent studies, the historian is thrown back constantly upon Ellison's work of 1886.[1]

The historian who has done most to fill the gaps of knowledge is Nigel Hall.[2] His research on Liverpool provides a backdrop to the commentary in this book and makes use of many of the surviving primary sources. This book builds upon his research by using additional primary sources and by considering in detail aspects of the cotton trade that he has not examined. Other literature is not entirely absent. Douglas Farnie devoted a chapter of his book on English cotton in the nineteenth century to the civil war period.[3] There is a plethora of secondary sources on discrete aspects of the war as it affected Britain – alternative sources of cotton supply; the Lancashire famine; public opinion; political and diplomatic manoeuvres. There are enough books on the post-war period in America to fill a substantial library. These various contributions focus in detail on entirely disparate aspects of the overall subject, so that to discuss them collectively at this stage seems premature. Instead, they are considered within the individual chapters that deal with each topic.

Beyond these studies, aspects of the raw cotton trade during the civil war, as well as the role of Liverpool, have been mentioned in countless works. However, because neither topic has been central to the focus of the book or article in question, the writers concerned have almost never conducted original research into them, but have relied on ancient judgments, handed down from one generation of historians to the next like family heirlooms. Constant, unexamined repetition has undeservedly bolstered the authority of the original judgment. The consequence of this neglect has been a distortion of history in two key areas: the assertion that a pre-war over-production of cotton goods was a principal cause of the Lancashire cotton famine and the allegation that Liverpool was an uncritical cheerleader for the Confederacy. The detailed evidence presented in this book will show that the first assertion is completely untrue and the second greatly exaggerated.

Time and again in the research for this book it has become apparent that the statistical and the human components of this particular subject need equal emphasis but have seldom received it. This study makes use of all the relevant cotton trade statistics, of which there are many. The Victorians were meticulous collectors of information: if something counted, they counted it. But it also makes extensive use of contemporary comment, to enable a greater understanding of the human psychology of the circumstances and of how events unfolded as they did.

Many primary sources underpin this study. The description of the search for alternative sources of supply relies on the minutes and annual reports of the Cotton Supply Association (CSA), as well as on Isaac Watts's published history of the CSA.[4] The statistics on the raw cotton supply, crucial to an understanding of the over-production issue, are based on the weekly reports of the Liverpool Cotton Brokers Association (LCBA) as summarised in the annual circulars of George Holt, and with additional detail from John Pender and Thomas Ellison, together with the weekly data (from the same original source) reproduced by Ezekiel Donnell. Full references for these sources are given in Chapter 4 and in the Bibliography. In view of the paramount importance of these statistics, the Appendix gives more detail on the sources and on the precise methodology used in interpreting them. The study of the cotton brokers and, in particular, the vicious dispute between the LCBA and the Cotton Spinners' Association, is based primarily on what survives of the LCBA membership lists and minute books, the latter covering the period from April 1864 to August 1870.[5] Minute books from earlier in the civil war are sadly missing. The investigation into who received cotton shipments at Liverpool during the civil war, and the role of speculators and of the cotton brokers, is founded on an examination of the B Lists of the Custom Bills of Entry for the port of Liverpool, a source not known to have been used previously by historians.[6] The contemporary understanding, constantly evolving as the civil war progressed, of the effect of the war on present and future raw cotton supplies is based largely on the end-of-year circulars of the Liverpool cotton brokers, many of which, to judge from their uncut state in the Liverpool Record Office, have not been read, and on the more numerous circulars of Neill Brothers & Co., not known to have been examined by historians until now.[7] More needs to be said about both sources.

Not all cotton brokers chose to offer personal comments on the market in their circulars. However, many wrote lengthy and articulate pieces, at varying intervals, but always at the end of each year. The only ones that appear to have survived are some of the end-of-year circulars. These commentaries are of great value for the insights offered, and especially those of Samuel Smith, which are quoted extensively in this book. Ellison remarked that Smith's circulars "gained for their author a great reputation in all the cotton markets of the world". Smith was born in Scotland in 1836 and came to Liverpool at the age of 18, apprenticed as a cotton broker. He was still a young man when he started his own cotton brokerage, Smith, Edwards & Co., in January 1864 and when, three months later, he became head of the Liverpool branch of the merchants James Finlay & Co. of Glasgow and Bombay. He later added cotton spinning and weaving to his activities through the purchase of Millbrook Mills, Stalybridge. In the winter of 1862–63 he visited India on behalf of the Manchester Chamber of Commerce to evaluate the prospect of increased supplies. His report, which is quoted in detail in Chapter 2, must have come like a cold bath to Manchester, as Smith demolished each and every cherished delusion of the CSA.[8]

The Neill brothers, William and Henry, were born in Belfast in 1824 and 1828 respectively. Henry emigrated to America in 1847, where he was joined by his older brother in 1854, styling themselves as 'Messrs. Neill Brothers and Co., Cotton Merchants of New Orleans, Mobile, and New York'. Henry was the cotton expert, based in the South, and William the commercial expert, based in New York. The value of their circulars comes in several parts. They were Irishmen based in America, although in Britain for most of the war, with a good understanding both of the cotton trade and of political realities and emotions on both sides of the Atlantic. They issued the most significant circular which was not written by a broker, did not emanate from Liverpool, and which survives at other than year-ends. Their father, a Belfast jeweller, was a fervent abolitionist: Frederick Douglass, William Lloyd Garrison and Henry C. Wright had all been his guests, and his sons found that this gave them an entrée to the abolitionist elite of New York and Boston. By the middle of the war, Henry Neill – having lost his first wife and then remarried – had acquired two American fathers-in-law: Daniel C. Lowber, a Confederate spy for Jefferson Davis, and Alexander Schultz, a close associate of US Secretary of State, William Seward, and his courier on several wartime missions to Britain. The brothers therefore had family links to both camps and were politically well connected in New York and New Orleans. Their circulars received extensive press coverage. In the four years of the war, the Neills accounted for nearly half of all British press mentions of cotton circulars and were often quoted at considerable length.[9]

But, however useful the Neills, Samuel Smith and other commentators are as sources, they collectively leave gaps in what one would ideally like to know, particularly in relation to sympathies in Liverpool during the war, the issue of speculation in raw cotton and the role of the cotton brokers. Where possible, these gaps have been plugged by a series of other primary sources, many of them anecdotal. While these sources are by nature subjective, the collective impression they give is often persuasive. The most valuable and frequently used of such sources is the *Liverpool Mercury*, the newspaper with much the largest circulation in the town at the time. (Although the word 'city' appears in several quotations in this book, Liverpool was in fact a town in the 1860s.) Every issue of that paper from January 1860 to December 1865 has been examined for this study.

This review of primary sources leaves the two most contentious figures till last: Arthur Arnold and Thomas Ellison, who between them have been responsible for most of the subsequent disinformation. Two contemporary, full-length histories of the cotton famine were written, the first by Arnold,

William and Henry Neill of Neill Bros & Co.:
cotton commentators and merchants
(WN held by the author; HN reproduced by permission
of the Wisconsin Historical Society, WHS-144668)

the second by John Watts.[10] Arnold was a versatile man: a surveyor, land agent, journalist, sensational novelist and later a Member of Parliament (MP). What he was not was a historian or an economist. He had received no formal education and wrote *The Cotton Famine*, at breakneck speed, when he was 31. He had first-hand experience of the famine, but none of the cotton trade, or of any trade. Watts, on the other hand, was a trained political economist and a member of the Central Relief Committee during the famine. What he thought of Arnold's book can be gauged by this barbed remark in his preface, justifying a second account: "A hurried compilation, got up to hit the humour of the passing hour, could not possibly meet the want." Yet despite this, or possibly because of it, Arnold's history of the famine is the one that is remembered and relied upon. According to Farnie, the resentment against Arnold's book in Manchester forced its author to withdraw his dedication to the Central Relief Committee in the second edition, while Watts "deliberately gave his own history the polemical title of *The Facts of the Cotton Famine* in order to rebuke Arnold and to vindicate the political economy of free trade". However, Farnie was hostile to the free traders himself, which may have persuaded him to prefer Arnold's version of events. As will be seen, it is Arnold's book, with a helping hand from Ellison, that is almost single-handedly responsible for the historical persistence of the over-production fallacy.[11]

Ellison's shortcomings as a reliable source have more to do with sins of omission. His standard work, *The Cotton Trade of Great Britain*, is in fact two works. The first part is a history of the British cotton trade in general, which is full, informative and above reproach, as are the tables in the appendices that, like this book, make use of Holt's statistics. The second part is a history of cotton broking in Liverpool from its beginnings in the late eighteenth century to the time of the LCBA's amalgamation into the Cotton Association. (The Liverpool Cotton Association was a successor body to the LCBA from 1882. It is referred to as the 'Cotton Association' throughout the text.) Again, there is little wrong with what Ellison says, and much of the detail he has supplied on cotton brokerages has been used extensively in Chapter 7. The problem lies in what he does not say. Developments on the Liverpool market are reported passively. Scarcely a name is mentioned in these sections. Events just happen; they do not appear to arise through human agency, so it is impossible to know who drove them. Anything that might reflect badly on broking as a profession, anything that might hint at conflict between Liverpool and Manchester, anything that might lift the lid on the orgy of speculation in the Liverpool cotton market is excluded from his account altogether. This is perhaps why Ellison made barely a mention of the American Civil War. It had ended only 20 years earlier, with consequences that were devastating to the industry, yet amnesia appears to have set in. The Liverpool cotton market during the war was a casino. The more reputable brokers, of whom Ellison himself was one, failed to prevent their trade from being overrun by spivs and interlopers, many of them members of the LCBA. When Ellison wrote his history, he was still a broker and still a member of what had been the LCBA and was now the Cotton Association, as no doubt were many of those whose conduct during the war he abhorred. This may reasonably explain his reticence. His subsequent autobiography lets the mask slip a little, but only by a few millimetres.[12]

However, in addition to his books, Ellison wrote two extensive series of articles for the *Liverpool Post*, published anonymously in 1881–82, much of the content later appearing verbatim in *The Cotton Trade of Great Britain*. At that time, immediately prior to the formation of the Cotton Association, the Liverpool cotton market was in turmoil, with the rival Cotton Exchange challenging the monopoly of the LCBA. One series consisted of four articles headed 'Cotton Merchants, Brokers, and Spinners', which traced the development of the dispute.[13] Some of Ellison's remarks were far more forthright than anything he allowed to appear in his book, published four years later. In fact, all the most contentious comments were later deleted. It would seem that, in the heat of the moment, a combination of Ellison's strong opinions and the protection offered by anonymity allowed him, on this rare occasion, to say what he really felt. When these articles are quoted in this book, the word 'anonymous' is used in conjunction with Ellison's name to distinguish these remarks.

One feature of this study is the disaggregation of interests. Any period of intense pressure reveals cracks in what, in gentler times, may look like a smooth and impermeable facade. Historians have often written about 'the cotton trade' as if it was a single industry, its constituent parts performing different functions, but working harmoniously towards a common end. This was not the case at any time, and especially not during the civil war. Those who earned their living from raw cotton had interests diametrically opposed to those who earned it from spun cotton. The attitudes and interests of the component parts of the trade need to be teased out and distinguished.

In summary, Chapters 1, 2 and 3 give the context for an examination of the main issues of the book. Chapter 4 quantifies the cotton supply and evaluates the over-production claim. Chapters 5, 6 and 7 describe events in Liverpool during the war. Chapter 8 relates what happened after the war and summarises the conclusions of the book.

Chapter 1 ('Feast and Famine') presents a picture of the British cotton trade on the eve of the American Civil War, describing both the pre-eminence of that trade and how it had been attained over the previous century and a half. In doing so, the relative merits of three major recent studies of the history of cotton are discussed. This is followed by a consideration of how the issue of slavery, and the threat to its survival, influenced the British trade before the war. There is then a detailed description of how the trade in raw cotton operated in Liverpool, or at least was intended to operate.

Chapter 2 ('The Saturday Afternoon Syndrome') examines what was done to reduce the dependence on American cotton before the war, and to replace the supply lost during the war. It is rash to use the word 'impossible', but the conclusion will be that, for all practical purposes, both these tasks were indeed impossible. The reliance on American cotton was not a historical accident. It was a reflection of the fact that – although cotton could be grown in many parts of the world – only in America did all the elements come together that made it both commercially viable and available to Britain in high volume. Without minimising the increase in cotton received from India and elsewhere during the war, other sources did not and could not replace the volume lost from America, and the augmented supply was entirely the result of an inflated price. The belief that India could replace America was the brainchild equally of naivety and desperation.

The raw cotton market in Britain during the four years of the war can be divided into three phases, and this is the subject of Chapter 3 ('A

Three-Phase Supply'). The first phase ran from Abraham Lincoln's election in November 1860 to the end of June 1862. It was characterised by a complacency in the trade, which failed to appreciate the likelihood, first of a civil war, then of a cotton scarcity. This is contextualised by looking at the Confederacy's 'King Cotton' strategy and its failure, and by examining attitudes in Britain towards the civil war, as well as the policy of the government of Viscount Palmerston (British Prime Minister from 1855 to 1858, and again from 1859 until his death in 1865). The price of raw cotton rose steadily through this period but, from July 1862, when the full scale of the impending catastrophe was belatedly recognised, it soared. This marked the start of the second phase, which lasted until the end of August 1864. In this phase, speculation – always present in the Liverpool market – became endemic. The collapse of prices in September 1864 marked the end of the phase. Thereafter, confusion was widespread and prices oscillated violently, as did speculation. This third phase lasted well beyond the end of the war, arguably until 1876. The conclusion of this chapter is that, although external influences shaped the market, an equal part was played by greed and irrational sentiment. The civil war period in Liverpool can best be seen as an extended series of bets on whether a war would start and how long it would last.

Chapter 4 ('Unfathomed Depths; Uncharted Mountains') investigates the facts and figures of Britain's cotton imports and usage during the war. There is no lack of contemporary statistics to enable this study; no doubt has ever been cast on their broad accuracy; there is no reason why this analysis should not have been made a long time ago. Instead, statements have been made based on an arbitrary choice of data, justifying Farnie's observation that "no other industry has generated so much punditry upon the basis of so little real evidence" – a charge of which he is guilty himself in the civil war period.[14] The reality of the British cotton market during the war, as set out in this book, contradicts much that has been written about it, and in particular the claim that the Lancashire cotton famine was wholly or mainly the result of pre-war over-production, rather than of a scarcity of cotton. There has been a citation chain on this subject of prodigious length and tenacity, resting on the most tenuous foundations.

There was nothing abnormal about the cotton market in 1859–61. Had the war never taken place, there would have been no allegation of over-production, no assertion of the glutting of overseas markets. Stocks of finished goods were indeed high when the war started, but not hugely so, given the growing demand. Some overseas markets may have been slightly overstocked, but they were balanced by others with an unfilled demand. There was nothing unusual in varying stock levels of finished goods. Indeed, manufacturers – in trepidation for many years of an interruption to the American supply – had developed the habit of manufacturing what was available when it was available.

If this resulted in periods of high inventories, they were not worried: they trusted in their expanding market to move the stocks, which it always had, and which it would have done again after 1861, but for the war.

It is not enough to disprove the existing explanation for why the shift to short-time working, leading to mass unemployment and the famine, began in October 1861, when there was not yet a cotton scarcity. An alternative explanation needs to be offered. The reason why Farnie was persuaded to swallow Eugene Brady's justification of the over-production argument was that it "explains so much that would otherwise remain inexplicable".[15] But it is not inexplicable, if the market is considered in a global, not purely a British, context. The international cotton trade needed a pipeline of stock at every stage. The outbreak of war, followed by the Confederate embargo on cotton exports and the Union blockade of the cotton ports, paralysed the world market. The price of raw cotton started to rise. Post-civil war commentators have minimised the immediate increase, but that is perhaps because they knew the scale of what was to follow. Ezekiel Donnell's tables of weekly Liverpool cotton prices show that the price of the cotton description Middling Orleans in mid-October 1861, when short-time working began, was 58 per cent higher than at the end of February, and higher than at any point since 1836. In an industry where the cost of the raw material was the largest single expense, this was a considerable increase. Spinners carried low stocks of the raw material: the pre-war average is thought to have been a supply of about three weeks. Yarn spun from cotton at the new price would be more expensive, and likewise cloth woven from that yarn. Why would anyone in the world pay an increased price when they held stocks at the old price? Why would they do it anyway? And why would they do it particularly when the near-universal expectation was that the war would be over in two or three months, before stocks ran out, whereupon American shipments would resume and prices would revert to pre-war levels?

This is an original explanation in terms of all the post-civil war historiography, but it is not new: several commentators made the same point during the war. The rebuttal of the over-production argument makes it easier to estimate what the course of the British raw cotton market might have been but for the war, and to quantify the cotton lost to Britain as a result. The conclusion reached is that, for the three main years of the war, 1862–64, British yarn production was at 36 per cent of the market requirement, and that about 4.5 billion lb of raw cotton was denied to British manufacturers in the seven years to the end of 1867.

For the next three chapters, the viewpoint moves to Liverpool. Chapter 5 ('Liverpool, Louisiana?') considers the other unexamined myth of the war years: that Liverpool was overwhelmingly Confederate in its sympathies. This question is studied from the point of view of public and press opinion in the town, and of the attitudes and activities of Liverpool merchants. Much contrarian evidence emerges: the port of Liverpool weathered the civil war remarkably well, despite the halving of its cotton imports; the trade of the port was always more dependent on the Northern States of America than on the Southern; the depredations of the CSS *Florida* and the CSS *Alabama*, warships built on Merseyside for the Confederacy, far from being a source of pride for Liverpool merchants, were for most a threat and an embarrassment. A noisy and partisan support for the Confederacy certainly existed in the port, as it did elsewhere. But perceptions have been clouded by the romance of blockade-running – which, during the war, accounted for less than 1 per cent of the port of Liverpool's trade – and by the public furore over the building of Confederate warships. This chapter produces detailed and original evidence that Laird Brothers, the Birkenhead firm that built the *Alabama* and the notorious Laird 'rams', was also approached to build warships for the Union and agreed to do so. The conclusion is that, while the opposite view cannot be maintained either, the idea that Liverpool was overwhelmingly pro-Confederate is unsustainable.

The focus of the book now switches to the value of the cotton trade, to the trade in Liverpool, and to who made and lost money out of cotton during the civil war. Chapter 6 ('A Toll Booth on the Mersey') begins with a description of how the raw cotton trade was financed, before showing that – despite a drastically reduced volume – the vast rise in price meant that raw cotton imports had a greater value than at any time in the nineteenth century and, in terms of the cotton actually traded, possibly the highest value ever. The implications of this for the earnings of the cotton brokers are demonstrated, together with the fury in Manchester that Liverpool was enriching itself while the rest of the industry was in crisis. Two of the key elements of Ellison's etiquette are considered: that cotton brokers were not usually both buying and selling brokers simultaneously, and that they did not trade cotton on their own account. A wealth of contemporary detail, all of it anecdotal, is produced to suggest that both contentions are false. The chapter presents plentiful evidence of how speculation infested the market during the war, but also how the spinners were implicated in it themselves. It concludes with the conflict that erupted towards the end of the war between the LCBA and the Cotton Spinners' Association.

Chapter 7 ('The Brokers and the Broken') provides substance for the mainly anecdotal evidence in Chapter 6. A study of the lists of LCBA members, together with the entries for cotton brokers in *Gore's Directory*, suggests that brokers were not a rarefied species *sui generis*, but an integral and influential part of Liverpool's wider merchant community. In a shadowy world, where it was not known at the time, and will never be known, who owned which consignment of cotton, the conclusion is that the two most powerful factions in Britain's trade in raw cotton were the selling brokers and the bankers – each more powerful than the importing merchants or the spinners. This is corroborated, in as far as it can be, by a detailed study of the B Lists of the customs entries for the Port of Liverpool, which provide a complete inventory of who received every consignment into the port. All cotton consignments for the years 1860 and 1864 have been tabulated – more than 21,000 entries in total – and they provide the scope for further historical investigation beyond this book. For present purposes, data are produced which show the huge changes wrought by the civil war to cotton shipments, and which prove that 91 per cent of LCBA members were direct recipients of cotton from Liverpool docks. This is surely the final blow to the notion that there was a scrupulous dividing line between buying and selling brokers. At least during the civil war, and probably for some time before it, brokers were traders. They were not necessarily successful traders, however. Some, tempted by the riches on offer, flew too close to the sun and were burned. The chapter ends with an account of some of the failures.

Quite apart from the magnitude of the loss of raw cotton to the British market during the civil war, there was the magnitude of the question as to what would happen afterwards. Chapter 8 ('When Johnny Went Marching Home') considers the aftermath of the war, both in Liverpool and in the Southern States of America. In Liverpool, a combination of rampant speculation, financial crises, the advent of the transatlantic telegraph and the formal establishment of futures trading created a cauldron of turmoil and disruption. Eventually, these changes would lead to a raw cotton market substantially different from the one that had operated before and during the war. For Britain's cotton trade, the immediate question was whether American cotton could be produced in the pre-war quantity at the pre-war price when the slaves had been emancipated and cotton was grown by free labour. In the latter stages of the war, this question came to overshadow the war itself as it became increasingly apparent that slavery was doomed, whatever the outcome.

The reality was that, after all the evils of slavery and all the sacrifices of the war, things did not get a great deal better afterwards for anyone who produced cotton in America. Yes, more and more cotton was grown. Yes, the price was not only as low as it had been pre-war but became considerably lower. But these were the consequences, not of more efficient production, but of the inability of the South to organise itself collectively, to diversify its industry, or to escape the stifling control of the credit merchants. None of this mattered to the British cotton trade, any more than slavery had mattered to it before the war. But the result was endemic poverty in the American South. There was no demonstrable failure of free labour, but there was a catastrophic failure of the free market.

The conclusion of the book is that the civil war years were, except for a handful of successful speculators and some brokers, a time of unmitigated catastrophe for Britain's cotton trade, and ultimately for America's cotton producers. They were also a watershed in the history of that trade. In retrospect, 1861 marked the end of the largely Anglo-centric era in which British cotton goods, using a raw material produced by American slaves, dominated the world market. It marked the beginning of a more diverse global cotton community, with the first commodity futures market evolving out of the unregulated chaos of the war. Britain still dominated the new order, but progressively less so as time went by.

A sceptical reader may wonder, if the evidence presented in this book is accepted, how so many historians can have been so mistaken about key aspects of the British cotton market during the war. One reason has already been given: the lack of original research. There are two others. Most sources, both primary and secondary, consistently underplay the role of price. The reports of the CSA seldom allude to price in relation to the efforts to find an alternative source of supply. Arthur Silver managed to write an entire book on the attempt to get more cotton from India without examining price. Sven Beckert, in explaining how America rather than India came to supply Britain with most of its cotton, does not emphasise price either.[16] These are not isolated examples: time and again, price is either minimised as a consideration or not mentioned at all. Pre-war, the cost of the raw material accounted for about 36 per cent of the selling price of cotton goods: it was much the most expensive individual item. The worldwide market for cotton cloth, as reinvented in Britain in the early part of the nineteenth century, had reached maturity by 1860. It was predicated on high volumes and on a low, and relatively stable, cost of the raw material. Keeping that cost low was essential.

The second point flows from the first. When the price of raw cotton first doubled, then trebled, then quadrupled during the civil war, that effectively ended the global market for cotton goods as it had existed before the war. Instead, it created a new, temporary market that lasted until prices once again returned to their pre-war level. These two markets cannot, or should not, be spoken of in the same breath, as if they were the same market. Yet, time and again, in both contemporary and subsequent commentaries, they were, as will be evident throughout this book. From the standpoint of 1862, too many goods had indeed been produced in 1860. From the standpoint of 1860, they had not. One market was being judged by the standards of a completely different one.

Throughout the book, some shorthand references are used, which need to be explained. In the terminology of cotton, there were three branches of the manufacturing trade: spinning (the turning of the raw cotton into yarn or thread); weaving (the turning of the yarn into cloth); and finishing (dyeing, printing, sizing etc.). Traditionally, the spinners were not referred to as 'manufacturers'. Here, the word is used to encompass all parts of the process: if the reference is to only one of the branches, 'spinners', 'weavers' or 'finishers' is used. Where the words 'consumers' or 'consumption' appear in the text or in quotations, they refer to spinners and their use of cotton and not to what we mean by 'consumers' today. 'Manchester' is used collectively to describe the manufacturing arm of the trade, just as 'Liverpool' is used to describe its raw material arm. In practice, by the time of the civil war, there was little manufacturing in Manchester. That now took place in the nearby cotton towns of Lancashire and Cheshire, while Manchester had become a city of merchants and warehouses. It nevertheless remained the acknowledged centre of the manufacturing trade. Values smaller than one pound have been expressed in decimal currency in the tables and figures, and also in the text, rather than in shillings and pence. Finally, in converting sterling values to their modern-day equivalents, a multiple of 100 has been used. This is sufficiently accurate for the purpose, and a great deal clearer.*

---

* The Bank of England inflation calculator gives a multiple of 119; other sources tend to be lower.

CHAPTER I

Feast and Famine
Britain's cotton trade on the eve of the American Civil War

At no time since the industrial revolution has one industry dominated the British economy, British employment and British exports in the way that cotton did for most of the nineteenth century. In 1850, Britain possessed 60 per cent of the world's spindles and 53 per cent of its power looms. In 1853, it supplied 45 per cent of the world's consumption of cotton cloth. By 1860, cotton accounted for 11.5 per cent of national income, and nearly half the factories in the country were for cotton production. Raw cotton accounted for 18 per cent of British imports, and cotton goods for 38 per cent of British exports. In 1861, the number of people directly employed in the industry was about 646,000. Those not directly employed, but still dependent on cotton for their livelihoods, took that figure into the millions. About a sixth of the population of England, Scotland and Wales was, to a greater or lesser extent, reliant on cotton for its income, including most people within the borders of Lancashire and Cheshire.[1]

Then, in August 1861, the raw cotton stopped coming. The American Civil War, which had started in April, switched off 80 per cent of Britain's supply, almost overnight. Cotton feast turned to cotton famine. From then until April 1865, when the war ended, the country was starved of most of the raw material for its largest industry. All aspects of Britain's cotton trade were profoundly affected by the war. There are no cotton indices for the nineteenth century that fail to show these four years, and the ones immediately after them, as an anomalous period. The market, as it had existed prior to 1861 and would exist again later, ceased to function. The civil war created a crisis for cotton. However, as Brian Schoen has written, "without cotton and the international demand for it, there would not have been secession or a Civil War."[2] Schoen's remark is a reminder that, even at this early stage in the world's industrialisation, cotton was part of a transatlantic and indeed a global network. If, by 1861, Britain had come to dominate that network, it was a comparatively recent development. It is important to understand the global influences that had enabled the growth and dominance of the British cotton trade.

Three recent works have challenged earlier, more national, views of this issue. How convincing one finds each of them depends to a large extent on whether one views history as a controlling process, in which powerful figures and interest groups impose themselves on events to produce their desired outcomes, or whether – while giving due weight to the role of elites – one views it more as an organic process, whereby a number of elements come together and sometimes produce momentous change as a result. Adherents of the first approach will be attracted to Sven Beckert's *Empire of Cotton: A New History of Global Capitalism*. Adherents of the second will be attracted more to the works of Prasannan Parthasarathi and Giorgio Riello.[3]

Empire of Cotton provides an overarching narrative of the development of cotton, more or less from the dawn of time to the present day. It also, as its full title implies, seeks to explain the emergence of modern-day capitalism through the history of cotton. Beckert's thesis is that cotton's industrialisation was first enabled by mercantilism, which he prefers to call 'war capitalism', to emphasise its permanent recourse to violence, enslavement and land expropriation. The opportunity for cotton manufacture in Europe that war capitalism had created is then held to be principally responsible for the industrial revolution, which in turn enabled a new phase of 'industrial capitalism', whereby "enterprising entrepreneurs and powerful statesmen in Europe recast the world's most significant manufacturing industry by combining imperial expansion and slave labour with new machines and wage workers." As a result, "Europeans came to dominate the centuries-old worlds of cotton, merge them into a single empire centered in Manchester, and invent the global economy."[4]

These are big claims and they need to be picked apart. There were indeed many 'enterprising entrepreneurs' and some 'powerful statesmen' in Europe, but no evidence that they colluded to 'recast' the cotton industry. Imperial expansion was of course the ambition of many European nations, including Britain, but most such expansion took place in the latter part of the nineteenth century, well after cotton production had been industrialised. Moreover, most leading members of Manchester's cotton trade were opposed to imperial expansion on principle. The minutes of the CSA reveal the agonised conflict between commerce and conscience that arose when the King of Fiji offered to cede his islands to Britain, together with their potentially vast cotton fields. Manchester was desperate for the cotton, but adamantly opposed to imperial aggrandisement, even when it was voluntary.[5] That same conflict between commerce and conscience was evident in attitudes towards slavery, which will be considered shortly. But, however hypocritical the behaviour of the cotton trade in this respect, it surely cannot be denied that, during the most crucial phase of cotton's industrialisation, when British manufacturers were dependent on slave-grown American cotton, the political force that was doing more than any other in the world to eliminate slavery, however haltingly, was the British government.

Similarly, while 'new machines' were indisputably at the centre of the cotton revolution, they were not the consequence of 'enterprising entrepreneurs and powerful statesmen' recasting the industry. Beckert creates the impression of an elite project to revolutionise cotton manufacture. But all the great cotton inventions were the work of humble men, divorced from the world of wealth and investment, whose breakthroughs stemmed from an uncoordinated and fortuitous process. Richard Arkwright had been a wig-maker, John Kay a reed-maker, Edmund Cartwright a clergyman; only James Hargreaves and Samuel Crompton had a background in the cotton industry, and that in a relatively small-time way. Beckert later acknowledges that the cotton inventors were "tinkerers", who were "to stumble upon a new way of spinning cotton", yet he does not appear to accept that the haphazard nature of much of what he describes contradicts his underlying thesis.[6]

The reality behind all these issues, as so often, was more messy, and not amenable to the sort of intellectual straitjacket that Beckert imposes. As Alan Olmstead and Paul Rhode have written in their critique of *Empire of Cotton*: "Beckert paints a top-down view of history that ascribes almost omnipotent powers to 'cotton capitalists' to manipulate events around the world."[7] As a result, the part played by chance or serendipity, the part played by individuals acting independently, the part played by imperfect markets, and the imperfections and shortcomings of those attempting to influence them, are all minimised as contributing factors. This will become apparent in Chapter 2, where Beckert's claim that – by the mid-nineteenth century – politicians were using the machinery of government to advance the interests of the capitalists of the cotton trade will be examined closely in relation to Britain's response to the American Civil War and will be found to be utterly untrue.

Riello and Parthasarathi have each taken a different approach to Beckert's. Their books offer an evolutionary account of the growth of the global cotton industry, explaining how and why the centre of world cotton gravitated from India to Britain over the course of the eighteenth and early nineteenth centuries. Riello emphasises the worldwide interaction of a multiplicity of elements, which combined to work in favour of Europe and of Britain. Inventions are given their due place, but it is not an exalted one. The role of active government is discussed but, again, not given excessive weight. Parthasarathi provides a damning indictment of the role of the East India Company (EIC) in enabling the ascent of Britain's cotton industry at India's expense. The EIC may not have actively suppressed Indian economic development, but it did nothing to encourage it, or to protect the Indian economy from changes that were detrimental to it, most of them instigated by Britain. While Europe advanced prodigiously in the first half of the nineteenth century, India regressed.

Both books portray an organic process of change and development. Three quotations exemplify how they differ from *Empire of Cotton*. Beckert presents the growth of the British cotton industry as a deliberate and *dirigiste* programme: "Managing to acquire [raw cotton] meant [Britain] building the first globally integrated manufacturing industry." In contrast, Parthasarathi concludes that "industrialization in Western Europe did not emerge from an effort to industrialize. It was an unanticipated, unforeseen and unintended outcome of the economic and social needs that were found in that part of the world." And, in Riello's words, "cotton did not become a global commodity because its production was mechanised and industrialised; on the contrary, it became mechanised and industrialised thanks to the fact that it was a global commodity." This is an important point: cotton did not suddenly become global because of the intervention of Europeans; to a large extent it was already global and had been for centuries. Parthasarathi and Riello have presented altogether more subtle, more credible accounts of the development of the cotton industry, and ones that take fuller account of the historical continuum. They have taken both the British and the global contexts and fused them into a single, coherent narrative of the birth of the British cotton industry.[8]

Despite the persistent belief that Britain's industrial ascent was enabled by free trade policies, all three historians emphasise the role of protectionism in the growth of the British cotton trade. Another recent work offers more detail on how, from the early eighteenth century, Britain was able to progress from being an insignificant force in the production of cotton goods to dominating the world market. William Ashworth demonstrates that the cotton industry embraced free trade only later in its development, when it became convenient, and that what enabled its ascent was protectionism.[9]

In synthesising these assorted histories into an explanation for the take-off of the British cotton industry, the starting point is to establish that, at the beginning of the eighteenth century, cotton was already a semi-global commodity. The trade was largely Indo-centric in terms of the cultivation of cotton and the production of cotton goods, which were traded through networks long established in Asia and the Middle East. The formation, at the beginning of the seventeenth century, of European companies trading with the East Indies began to create a demand for cotton goods in Europe, where previously the available fabrics had been made of wool, linen, fustian or silk. So concerned were European governments at the popularity of brightly coloured Indian cotton fabrics, with the consequent flow of bullion to pay for them, that protectionist legislation was enacted in several countries. In Britain, two acts were introduced, in 1701 and 1721, with the combined effect of prohibiting the import of all decorated Indian cloth, unless it was kept in bonded warehouses and re-exported. The law allowed the import of plain Indian calico and its subsequent printing in Britain, as long as the finished cloth was also re-exported. The intention of these measures had nothing intrinsically to do with cotton. They were enacted to protect British wool and silk manufactures, as well as its textile printing industry, without damaging the export trade. The effect, however, was to whet still further the country's appetite for a banned fabric, to encourage the growth and refinement of cotton printing, previously a rudimentary process in Britain, and eventually to stimulate cotton manufacturing.[10]

Of equal importance to this unintended promotion of a British cotton industry was the Atlantic trading network that Britain was developing, also founded partly on cotton. Before long, this network would unite with the existing Asian network to create a worldwide web of cotton – "the first truly global commodity", in Riello's words. Much of this Atlantic trade was connected with slavery, with cotton fabrics used as the currency to purchase slaves in west Africa. Initially, these fabrics were Indian but, as the demand for them grew, merchants supplemented them with British-made cotton fabrics. At this point, in the third quarter of the eighteenth century, the British product was both inferior to the Indian and more expensive. In the view of both Riello and Parthasarathi it was this, and the need to produce cotton warp, the stronger, longitudinal thread used in weaving, that created the pressure to innovate that led to the great inventions of Hargreaves, Arkwright and Crompton, and paved the way for the industrialisation of the British cotton manufacture.[11]

Thus, three elements with different roots came together haphazardly in the late eighteenth century to create the possibility of a transformational change. The first was the fact that a global demand for cotton goods already existed, created largely by India. The second was that major markets and trading routes had already been opened by British merchants. The third element, and the one most neglected by historians, was that, during the long incubation period of Britain's cotton manufacture, the industry was protected, first by an outright ban on the competition and then, later in the century, by a tariff wall. Even at the end of the eighteenth century, Lancashire merchants and manufacturers still feared competition. In the 1780s, Manchester successfully demanded continued government protection from Indian cottons: a 100 per cent duty effectively shut them out of the British market. By the end of the century, with the main inventions now in place, British cotton yarn and cloth were the cheapest in the world, arguably the best, and certainly capable of being produced in the greatest quantity. And Britain, through its control of India, could now prevent that country from creating the same protective wall against British imports that Britain had created against Indian imports. In this way, the cuckoo in the nest was able to fledge. Britain did not create the global market for cotton goods; it usurped India's role in it. The stage was set for explosive growth.[12]

Before it could be realised, a further element was required: a reliable high-volume source of the raw material. As Beckert has pointed out, "British cotton manufacturing ... was the first major industry in human history that lacked locally produced raw materials." In the early years of Britain's cotton manufacture, raw cotton had been imported mostly from the Ottoman Empire. Volume and price were erratic. Then, cotton began to come from the slave plantations in the British West Indies. For Britain, slavery was not so much a triangular trade as a circular one. Cotton cloth – both British and Indian – was sent to Africa to pay for the slaves who were transported to the West Indies, where they grew the cotton that was shipped to Britain to make the cloth that was sold to Africa to buy more slaves.[13]

American raw cotton began to be imported into Britain on a regular basis in 1791 and assumed a progressively dominant share of the market, enabled by Eli Whitney's invention of a cotton de-seeding machine, the saw-gin, which was an innovation as important as any of the British cotton-processing inventions. William Phalen has argued that it was the saw-gin that kick-started the volume export of American raw cotton to Britain. America rapidly became the answer to Britain's need for a raw cotton supply that was large, dependable, capable of keeping pace with the demand for finished goods and, crucially, at a price that grew steadily cheaper through to the middle of the nineteenth century. From small beginnings, raw cotton imports advanced through the century, while prices tumbled (Figure 1). The growth in the demand and the reducing cost of the raw material fuelled each other constantly. Much of this growth came from overseas markets: at the start of the civil war, nearly 80 per cent of Britain's production of cotton goods was exported.[14]

By 1861, the growth rate of the British cotton trade had passed its zenith, but it was still growing, and cotton was still by far the country's foremost industry. The years immediately before the war were some of the most profitable the manufacturing trade had ever known: margins averaged 21 per cent between 1856 and 1860. After a poor American crop of 1856–57, supplies had been good, and the 1859–60 harvest spectacularly so. Exports were running at record levels and prices were firm. In fact, the market for British cotton goods was so strong that the greatest concern of all sectors of the trade was whether the supply of raw cotton would continue to keep pace with the demand. Viewed with hindsight, the years before the outbreak of war were a golden age for the British cotton trade – if not for those who grew its cotton – set at the heart of a golden century. Farnie referred to the period from 1849 to 1861 as "the halcyon decade".[15]

Cotton's pre-eminent position came at the price of two endemic problems. In a global market that was growing rapidly, it was difficult for the manufacturing trade to know precisely what the demand for its goods was at any

Figure 1 British raw cotton consumption and prices, 1800–1900
consumption (solid line); prices (dotted line)

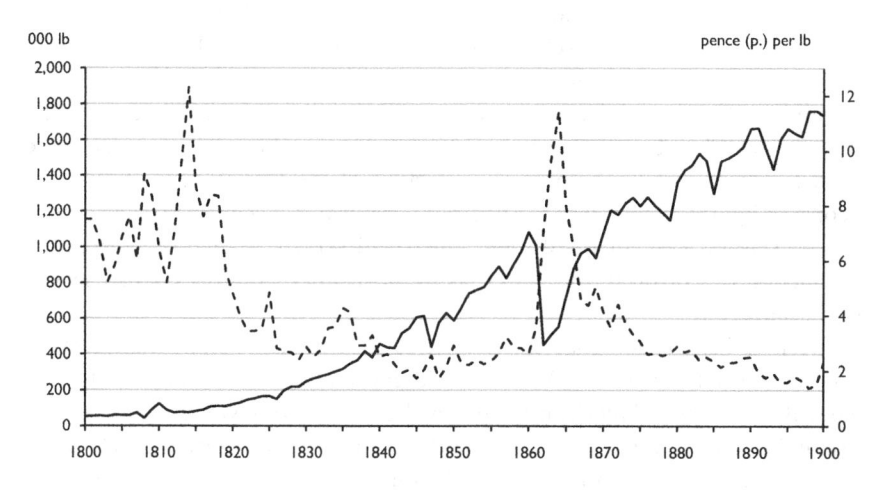

Source: B. Mitchell with P. Deane, *Abstract of British Historical Statistics* (Cambridge: Cambridge University Press, 1962).

moment, or what it would be in a year or two's time. Acting on market intelligence from the far corners of the world at a time when goods could take six months to reach their destination was an almost impossible task. It was hard, therefore, to keep the supply of cotton goods in equilibrium with the demand, and hard to know how much to invest in new capacity, and when. These problems were not helped by the multiplicity of firms within the industry, many of them large, but even more of them small. Imbalances between supply and demand did occur and, as will be explored in Chapter 4, the greatest of them is widely believed to have occurred immediately before the civil war, which has made the impact of that conflict harder to assess.

The other endemic problem for the industry was that it had no jurisdiction over its raw material. As John Chapman noted, "Lancashire may any year be laid prostrate by causes from whose action she has no escape, and over which she has no control." In any given year, the imports were what they were, and there was no immediate way of obtaining more. Price regulated demand to match supply, and never more so than during the civil war (Figure 1 illustrates this clearly), but the country's largest industry was still a hostage to forces beyond its control. Although the years of the civil war were, by a distance, the most disruptive period of the century, they were not the only such period. The vagaries of the American crop; variable imports from other sources; wars and disturbances: all these had an effect on the market. This unpredictability of imports, and the periodic imbalance between the supply and demand of finished goods, meant that the cotton industry – even in the midst of its greatest prosperity – was no stranger to short-time working.[16]

The cotton trade was well aware of the danger of over-dependence on a single source of supply, and on one that was based on slave labour. "Never before," wrote Henry Ashworth, a major mill-owner and later President of the Manchester Chamber of Commerce, "has so large and perilous a dependence been found to rest upon so small a portion of the human race, or upon a people so lightly esteemed as the negroes usually are." According to one cotton broker, slavery was "an Institution which had served as much to foster the production of Cotton in the States, as in most other Countries it had served to discourage it".[17]

Beckert has argued that the growth of the British cotton manufacture was inextricably linked to American slavery, and it is hard to dispute this view. By the 1820s, American slavery had become synonymous with cotton, expanding only to regions in which cotton could be grown. By 1850, about 70 per cent of the American slave population was involved in growing cotton. It is nevertheless ironic that the British dependence on slave-grown cotton accelerated at precisely the time that Britain was committed to ending the slave trade, which tends to undermine Beckert's wider thesis of collusion between manufacturers and governments. In Riello's view, "cotton production came to rely on slave cultivation not out of rational calculations on its efficiency, but because it followed a model already adopted by sugar, cocoa, coffee and tobacco cultivation." While this is true, it is simpler and sufficient to say that, after Whitney's invention, America produced the best cotton, and it was available to Britain cheaply and in volume. The fact that it was slave-grown was excoriated in principle, but conveniently overlooked in practice.[18]

It remains a moot point whether Britain's increasing demand for raw cotton could have been supplied without slavery. America would eventually, later in the century, grow more cotton with free labour than it had with slave labour. Even in the pre-war period, the free labour that produced Indian cotton was cheaper than slave labour in America.[19] It is also undeniable that America came to be the predominant producer of cotton for reasons other than slavery: product quality, superior transportation, the almost unlimited availability of new land (much of it expropriated from Native Americans) and, perhaps most of all, the fact that cotton was grown as a commercial, not a subsistence, crop. However, it remains highly unlikely that, at the precise moment when Britain required a rapidly expanding volume of raw cotton, that cotton could have been supplied from anywhere other than America, or on any basis other than slave labour.

"The intimate connexion between the growth of our cotton manufacture and the extension of slavery in the United States, is not a very pleasant subject for contemplation," declared one commentator. The threat posed by this connection had at least as much to do with the economic as with the political future of slavery. The number of slaves, and hence the size of America's cotton crop, was growing more slowly than the British demand for raw cotton. In 1856, the *New York Herald* concluded: "Viewing ... the question of labor available for increasing the crop of Cotton to meet the increase of consumption in ten years ... in no point of view can we arrive at the conclusion that adequate labor for its production can be found." The British cotton trade thus found itself in the position of wanting no slaves in America in theory, while requiring a great many more of them in practice. The Liberal MP Thomas Bazley ruefully told a CSA meeting that "whilst we wait for an increase in the number of negroes, we have to wait in the same proportion for an increase in the supply of cotton."[20]

The growing demand for cotton prompted a rise in the value of slaves. The price of a prime field hand had risen from $600 in 1802 to $1,800 in 1860. This was equivalent to a British farm labourer's wages for fifteen years. By the time the costs of food, clothing and housing, however primitive, were added, it was arguable that slave labour had become nearly as expensive as wage labour – in fact, more expensive than wage labour in some countries – and it was certainly more capital-intensive. Much of the capital of individual planters, and of the Southern States in general, was tied up in slaves. The significance of this fact should not be underestimated. Slaves were the largest single asset that wealthy Southerners possessed; the value of that investment was as important as house prices are to home-owners today. While the rise in the price of slaves was a problem for slave-holders in the sense that it increased the cost of cotton cultivation, it was otherwise welcomed because it boosted their asset wealth.[21]

There were two main threats to the maintenance of slave values. The first, as demanded by the more radical secessionists, would have been the reopening of the African slave trade, ended by the USA (at least theoretically) in 1808. However, most slave-holders perceived that the consequence of this would be to depress the price of slaves by increasing their availability. The Confederacy's Montgomery Constitution of 1861 specifically banned the African trade and even authorised the Confederate Congress to stop the importation of slaves from the Northern States. The second threat came from the constant drip-drip of Northern hostility to slavery. The market for slaves, like any other, was subject to investor sentiment and confidence. Even if slave-holders believed that Lincoln lacked the power, the public support and the will to end slavery, they feared that his Administration would reduce confidence in its long-term future, thereby causing a fall in the market. In October 1860, the *Charleston Mercury* predicted that Lincoln's election would cause an immediate drop of $100 in the value of a slave. That would have equated to a depreciation of $400 million (about $12 billion today) in the capital wealth of the South. The economic historian Gavin Wright has argued that it was these fears that were the catalyst for secession, rather than any belief in the imminence of emancipation.[22]

In Britain, the issue for the cotton trade was whether, if slavery were to be abolished, a commensurate volume of cheap cotton would continue to come from America. What had happened to West Indian sugar after the British abolition of slavery offered a disturbing precedent. Former slaves were unwilling to return to the sugar plantations as freedmen; there was a shortage of labour; slave-grown sugar from Brazil and Cuba became cheaper than West Indian; and there was a heated political debate over the implications of abolition for free trade. As Richard Huzzey has wryly put it, "anti-slavery was still identified with the historical forces of progress, morality, and civilization, but not necessarily immediate economic gratification." No one could know whether, in America, there would be continued availability of cotton without slaves.[23]

Britain and its cotton trade remained opposed to slavery in principle but, by 1860, the majority view was that what a British government could not control should not affect British behaviour. The consequence was that the trade turned a collective blind eye to how its cotton was produced. In Eugene Dattel's words, "most New Yorkers did not care that the cotton was produced by slaves because for them it became sanitized once it left the plantation." For New Yorkers, one could read Mancunians.[24]

The British cotton trade, while professing itself outraged by slavery, was more than content to profit from it. Some people advocated a boycott of cotton produced by slaves, but only once an alternative source of supply had been established. This sentiment carried more than a whiff of St Augustine's prayer: 'Please God, make me good, but not just yet.' There was a cognitive dissonance amongst the cotton manufacturers and merchants. Many mill-owners were convinced abolitionists, yet they had earned a collective fortune on the back of slave labour. During his tour of the USA in 1860, Henry Ashworth was under pressure to explain his own moral stance and that of his fellow mill-owners. He was told:

> If the raising of cotton and sugar by slave labour does constitute a theft, as the English abolitionists have insisted, surely the receiving of goods so stolen, whether by purchase or otherwise, must constitute a participation in the crime; and in this case the British people themselves were the greatest of moralists, and the greatest of sinners! ... We may have had the worst of it in the discussion, yet we do not hesitate to give the substance of the remarks.[25]

Thus Ashworth admits to having had the worst of the argument, yet takes pride in his honesty in repeating the criticism while feeling under no obligation to provide any sort of answer to it. The degree of both hypocrisy and moral disconnection is extraordinary, yet it was commonplace within both the British cotton trade and British society at the time. Slavery was evil, but eliminating it in America was someone else's problem, to be achieved at some undefined future point. It is not surprising that John Watts, historian of the cotton famine, should remark that "it may safely be affirmed that, if the annihilation of slavery had depended upon the people of this Christian land paying knowingly one farthing per yard extra for free-labour calico, slavery would have gone on for ever."[26]

So, while there is no evidence that the British cotton trade positively fostered slavery as the most economical means of producing cotton, there is abundant evidence of an indifference as to how its cotton was produced, cocooned in a wrapper of self-serving moral humbug that excused it from confronting the issue. The trade was amoral: it did not really mind where its cotton came from, as long as it came, and as long as it was cheap. When it failed to come, the cotton trade did not look specifically for non-slave-grown cotton, it looked for any cotton. Henry Ashworth declared that spinners would buy cotton anywhere and "asked no questions as to whether it was slave-grown or not".[27]

In considering why Britain – a country that was strongly abolitionist – underwrote the perpetuation of American slavery, it is pertinent to consider the textile industry of today. Most people in the western world wear clothes produced under working conditions that would be anathema to them if they existed in their own countries, including the widespread use of child labour. Yet few people refuse to buy such clothes because, unsurprisingly, they are cheap. They thus tacitly enable atrocious working conditions in Asian countries, as once they tacitly enabled the continuation of slavery in America. It might be thought that, in this context at least, moral progress in the past century and a half has been negligible.

There was thus no ignorance within Britain's cotton trade of the looming threat to its supply, but, for a variety of reasons, no effective measures were taken to spread the risk. The emphasis is on the word 'effective': there was no shortage of measures. The reasons for their failure will be discussed in Chapter 2. The result was that, when the civil war started, America was still supplying most of Britain's raw cotton, and Britain's largest industry was wholly vulnerable to the calamity about to befall it. Table 1 shows the level of imports in the years before, during and immediately after the war. The American share of those imports averaged 80 per cent in the three years before the war. They were to average 8.2 per cent of a much smaller total in the period from August 1861 to August 1865.

Table 1 British raw cotton imports, 1853–1867 (000 lb)

	All imports	American	percentage
1853	902,300	664,100	74%
1854	886,600	722,500	81%
1855	901,100	689,000	76%
1856	1,021,100	779,300	76%
1857	976,100	660,800	68%
1858	1,025,500	826,200	81%
1859	1,190,800	934,400	78%
1860	1,435,800	1,152,800	80%
1861	1,261,400	822,900	65%
1862	533,100	22,300	4%
1863	691,800	56,800	8%
1864	896,100	82,100	9%
1865	966,400	187,700	19%
1866	1,353,800	512,600	38%
1867	1,273,800	533,500	42%

Sources: George Holt & Co., annual cotton circulars (Liverpool Record Office, 380 COT/1/11/71); John Pender & Co., *Statistics of the Trade of the United Kingdom with Foreign Countries from 1840* (London: Simpkin, Marshall, 1869).

The historical consensus on Britain's supply of raw cotton during the war is not to be trusted. It can be summarised in three contentions. The first is that the Lancashire cotton famine was caused principally by over-production in the pre-war period. The second is that the shortage of raw material was overcome by the industry finding other sources of supply. The third is that, by the time the war had ended and before the American supply had resumed, the trade had returned to normal. In disproving each part of this consensus, a more precise definition of what is meant by 'the cotton famine' is required. There were in fact two famines, which have been conflated into one. The first was the starvation of work, income and stomachs for those employed in cotton manufacturing. The second was the starvation of raw material for the entire industry. The extent to which the two starvations were related forms the substance of a future chapter, but they were not the same thing. In this book, the phrase 'the cotton famine' will be used to refer only to the first circumstance. The starvation of the raw material will be referred to as 'the cotton scarcity'.

Since the operation of the Liverpool raw cotton market and its brokerage system is of crucial importance to this book, and especially to Chapters 6 and 7, a summary of how the system was intended to work, and how Ellison alleges that it did work, is needed. Raw cotton was shipped into Britain, 94 per cent of it into Liverpool, by importing merchants. The merchants hired cotton brokers, referred to as 'selling brokers', to sell the cotton exclusively on their behalf, at a fixed commission rate of 0.5 per cent. The cotton was sold by the selling brokers to 'buying brokers', appointed by spinners to buy exclusively on their behalf, also at a fixed commission rate of 0.5 per cent. All the cotton that came into the country passed through the hands of these two sets of Liverpool brokers and all that cotton attracted a compulsory charge of 1 per cent by value. The rate of commission may not sound large, but the value of cotton imports became increasingly vast, and the number of brokers was comparatively few. Even in lean times, they were rich men.[28]

The fundamental truth about the buying and selling of raw cotton was that, with any consignment, there was a finite buying price that someone, usually in a producing country, was contractually due and a finite selling price that the end user, the spinner, would eventually pay. The difference between the two prices was the profit (or loss) on the consignment, and the battle concerned how big that profit should be and who should receive what share of it. Although the cotton market, whether in its raw or manufactured state, was enormous, the margins were not, or not always, and they fluctuated greatly. Even allowing for special pleading by different interest groups, it seems that it was hard for both importers and manufacturers to be simultaneously satisfied with their profits. Before the war, it was the importers who were struggling to make money from cotton, not the spinners. The large import, and low prices, of 1860 were especially ruinous. "The year has been a disastrous one to importers," said broker Francis Hollins. William Clare & Sons claimed that: "The importers of the raw material have had three years of profitless business here, and ... almost brought to the verge of ruin."[29]

There were four principal contenders for a share of the spoils: the importing merchants, the selling brokers who represented them, the spinners, and the buying brokers who represented them. In addition – at all times, but especially during the civil war – there was a fifth group: the speculators. Self-evidently, the importing merchants wanted a high selling price for their cotton, and the spinners a low buying price. There is no evidence of friction between these two groups. There should have been no friction between either of these groups and the brokers, since the latter in theory earned their income from a fixed percentage of each contract. However, in practice there was huge friction: not – until after the war – between the importing merchants and the brokers, but between the brokers and the spinners.

Three of the five groups, the merchants and both sets of brokers, were based in Liverpool and had a vested interest in high prices. The spinners were based around Manchester and had a vested interest in low prices. Speculators could be based anywhere, although their trade was conducted through Liverpool. They mostly had a vested interest in rising prices, unless they were trying to bear the market, when their interest became falling prices. In the decades before the civil war, as the relative balance between supply and demand see-sawed, there appears to have been a rough equilibrium between Liverpool and Manchester, placing the relative strengths of seller and buyer on something close to a par over time. But Liverpool was never Manchester's "closest ally", as David Olusoga has claimed. There was a permanent, if not a permanently visible, conflict of interest between the two, as well as a hostility which is still evident today, as any football supporter can testify. When times were good, the hostility simmered beneath the surface. When they were bad, it erupted. Never were times worse, never was there a greater dichotomy between the fortunes of Liverpool and the rest of Lancashire, than during the civil war. At least until prices tumbled for the first time in September 1864, holders of cotton held the whip hand. Manchester had no alternative but to pay what Liverpool demanded.[30]

Not that anyone would know that from reading Ellison. Instead, he presented a sanitised account of how the system worked:

> The business of the cotton market was conducted on the lines of an unwritten, but popularly accepted, code, which clearly defined the functions, and plainly set forth the rights and duties, of both merchants and selling brokers on the one hand, and of spinners and buying brokers on the other. The merchant sold his cotton through a selling broker: the spinner purchased it through a buying broker. There were brokers who both bought and sold, but they were an exception to the rule, and comparatively few in number. No merchant thought of selling his imports except through the intervention of a selling broker, and no broker attempted to import cotton in competition with the merchant.[31]

Ellison did not explain how an 'unwritten code' could 'clearly define' anything. He went on to say that "this happy-family condition of things ... was not seriously jeopardised until the laying-down of the [transatlantic] cable." It is pertinent to ask which laying-down of the cable he was referring to: the abortive attempt of 1858 or the successful attempt of 1866. These two attempts sandwiched the civil war, meaning that all news of the war took about a fortnight to reach Britain. In his memoirs, Ellison alluded to "the gigantic speculative transactions developed by the occurrences incidental to the American War". This may suggest that he was referring to the 1858 attempt, but the context makes it clear that he was not. The statements above stand on their own: they are not amplified. In other sections, Ellison frequently refers to the respect held for individual brokers, but with anything that is negative, anything that is to do with the period of the civil war, he operates a strict code of *omertà*. Fortunately, enough other evidence exists to fill in most of the missing colours in Ellison's portrait. A better text for the period was provided by the Liverpool satirical paper, the *Porcupine*: "During the war, Liverpool literally festered and rotted with false trade. Huge commercial imposthumes and bails sprang up and ripened into horrible rankness, which never could have existed but for the uncertain condition and suddenly varying humours of the public mind."[32]

At the end of 1860, those 'imposthumes and bails' still lay in the future. The British cotton trade had enjoyed an Indian summer before disaster struck. If earlier warnings had been heeded, it might have enjoyed a few more Indian seasons. "When the fatal contest between the United and Confederated States of America unfortunately commenced," wrote Leone Levi, "it found us as unprepared as ever to meet the dire calamity."[33] No one in the British cotton trade was unaware of what might happen, so why was it so vulnerable when it did?

CHAPTER II

The Saturday Afternoon Syndrome
Why nothing was able to replace American cotton

"Saturday afternoon," wrote W. S. Gilbert to a London newspaper, complaining about the Metropolitan Railway, "although occurring at regular and well-foreseen intervals, always takes this railway by surprise."[1] Much the same could be said of the cotton trade and its shortage of raw material. The civil war was far from its only crisis. The Anglo-American War of 1812–15 had been a dress rehearsal for what was to happen 50 years later: imports slumped; prices soared; there was distress in the manufacturing districts. The intervals between crises were not regular, and the precise timing and nature of the next one could not be forecast, but the fact there would be a next one, and probably quite soon, was foreseeable. And, in fact, foreseen – just not effectively acted upon. No other aspect of the cotton trade absorbed so much time and energy to so little effect as the attempt to find at least one major alternative to America as a supplier of raw cotton. Much of that effort was conducted under the auspices of the CSA. To succeed in its objective, its members needed first to persuade themselves that it was attainable. Only then would they stand some chance of convincing others and persuading them to contribute money to the cause. Soon, like the Red Queen in *Alice Through the Looking Glass*, they learned to believe six impossible things before breakfast.

The search for at least one other substantial source of raw cotton pre-dated the civil war by decades. Its starting point was the danger of such a large industry depending on a single source of supply. That reliance was all the more perilous when the supply was subject not only – as with all crops – to unpredictable harvests, but to a dependence on slave labour. The scale of the problem is shown by the fact that, in 1860, America grew 66 per cent of the world's cotton and more than 75 per cent of all cotton entering world trade. It produced it at a landed price in Liverpool that other countries could not undercut, and that gave them no incentive to expand cotton cultivation. The dominance of American cotton meant that it set the price for the world market. When there was a short American crop and prices rose, that was of little avail. It would take several years for any country substantially to increase its production; one year of artificially high prices was not a sufficient temptation to begin the process. Capitalists could see no profit from investing in cultivation in some as yet untested country and, *pace* Beckert, government intervention on the scale required to make a difference was out of the question in the mid-nineteenth century. For these general reasons, no significant progress had been made in replacing American cotton before the civil war.[2]

When the war started, the nub of the problem was this. It had proved impossible to find a long-term solution to the supply problem without a short-term crisis. When the short-term crisis arrived, there was insufficient time to find a long-term solution. Because the world knew it was a short-term crisis, and that any gain that might accrue to other suppliers was likely to be fleeting, it was not possible to find much of a short-term solution either. The CSA had hoped to circumvent this vicious circle by asserting that "if the supply is to wait for the demand, the latter may have ceased to exist by the time the former has been created."[3] Others took the view that, if the supply was created before the demand was known to exist, it might turn out not to exist. In this instance, the demand did exist, but only during the cotton scarcity and not before or after it.

The search for an alternative supply focused on India: the cradle of cotton, a British possession, and assumed to be the natural answer to the problem. India was the second largest cotton-producing country, but produced less than 30 per cent of the volume of the USA, much of it retained for domestic consumption.[4] Two secondary sources describe how Manchester tried to pressure the EIC, the British Government and – from 1858, after the dissolution of the EIC – the Government of India into enabling an increase in cotton supplies from India, especially during the civil war.[5] Together, they present a different picture from the one that Beckert has painted. Far from 'cotton capitalists' working hand in glove with government to enforce Manchester's will, the Government frustrated Manchester's demands at almost every turn. Substantial extra supplies did come from India during the war, but that was due to price alone.

This chapter will draw together the narratives from these secondary sources and those from the main primary sources: the archives of the CSA, Isaac Watts's history of the CSA and Samuel Smith's 1863 report to the Manchester Chamber of Commerce on the prospects for receiving more cotton from India.[6] Although these sources have been referenced in other works, they have not been considered in detail by historians, nor used to give a coherent overview of the issues. Together, they present a portrait that is heroic, comical and hypocritical in turn. They explain fully why the outbreak of war found the British cotton trade helpless, and why its continuation left the trade without anything like the volume of cotton it needed.

The sense that events in America were coming to a head impelled the trade to make a fresh attempt to solve the supply problem in the late 1850s. This was the latest in a long chain of attempts, mostly centred on India. Until 1858, the responsibility for developing cotton cultivation in India belonged – in as far as it belonged to anyone, which was itself a contentious point – to the EIC. Isaac Watts wrote that, from 1788 to 1850, "numerous attempts had been made [by the EIC] ... to improve the culture of cotton in India", allegedly no fewer than 28 measures. This was not a view shared widely in Manchester, where the belief was that the EIC had done next to nothing. According to the *Manchester Examiner & Times*, "the very name of the East India Company ... stinks in the nostrils of the community." This was not surprising. A major objective of the EIC was to export cotton goods *from* India, so it needed to encourage manufacture there, along with India's own use of its raw material. A major objective of Manchester was to export cotton goods *to* India, which required both the curtailment of indigenous manufacture and the export of the raw material to Britain. The interests of each were opposed. In addition, as Arnold wrote, "it was not possible for the EIC to force the native farmers to produce cotton, which, for ten successive years perhaps, must be allowed to rot, in order that in the eleventh it might rescue Lancashire from the consequences of a deficiency in the cotton crop of America."[7]

In 1848, John Bright, then a Manchester MP, instigated a select committee of the House of Commons, which he chaired himself, to enquire into the growth of cotton in India. That committee having achieved no tangible results, in 1850 Bright attempted to establish a Royal Commission on the subject. The reply to Bright's motion by Sir John Hobhouse, President of the Board of Control and the Government minister responsible for India, covered most of the issues that were to dominate the debate over the next two decades. The heart of his argument was that, no matter what was done and by whom, Indian cotton could not compete with American. Events were to prove him right.[8]

There was a hard core of the cotton trade that agitated permanently on the supply issue, centred on radical Manchester. In 1845, the capture of the Chamber of Commerce by what Farnie termed 'free trade fanatics' prompted the establishment of the less radical Manchester Commercial Association and led to a 13-year schism in the commercial representation of the city. To emphasise the distinction, the term 'Cottonopolis' will be used in this chapter to identify the polity of radical Manchester cotton men, although the original meaning of that word was broader. In the present sense, Cottonopolis was epitomised by the Chamber of Commerce, by a handful of MPs – of whom Thomas Bazley and J. B. Smith were the most vociferous – and by the CSA. The formation of the CSA represented the most committed, most enduring attempt by the cotton trade to find a solution to its supply problem. It was founded in

Manchester on 21 April 1857. It consisted of the great and the good of radical Lancashire. Its President was John Cheetham, MP for Lancashire South. Six other MPs were ex-officio members and three more were on the Council. The CSA saw itself as the successor to the Anti-Corn Law League. Fifteen of the top 35 subscribers to the League were among the leading subscribers to the CSA. This was an attempt by Cottonopolis, its numbers now depleted by defections to the ranks of the complacently wealthy, to show that it still had fire in its belly. And, for a while, it did. At successive annual meetings, brimstone rained down upon the CSA's perceived enemies – usually the Government, frequently the backsliders in the cotton trade, and always the EIC and its heirs and successors in indolence.[9]

Two blows to the chances of the CSA's success were struck within days either side of its inauguration. In the General Election of April 1857, cotton's main protagonist in Parliament, John Bright, lost his Manchester seat. Thereafter, his interventions on behalf of cotton were few and far between. The second blow was the outbreak of the Indian Rebellion on 10 May. The cost of suppressing it, and of an increased military presence afterwards, wreaked further havoc on India's parlous finances. The determination of the Government to achieve a balanced budget resulted in cuts to public works and infrastructure projects intended to facilitate an increase in India's cotton exports.[10]

According to its 1862 annual report, written at the height of the famine, "the [CSA] originated in the prospective fears of a portion of the trade that some dire calamity must inevitably ... overtake the cotton manufacture of Lancashire, whose vast superstructure has so long rested upon the treacherous foundation of restricted slave labour."[11] The phrase 'a portion of the trade' was well chosen: most of the trade believed that, if war did come, it would neither last long, nor cause a dire calamity. From the outset, the CSA was bedevilled by the lukewarm support it received from its own industry:

> The Executive Committee ... are surprised at the apathy shown by those who ought to have been the principal supporters of the Association. The cotton brokers and mill owners most directly affected by the short supply of cotton, and most likely to be first benefited by the exertions of the Association, have withheld that measure of support which was naturally expected at their hands. ... The Executive Committee are willing to believe that this has arisen from a misapprehension of their intended objects.[12]

The cotton brokers apprehended the 'intended objects' of the CSA all too well. As Chapter 6 will show, they were 'directly affected by the short supply of cotton' only in the sense that it massively enriched them.

The CSA was funded by voluntary subscription, so it was under permanent pressure to justify itself to its subscribers. It was proposed to call for a maximum of 12.5p per horsepower as a yearly subscription, with the probability that the actual call would not exceed 5p. Since there was about 300,000 horsepower in the cotton industry at the time, the CSA had a potential revenue of between £15,000 and £37,500, depending on the levy. In its foundation year, the subscription income was £1,372, suggesting that it had the active support of 9 per cent of the trade at best. In practice it would have been less since the CSA had several major subscribers from outside the industry. In 1862, at the height of the famine, income was only £4,123. Liverpool contributed the grand sum of £56. As a Mr Ryley put it, "my fellow-townsmen of Liverpool are not quite so hearty in this cause as I think they might be. They state that they think it is purely a manufacturers' and spinners' question."[13]

The CSA's efforts from 1857 through to its dissolution in 1872 were directed to two ends: a general attempt to encourage cultivation wherever cotton could be grown, and a specific attempt to attract greater supplies from India. According to one of its members, the CSA was "essentially missionary in its character", and it certainly pursued its aims with a missionary zeal. An essay was procured on the best practice of cotton cultivation in America and circulated around the world, together with the provision of seeds and, later, cleaning machinery and agricultural implements. The CSA produced a grow-your-own cotton kit and was granted the use of British consular offices to promulgate it. There was no shortage of suitable recipients. "The Cotton fields of the world may be regarded as almost illimitable," declared the CSA, and for once it could not be accused of exaggeration, as this *tour d'horizon* shows:[14]

Heading south from the Mississippi, "in Central America there is a larger area of land suitable to cotton than ... in the whole of the Confederate States." Further down, "British Guiana ... was capable of growing as much Cotton as Great Britain required." Then, "with the aid of foreign capital the cotton trade of Brazil would be capable of almost unlimited extension. ... The port of Bahia would ... become ... a second New Orleans." Other parts of South America were equally promising: "Bogota, La Esmeralda, Callao, Carracas, Lima, Tacna, and Baranquilla ... could produce Cotton sufficient for the entire consumption of the world." Crossing the Atlantic, "cotton will yet come in abundance from Africa, there are immense districts that could supply all that Lancashire requires." Dr Livingstone discovered a source of cotton near the former Lake Nyasa that "presents a reasonable hope of a solution of the problem of supply". In the Mediterranean, aside from Egypt, "[no] other country ... offers anything like to the prospect of a large continuous and cheap supply of cotton as Italy." In the Middle East, "the whole northern half of Mesopotamia ... might be converted into one vast cotton field, extensive enough to place Manchester once and for ever in complete independence."

In addition, "Turkey possesses vast tracts of country, which by soil and climate are peculiarly adapted to cotton." Further afield, "half a million of well-directed labourers in Australia could produce more cotton than this country could consume." In Fiji, "one single island" – and there are 211 of them – "is capable of producing all the cotton that Europe requires at the present time." Crossing to western China, "under proper cultivation ... Pegu, Burmah, and the adjacent Shan territories ... could produce annually all the raw Cotton that England requires." Cotton could even be grown in England. "J. Blackburne, Esq., M.P., had a gown made from cotton grown in his own gardens, for a dress for his lady to appear at court." Finally, as always, there was India: "If the government were only ordinarily wise ... we could have the whole of our supplies of cotton from India", which "could supply all the cotton we require, and much more."[15]

The missionaries of the CSA did not pause to enquire why, if this endless vista of cotton fields had the potential to stretch across much of the earth's surface, it had so far failed to do so. They also neglected to notice that cotton production was labour-intensive and that many of these lands were populated sparsely, if at all. Cotton manufacture was becoming a mature industry in Europe. An increasing demand for raw cotton had existed for decades, a fact known throughout the world. No one seems to have asked why so few of these countries had grown and exported cotton on a significant scale. The CSA's annual report in June 1861 boasted that, "owing mainly to ... the efforts of your Association ... [there is] a total of 58 new, revived, or increasing ports from which we are now receiving cotton."[16] These 58 ports are proudly listed, together with the quantities shipped. Nowhere does the report mention that the combined shipments amounted to less than 2 per cent of the American supply in the process of being lost at that very moment. It is difficult not to be struck by the collective naivety of a group that included many experienced and successful businessmen.

The Cottonopolists displayed an ignorance about the wider world of cotton, accompanied by an equal arrogance. Their lack of confidence in anything told them by the EIC, or by the Government, prompted them to latch on to any idea that sounded hopeful, propounded by anyone who seemed informed. They were particularly susceptible to lesser officials from British India with large egos. At one moment, the situation would be transformed if American seed could be planted in India. A pamphlet that was a paean to the experiments of A. N. Shaw, the British Collector of Dharwar, concluded that "Mr Shaw's opinion that 'Indian cotton may ultimately oust the American from the English market' will not seem extravagant." The effect is somewhat reduced when one knows that the anonymous author of this pamphlet was probably Alexander Nisbet Shaw himself. In the end, as Isaac Watts conceded, "little or no permanent advantage can be expected from these attempts, and ... the improvement of indigenous cotton is the work which demands and will most reward exertion." Watts does not mention the time the CSA spent angrily arguing the opposite, nor that for many years it agitated for a reform of land tenure in India and for the Government to sell off waste lands. The Secretary of State for India from 1859 to 1866, Sir Charles Wood, was castigated for his failure to implement these measures which, Cottonopolis alleged, would transform the prospects for cotton cultivation.[17] Eventually, Isaac Watts admitted that:

> The subject of land-tenure occupied the earnest attention of the Association at an early period ... but the conclusion soon adopted [*in this context, 'soon' means after six or seven years of insisting on the opposite*] was that it did not interpose any serious obstacle to an extended cultivation of cotton. ... The utilisation of waste lands was also a subject which engaged much attention ... and some of the opinions once entertained on this subject have been considerably changed.[18]

As on almost every other subject, one might say.

The two illusions most sacred to the CSA were that India grew vastly more cotton than it actually did and that much of it was stacked in the interior, unable to find a way to market because of a lack of transportation. Leonard Wray, in an address to the Society of Arts in December 1858, declared that India already produced between four and five million bales of cotton annually, "a fact little dreamed of in this country". The reason it was little dreamed of is that it was not a fact, or anything close to one, as Samuel Smith was to demonstrate four years later. At the 1859 annual meeting, Henry Ashworth told the CSA how the 1846 crop of Berar – more than 400 miles from the sea – was so plentiful and so good that efforts were made to sell it in Bombay, but "they had to employ 180,000 bullocks to carry that cotton to market." It is true that transportation in parts of India was appalling, but the idea that there were vast quantities of cotton trapped in the interior, just waiting for someone to gather it, was a fantasy. The *ryots* – the Indian peasant farmers – were not in a financial position to grow crops speculatively. If they produced cotton, it was because they had a market for it, whether in the ports or among the local hand spinners and weavers. Not only was there much less cotton in India than Cottonopolis thought, but most of it was spoken for already.[19]

A strange aspect of the attempts to find other sources of cotton was that the issue of price was barely mentioned. Manchester had a fixed idea that the 'correct' price for raw cotton was 1.67p per lb. One of its concerns was that producers in America were levering the price above this 'natural' level to line their own pockets excessively.[20] But nowhere in the discussion of the cotton supply has there been found any extensive reference to price. The CSA claimed to be researching the prospects for cotton cultivation throughout the world. Surely any competent botanist could have answered that question well before 1857. The cost of the supply was critical, but this is never mentioned as an objective.

Someone who did grasp the centrality of price was Alexander Mackay, a journalist. When Bright failed to persuade the Government to set up a Royal Commission into cotton growing in India, he instigated a private enquiry. Mackay was its Commissioner. He died on the journey home, and his posthumous report in 1853 was by then an anti-climax. It included this telling question:

> Can Indian cotton, of good quality, be laid down in Liverpool at prices remunerative to all legitimately engaged in the trade, in successful competition with American cotton, not only when prices are high, but ... when they are at the lowest point at which cotton can be supplied from America at a profit?[21]

This was the right question. It is strange that no one else in Cottonopolis thought to ask it, or to realise that the answer to it was 'no'.

The position of the cotton supply on the eve of the civil war, therefore, was identical to its position at the formation of the CSA four years earlier, and identical to its position for a long while beforehand. The American share of the British raw cotton market was the same as it had been 20 years earlier. The Indian share of the market was variable, growing only when the American harvest was bad and the price rose above its normal level. No significant new sources of supply had been established. The two fundamentals remained unaltered: America produced two-thirds of the world's cotton; and no other country could, or would, land cotton in Liverpool in quantity at a competitive price. The CSA had achieved nothing of substantive value. Now it was faced with the crisis it had long dreaded.

In January 1861, the growing possibility of a civil war in America prompted two letters from the Government. Earl Russell, the Foreign Secretary, wrote to the Manchester Chamber of Commerce asking for an estimate of the additional cotton required in the event of an interruption to the American supply, and pledging to request consular offices to discover how much of the shortfall each country could supply. On 28 February, Lord Canning, Governor-General, wrote to each local government in India that he was considering "the possibility of a ... suddenly increased demand for Indian cotton in England", and asked them to review how "the power of India to meet such increased demand for cotton may be augmented by help of Government". He then ruled out any measure "which in any way interferes with private enterprise". The

Government was happy to write letters, but not to do very much. The cotton trade would need to look to its own resources.[22]

"The most important country to which we have to look ... is India," CSA President John Cheetham had told the 1859 annual meeting. Yet Cheetham himself was only too aware of the problems in India. In 1862, in an unguarded moment, he was reported as telling representatives of countries showing cotton samples at the International Exhibition that "the example of India was to be avoided rather than imitated. [The CSA] had nothing to learn from India, except ... how to mismanage their business and produce the worst cotton grown on the face of the earth." Despite this, the CSA's obsession with India continued, because it had to. It was no use now relying on promoting cultivation in countries where little cotton had ever been grown. The crisis was at hand. The only hope lay in India, where there was already a large indigenous crop. It now became essential to discover how large that crop really was.[23]

In 1858, Leonard Wray had declared the crop at four to five million bales. In 1859, Dr John Forbes Watson, Reporter on the Products of India for the Secretary of State, asserted that India was producing more than eight million bales. Three years later, Richard Burn, editor of a Manchester trade circular, wrote to *The Times*: "Your correspondent ... endorses my statement that India ... produces 6,000,000 bales of cotton, and quotes Dr J. Forbes Watson as his authority, than whom no one is more competent to form an opinion." In September 1862, the CSA decided that "it is erroneous to suppose that a stock of 6,000,000 bales of cotton exists at this moment in India, only awaiting the means of purchase and export", and reduced the estimate to where Wray had placed it: between four and five million bales. It would seem that Manchester now began to doubt any of these estimates.[24] Its Chamber of Commerce took the unusual step of commissioning Samuel Smith, a Liverpool broker, to visit India and report on what he found. Smith's report consisted of a series of letters, written between 12 February and 12 May 1863, and first published in *The Times of India*. These excerpts are taken from three of his letters:

> A misty undefined notion prevailed that a vast amount of cotton was grown in this country; random estimates of four and six millions of bales had been propagated by theoretical writers. ... One million and a half of bales must have been a full crop for all India prior to this crisis [*subsequently modified to fewer than two million bales*]. ... It was also imagined that ... if a high enough rate was offered ... the immense stores in the interior would be unlocked, the obstacles of transit overleaped, and prodigious quantities shipped from the ports; while it was thought that a moderate increase in the cultivation ... would easily provide a substitute for the entire American crop.

> India is not able ... to supply the place of America. ... Large supplies of cotton can ... be drawn from India only by excessive prices, and whenever prices return to a normal level the production will recede correspondingly. ... No hope whatever exists of India being able to fill the void made by the stoppage of the Southern [American] trade. ... Were a lively picture of Indian customs and commerce before the mind of the British public, fewer utopian notions would prevail, and fewer impracticable schemes be advocated.[25]

Smith explained the reasons for his conclusions. The priority of the *ryots* was to grow food: cotton was seldom a profitable crop and there was always a high chance of it failing. The yield per acre was about one-fifth of that obtaining in America. Production methods were antiquated and laborious. Indigenous cotton was of poor quality and unsuited to British machinery. It was often picked when over-ripe and was frequently dirty and mixed with extraneous material. The slowness of the cleaning process exposed much of the cotton to the monsoon rains. The problems with transportation were immense. Different growths of cotton were mixed in the same bale, undetectable until the bales were opened in Britain. In the ports, corruption was endemic and quality control non-existent, so that "the English houses have to contend with trickery and fraud on every side." On top of all that, the cotton then took from four to six months to reach Liverpool. Other commentators have weighed in with similar observations. According to Beckert, "transporting cotton to the port added about 50 percent to its cost in India, but as little as 3 percent in the United States." The newspaper, *Friend of India*, referred to "the seven middlemen who stand between the Bombay merchant and the *ryot*". It was not the case that India failed to match America on one or two indices: it fell down on all of them. Smith's report proved to be unchallengeable. On the key question of the size of the Indian crop, his estimate would later be endorsed by both Ellison and Farnie.[26]

Now in a desperate situation, Cottonopolis hoped to bully the Government into doing things it had proved unable to do itself. But the Government refused to undertake activities that it considered the province of business. It was hamstrung by a lack of funds following the Indian Rebellion and it was under pressure to govern India for the benefit of Indians, not of Mancunians. If Cottonopolis considered that the Government had done far too little to help Manchester, many Indians considered that it had done far too much. All the fury that Cottonopolis felt towards the Government was vented on one man: Sir Charles Wood. Hugh Mason – mill-owner, later President of the Manchester Chamber of Commerce and an MP – called on the Chamber of Commerce, the CSA, the mayor of Manchester, and anyone else he could think of, to demand Wood's impeachment. If that demand was refused, he wanted

Samuel Smith: cotton broker, merchant and commentator (LRO 380 COT/1/14/1, reproduced by permission of the International Cotton Association)

the country to dismiss Lord Palmerston from his premiership. In return, Wood despised the Cottonopolists. "The cotton people try my temper sadly," he wrote. "They have no regard for anything but their own selfish interest."[27]

One can nevertheless feel sympathy for the Cottonopolists. They were under enormous pressure in 1861–63. Their mills were closed or on short time; their finances were parlous; their employees were starving in their hundreds of thousands. Some people were falsely blaming them for having caused the famine by over-producing cotton goods. The onus was on them to explain how things had got to this pass and what they were doing about it. Others who might have shown an active concern – the bulk of the manufacturing trade, Liverpool, the Government, anyone in India – declined responsibility. A Mr Clegg of Manchester asserted that "not one hundred thousand pounds has yet been paid up, from all sources in England put together, toward companies organized for the encouragement of cotton cultivation."[28] Cottonopolis was left alone to do something it could not do. The result was a series of hysterical demands, coupled with vitriolic criticism of the only scapegoat to hand: the Secretary of State.

Sir John Hobhouse had earlier made the point that, when there had been problems with indigo and opium supplies from India, the merchants in those trades had resolved them, not the government, so why did Cottonopolis not follow their example? Henry Ashworth had answered that question in 1859: "Would people ... undertake to tell a corn miller, if there happened to be a scarcity of corn, that he ought to go to India or some other country, and grow the corn that was needed?" (*The Times*, astonishingly, thought that this would happen: "[The mill-owners] will ... go earnestly to work to gather from the inexhaustible fields of India the raw material they require, and they will bring it home.") The Cottonopolists were not merchants: they were manufacturers. Exports were managed by overseas firms based in Manchester: in the 1860s, at least three-quarters of the trade was handled by these foreign companies. If there was one body that could have transformed the supply of raw cotton from India to Britain, it was the cotton merchants of India. The inexorable law of supply and demand, so beloved of Manchester, might have led the Indian trade to recognise the extent of British demand and ensure a far greater supply. This did not happen to anything like the required extent.[29]

Isaac Watts placed the blame for this on the hostility of the Indian press to what it regarded as Manchester's selfishness. This is unfair. Everyone knew that, when the war ended and American cotton came back to the market, the British trade would forsake Indian cotton and buy American again. It was universally, and correctly, believed that, when this happened, the price of raw cotton would plummet. In normal times, there was no incentive for India to increase its supply to Britain unless there had been a poor American harvest: the price was not high enough to entice existing cotton away from other destinations, whether export or domestic. If significantly more cotton was now to be planted, the consequent increase in the global supply would make prices even less attractive in the long term. It would have been madness to change the priorities of India's agrarian economy because of another country's short-term problem. It was a risk even to divert existing supplies to Britain, bearing in mind the time lag of up to six months. At no point of the civil war could anyone have a sure opinion that American cotton would not return within six months. The brokers Cunningham & Hinshaw asked: "Who will dare to import freely of Cotton from India at high prices, when long before it can be marketed here, we may be largely supplied by the release of the pent-up crops of the States?"[30]

The proof of how closely Indian merchants watched what was happening in Britain – not only during the civil war, but before and after it – is provided by Figure 2. This graph incorporates a 36-week time lag between the price and the import, to give time for information from Liverpool to reach India and be acted upon. The correlation is not exact, but it is striking. It suggests that everything was done at the last minute, in the hope that the civil war, and the prices of scarcity, would still obtain when the cotton arrived in Liverpool.

Despite the risks, many Indian merchants *were* seduced by the prices on offer: Indian cotton exports to Britain roughly trebled in the war years (see Table 2). Until September 1864, the profits were enormous. Then the

Figure 2 British imports of Indian cotton and its Liverpool price, 1859–1867
British imports (solid line: 52-week moving) and its Liverpool price (dotted line: 4-week moving), incorporating a 36-week time lag for imports

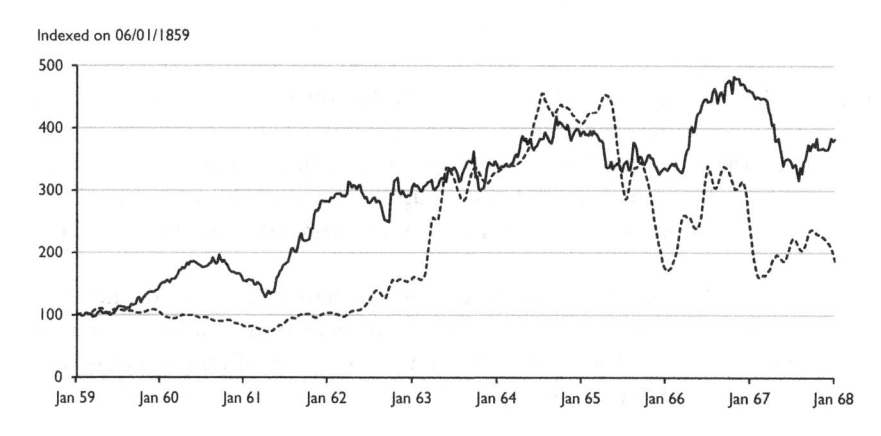

Source: Ezekiel Donnell, *The Chronological and Statistical History of Cotton* (New York: James Sutton & Co., 1872).

predictable happened. The broker Paul Hemelryk told of a cargo of 400 bales of Madras cotton, worth 8.3p per lb when shipped and 2p when it arrived.[31] Many of the merchants were bankrupted, either then or later. Smith reported that:

> The [Parsee merchants] profited greatly by the huge rise in the price of cotton. ... This wonderful prosperity ... led to a wild outbreak of speculation unparalleled in India. ... The trading community became intoxicated with sudden fortunes. And then the bubble burst! The American War came to an end; a terrific decline in prices occurred; and merchants, banks, and financial companies toppled over in a mass of hopeless wreckage.[32]

Discreditably, the CSA used the inflated wartime price to entice greater long-term cotton cultivation in India, despite knowing that this price was far higher than Britain was prepared, or would need, to pay when the war ended. It declared that "a prize of from thirty to forty millions sterling per annum, is at the present moment offered ... to ... all nations capable of growing cotton, together with innumerable social and commercial advantages. ... Never ... was so magnificent an opportunity for national aggrandisement afforded to tropical countries."[33] The key phrase is 'at the present moment'. Pre-war, non-American cotton sold for about £6 million p.a. in Britain, by no means all of it going to the producing countries. (See Table 8: the amount would have been about 20 per cent of the final column.) Had the *ryots* heeded this plea, they would have turned land over to cotton cultivation, enjoyed a few years of profit and would then have been told either that their cotton was no longer required, or that the price was a fraction of what it had been.

Egypt serves as an example. That country had previously exported surplus cereals. Now it subordinated all agriculture to cotton cultivation. It needed to import foodstuffs. There were famine conditions in the interior. Egypt was transformed from self-sufficiency to a one-crop economy dependent on exports. In India, some *ryots* did plough up their grain fields to plant cotton. But most of them had longer memories.[34] In the words of Ellison & Haywood:

> The stolid opposition of the cultivators to change of any kind, and their especial and hereditary distrust of the British Cotton market, are not to be got over in a day. Even at the end of two years of famine prices, the prejudices of the ryots have scarcely been affected, let alone eradicated.[35]

Smith observed that "[the *ryot*] is well aware that the price of cotton is exceedingly precarious; he knows very little of American politics ... but he has not forgotten the experience of the past, and remembers that extraordinary rises have generally been followed by seasons of ruinous depression."[36]

All else having failed, the free traders of Cottonopolis resorted to pleas for government intervention. Even Bright lacked sympathy for them: "When there comes this great calamity of the failure of the cotton supply, everybody runs to everybody else asking that something should be done." In 1857, the mill-owner John Baynes had declared that "the procuring of an increased supply of cotton ... must be left to the operation of the 'laissez-faire' principle, which has worked so beneficially in rewarding enterprise, enriching individuals, and promoting the national prosperity." A few years later, ravaged by the famine, Cottonopolis had changed its tune. The law of supply and demand did not operate properly in India, it said, so the Government must intervene to make it operate. If England demanded something, someone else should supply it.[37]

There is no reason to think, from an Indian perspective, that the law of supply and demand was not working. The role of cotton in the country's domestic economy made perfect sense, just not the sense that Cottonopolis wanted it to make. Some in Liverpool were apoplectic at the more extreme of Manchester's demands. Charles Holland, importer, cotton broker and former chairman of the Chamber of Commerce, declared that "if he were called upon to express his concurrence ... that the consolidated fund should be made available for the production of a larger supply of cotton in India – he should say at once that a more extraordinary and barefaced proposition was hardly ever put before any public community." Many in Manchester agreed with him.

Even its Chamber of Commerce opposed interference with trade through the compulsory purchase of cotton or by underwriting its price. Its Board declared that "any such proposals are utterly at variance with true trading principles, and amount to a direct renunciation of the law of supply and demand."[38]

In Beckert's view, "cotton had become a matter of state, a state empowered not least by decades of merchant political mobilization."[39] If this had been true, then, faced with a crisis in the country's largest industry and with hundreds of thousands of its citizens deprived of work and starving, there were two things one might have expected a British government to do. The first would have been to use the most powerful navy in the world to break the blockade of the ports that shipped 80 per cent of Britain's raw cotton. The second would have been to act urgently to help procure fresh supplies of cotton from other countries, notably India. During the American Civil War, the British Government did neither of these things. In Beckert's review of the attempts to secure more Indian cotton during the war, he is contradictory. His intellectual straitjacket demands statements like the one quoted above, but honesty compels occasional recognition of Manchester's extreme dissatisfaction with government measures, or the lack of them. He creates the impression of ceaseless joint Cottonopolis and government initiatives, while the fact that these efforts were all instigated by Manchester and led almost nowhere goes unmentioned. To give a specific example, he uses the 1862 reduction of the Indian import tariff on cotton goods from 10 per cent to 5 per cent to illustrate his claim that the Government pursued Manchester's interests. He does not mention that this reduction merely returned duties to the level they had been between 1814 and 1859, when they were raised to help cover the post-Rebellion costs. Nor does he mention that, in 1863, the cotton values on which the duty was calculated were increased considerably, to Manchester's fury.[40]

Beckert is surely correct in identifying the war as presenting "the world's first raw material crisis", but he is wrong to allege that state interventionism formed the British response to that crisis. The statement in the final paragraph of his chapter on the civil war – "cotton capitalists had learned that the lucrative global trade networks they had spun could only be protected and maintained by unprecedented state activism" – bears no relationship to actual events. Neither does his claim that, in India, "British colonial bureaucrats, and Manchester manufacturers embarked on a frantic race to grow cotton for world markets." Rather, the manufacturers demanded that the Government should do it for them, and the Government declined.[41]

Having previously advocated free trade to advance their interests, many Cottonopolists now needed to justify interventionism, without appearing to contradict themselves. Harnetty argued that the Cottonopolists were imperialist interventionists more than they were free traders. But they were businessmen first, not ideologues, and they viewed economic theory through the prism of their own experience and perceived self-interest, which varied over time. As the last chapter showed, the British cotton industry was built on the back of protectionism, cheered on by Manchester. The switch to a passionate defence of free trade happily coincided with the period when, by now the dominant force in the manufacture of cotton goods, Cottonopolists needed world markets to be open to their products. Even then, their enthusiasm for free trade did not usually extend to the export of textile machinery. In William Ashworth's words, "the enlightened minds spearheading Britain's Industrial Revolution were liberal free-traders as long as there was no competition." Now, with the main source of their raw material cut off, they reverted to their previous demands for government intervention. However, their earlier efforts to convert the government to free trade had been so successful that they were hoist with their own petard. There was no more stalwart defender of free trade during the cotton crisis than Sir Charles Wood.[42]

One could say that the Cottonopolists were hypocrites. More charitably, one could say that they were pragmatic businessmen trying to protect their businesses. In some ways, they were ahead of their time. A striking aspect of this economic debate was how it prefigured twentieth-century arguments, rather than exemplifying nineteenth-century ones. In Parliament, J. B. Smith asked the Government to buy up Indian cotton and to take it for three years in payment of rent. The proposal was thought outlandish at the time but, a hundred years later, it would have seemed commonplace.[43]

This chapter is the story of what did not happen and why it did not happen. It concludes with a summary of what did happen.

The cotton scarcity persisted throughout the war. At best, the manufacturing trade reached a *modus vivendi* with its new circumstances. An inflated price regulated the demand, and an improving, though still inadequate, supply allowed mills to work more normally than in the trough of the famine. But it would have needed a quintupling of the 20 per cent of the pre-war supply that was not American to replace the 80 per cent that was. That did not come close to being achieved.

The main source of the wartime supply was India (Table 2). The other main pre-war exporters, Brazil and Egypt, increased their supplies. A plethora of small exporters contributed their mites. According to Isaac Watts, "the increased supplies obtained from [Turkey] ... contributed in a very important degree to meet the scarcity occasioned by the American war." This was one of the many euphemisms, not to say untruths, which the CSA used to conceal the reality. At its wartime peak, Turkish cotton amounted to less than 3 per cent of the lost American supply. Britain attracted a larger share of the crop from countries with which it had an established trade. It attracted some of the crop from China and Japan, unparalleled before or since. Impetus was given to increased cotton cultivation in a few countries: Egypt, India and Turkey

Table 2 Source of British raw cotton imports, 1857–1868 (000 lb)

	America		India		Egypt		South America		China and Japan		West Indies		Turkey		Others		Totals
1857	660,800	68%	251,800	26%	25,200	3%	30,200	3%	0	0%	0	0%	0	0%	8,100	1%	976,100
1858	826,200	81%	131,900	13%	37,700	4%	18,800	2%	0	0%	0	0%	0	0%	10,900	1%	1,025,500
1859	934,400	78%	186,500	16%	36,900	3%	21,400	2%	0	0%	1,000	0%	0	0%	10,600	1%	1,190,800
1860	1,152,800	80%	210,700	15%	45,400	3%	18,600	1%	0	0%	0	0%	0	0%	8,300	1%	1,435,800
1861	822,900	65%	370,300	29%	41,100	3%	17,100	1%	0	0%	0	0%	1,000	0%	9,000	1%	1,261,400
1862	22,300	4%	399,100	75%	59,900	11%	25,400	5%	2,000	0%	1,000	0%	6,100	1%	17,300	3%	533,100
1863	56,800	8%	448,100	65%	97,100	14%	25,800	4%	33,000	5%	3,100	0%	14,500	2%	13,400	2%	691,800
1864	82,100	9%	507,600	57%	125,200	14%	45,100	5%	96,100	11%	1,000	0%	22,000	2%	17,000	2%	896,100
1862–64 average	53,700	8%	451,600	64%	94,100	13%	32,100	5%	43,700	6%	1,700	0%	14,200	2%	15,900	2%	707,000
1865	187,700	19%	440,700	46%	174,900	18%	69,200	7%	38,500	4%	2,000	0%	26,700	3%	26,700	3%	966,400
1866	512,600	38%	605,100	45%	116,100	9%	78,700	6%	5,900	0%	3,000	0%	10,800	1%	21,600	2%	1,353,800
1867	533,500	42%	502,300	39%	127,100	10%	80,700	6%	1,000	0%	4,000	0%	7,100	1%	18,100	1%	1,273,800
1868	559,000	43%	480,200	37%	125,400	10%	91,400	7%	0	0%	0	0%	0	0%	36,000	3%	1,292,000

Sources: George Holt & Co., annual cotton circulars (Liverpool Record Office, 380 COT/1/11/71); John Pender & Co., *Statistics of the Trade of the United Kingdom with Foreign Countries from 1840* (London: Simpkin, Marshall, 1869).

in particular. But the volume of cotton needed to replace the lost American supply did not exist elsewhere in the world. Due entirely to price, much of what did exist was enticed to Britain, but it was not enough. In India, the loss of raw cotton to local spinners and weavers was severe. According to Smith, "the small hand-manufactures which at that time were spread all over India were almost stopped, as they could not be carried on at the enormous prices which the starving mill-owners in Europe could offer for the raw material."[44]

Despite these readily available facts, some historians persist in painting a distorted picture. According to Jay Sexton, "alternative sources had been developed in India and Egypt since the 1840s and could sustain Britain's textile industry during the crisis in America." Howard Jones reported that "cotton continued to flow into England ... from expanded purchases in Brazil, China, Egypt, and India." And Beckert has said that "Indian, Egyptian and Brazilian cotton became a major presence on Western markets." None of these statements is technically untrue, yet all present a misleading view of the reality. As Chapter 4 will show, Britain received less than half the raw cotton it needed for the entire duration of the war. There is no truth in the contention that the lost American supply was adequately replaced. It was not.[45]

After the war, prices fell, American supplies resumed, and the world of cotton began its return to normality. Ellison reviewed what had happened in the meantime:

> The high prices caused by the "famine" brought increased supplies from the Brazils, Turkey, India, and China; but with the return of ante-war values the imports into Europe fell back almost to the level at which they stood in 1860–61. From the West Indies, Central America, South America (other than the Brazils), Africa, and the Far East (other than India, China, and Japan) the imports of 1865–6 showed an increase of ... less than one week's consumption for all Europe. ... China and Japan ceased to ship anything after Middling American fell to 15d. [6.25p] per lb.[46]

Price was the magnet, but there was a sell-by date: the end of the war. No one trusted the loyalty of the British cotton market once the magnet lost its attraction. Despite the CSA, despite the Manchester Chamber of Commerce, despite MPs such as Bazley and Smith, it is doubtful whether more than a tiny fraction of the increase in the cotton supply from other countries came as a result of their efforts. The rest was down to price. Henry Ashworth remarked that the increased Indian supply "was not the consequence of any change of policy, but of the magic effect of price." The CSA did not see it that way. "Your Committee," it declared, "cannot but attribute a very large proportion of this increased consumption of Indian cotton to the practical measures they adopted for encouraging its use."[47]

This, alas, was typical: the CSA was never slow to vaunt mythical achievements. In June 1861, it declared that "your Committee ... have reason to congratulate the subscribers upon the wisdom and sound policy which originated this Association four years ago." The civil war has started; 80 per cent of the cotton supply is in the course of drying up; the body self-appointed to deal with this prospect has failed to find an alternative to American cotton; but let us all congratulate ourselves. "What," the CSA continued, "would have been the present position ... had not this Association ... been familiarising the public mind with the present situation of affairs?" Not much different, one might think. Isaac Watts believed that "had there been a hearty, generous, and universal co-operation on the part of all ... the few years which elapsed between [the CSA's] formation and the breaking out of the American civil war might have sufficed to secure ... immunity from the sufferings and losses which ensued." This was wishful thinking on a monumental scale. Ellison was blunt in his verdict: "The ... Association ... entirely failed to accomplish the laudable object they had in view." Ellison's view may not have been shared by G. R. Haywood, his partner in the cotton brokerage Ellison & Haywood, and previously the Secretary of the CSA and a director of the ill-fated Manchester Cotton Company.[48]

However, it *was* a laudable object and much can be said in the CSA's defence. Correctly and far-sightedly, it foresaw an impending crisis for the cotton supply. Admirably and unselfishly, its members took responsibility for trying to avert the crisis when no one else was doing much to help. Failure was due to circumstances beyond the CSA's control. It was too small and too impotent to effect change on the scale it sought. It lacked the experience to develop new sources of supply itself, and the political clout to compel others to do so. Cottonopolis was too associated with laissez-faire to make a convincing plaintiff for interventionism. It must also be remembered that, while 15 per cent of the population was dependent upon the cotton trade for its livelihood, 85 per cent was not, and that this 85 per cent was doing rather well in the 1860s. As Richard Cobden observed in April 1863, "this partial breakdown in the Cotton Manufacture has been attended with less injury to the Country ... than we had expected. ... So long as food is plentiful, and the interest on money low, the nation can bear ... the derangement of any one of its manufacturing industries."[49]

A wag at the CSA's annual meeting in 1859 suggested that "there should be a treaty between governments for securing a constant and sufficient supply [of cotton] at an unvarying price. (Laughter.)"[50] That was exactly what Cottonopolis did want. It wanted several cotton exporting countries, all at a permanent readiness to raise their production to compensate for a temporary shortfall from America. This was impossible, and against the interests of the producing countries. There needed to be a long-term equilibrium between global supply and demand. Despite short-term vicissitudes, that was more or less the case at the time. America was not about to cease its cultivation. Raising an equivalent or greater production from India or from anywhere else would have inundated the world market with cotton, depressing prices and preventing a return on the investment in new cultivation – as, ironically, America was itself to prove after the war. Cottonopolis was seeking a tap it could turn on and off at its own convenience.

Table 3 Long-term share of British raw cotton imports, 1840–1900

	1840	1860	1880	1900
America	82%	80%	75%	78%
India	13%	15%	13%	2%
Brazil	2%	1%	1%	2%
Mediterranean	1%	3%	9%	18%
Others	1%	1%	1%	1%

Source: House of Commons, Parliamentary Papers, *Statistical Abstract for the United Kingdom in Each of the Last Fifteen Years* (various years).

Millions of words have been spilled on this subject. One table says everything. Table 3 shows the proportion of raw cotton imports to Britain at 20-year intervals from 1840 to 1900. That is, 60 years of upheavals, not least the American Civil War, and 60 years of change in the politics and industrialisation of the world. Nothing changed in terms of Britain's raw cotton supply except that, towards the end of the century, India developed a cotton manufacture that claimed most of its own raw material, and Egypt – which did not – replaced India as Britain's back-up supplier to America. And, by the way, the price of American raw cotton in Liverpool for most of the 1890s was below the 1.67p per lb that Manchester considered 'correct'.

So Saturday afternoon came around again in 1861, and this time it lingered. It had been foreseen, but still came as a surprise. The following four or five years were to be one long Saturday afternoon in Manchester, although not necessarily in Liverpool. Those years showed that, although the cotton market may have been global in its commerce, it had yet to become global in its understanding. In India, the increased wartime demand for its cotton was apparently attributed to the fact that "the Queen had given every one in England new clothes" on the occasion of the wedding of the Prince of Wales in 1863.[51] However, members of the CSA were no better informed about circumstances in India. Neither were many people in Britain better informed about circumstances in America. Narrow, insular perspectives were broadened slowly during the war, but British comprehension had yet to catch up with its commerce. In the Southern States of America, comprehension lagged still further behind.

CHAPTER III

A Three-Phase Supply
How the cotton trade reacted to the civil war

"The first demonstration of blockade of the Southern ports would be swept away by the English fleets of observation hovering on the Southern coasts, to protect English commerce, and especially the free flow of cotton to English and French factories," declared Colonel Chase of Florida in January 1861. In the previous month, Samuel Smith – in a rare lapse of sound judgment – wrote that "famine of the raw material so often dreaded but never yet encountered in Lancashire ... is highly improbable." The two main losers from the civil war – the Confederate States of America and the cotton trade of Great Britain – thus greeted its approach with a confident equanimity. This took a surprising length of time to evaporate. A year later, with the war in full flow, the Confederate embargo on cotton exports and the Union blockade of cotton ports both in place, and the Lancashire mills working short time, a cotton broker could still claim that "the crisis may be a trying one, and a change in the usual sources of supply may bring with it many losses, but in a short time the gap will have closed up."[1]

The war, as experienced by the cotton trade, fell into three distinct phases. The first lasted from Lincoln's election in November 1860 until the end of June 1862. The second lasted from the beginning of July 1862 until the end of August 1864. The third lasted from the beginning of September 1864 until the end of the war in April 1865 and well beyond it. All three phases were related entirely to the American Civil War and its assorted consequences and to nothing else. This – and the fact that the consequences were so severe and so disruptive – is what justifies regarding the civil war period as anomalous within both the British and the global cotton trade, demanding to be treated as a separate entity. During the period of the war and after it, a temporary cotton market existed which bore little resemblance to the relatively stable market that had preceded it or would follow it. This chapter charts the course of that temporary market in the context of an evolving political and military situation.

One could compile a running commentary, month by month, of all the influences that affected the raw cotton market during the war. This was in

Figure 3 Weekly raw cotton prices in Liverpool, 1861–1865 (Middling Orleans)

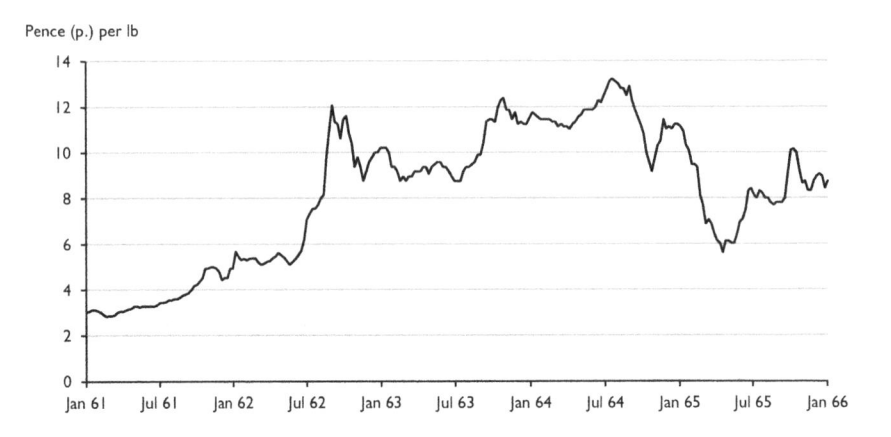

Source: Ezekiel Donnell, *The Chronological and Statistical History of Cotton* (New York: James Sutton & Co., 1872).

fact done by Maurice Williams in the monthly summaries contained in his annual circulars. Their cumulative effect is to reveal the bewildering, and often contradictory, array of information with which the cotton market had to contend. A more comprehensive overview has been provided by Nigel Hall. It is a fine attempt to make the switchback ride of those years amenable to rational comment but, as Hall himself acknowledges, this is a difficult task. Too many elements with opposite implications were simultaneously present in the market. The smallest event or rumour could have a disproportionate effect. Besides, the market was frequently not driven by reason but by sentiment, and sentiment could be capricious. Even when it was driven by reason, the judgments were often wrong. The market was permanently shrouded in the fog of war.[2]

The break-points between the first and second phases, and the second and third phases, are specific: to the week, almost to the day. The justification for them is provided by Figure 3, which charts the weekly prices of raw cotton on the Liverpool market. It can be seen that, after months of a steadily rising market, prices began to rocket at the turn of June/July 1862 and then, having reached their peak in July 1864, descended just as sharply from the turn of August/September. Yet no single, decisive event happened at either of these points to justify such a huge change in the course of prices. Market sentiment changed. In W. F. Machin's words, "the fluctuations in the price of cotton in Liverpool can be taken as a reliable barometer registering outside opinion, first of all on the chances of war and, subsequently, its probable duration."[3] But, since that opinion was often wrong, the barometer reliably registered only unreliability.

Rather than proceeding in strict chronology, this chapter will treat each of the three phases thematically, drawing out their main characteristics. These naturally changed over time, which is what created the three phases. However, there were some elements common to the period as a whole. The first was the opinion, held almost universally until late in the war, that it would prove impossible for the North to subdue the South and to re-establish the Union.[4] The second was that there was no means of knowing when the war would end.[5] The third was the belief that, when it did end, an abundance of pent-up American stocks would be sent to Britain and prices would collapse.[6] These opinions were of crucial importance to the behaviour of the cotton trade throughout the war. To them should be added a fourth influence. As the last chapter showed, the main source of British raw cotton in the war years was India. That country, together with China, which also supplied raw cotton to Britain during the war, were two of the main markets for British cotton manufactures. Shipping times between Britain and Asia were from four to six months. Consignments in either direction – raw cotton to Britain, cotton goods to Asia – would not arrive until at least four months after their despatch. At no stage of the civil war was there a certainty that hostilities would last that long. Anyone with a financial stake in either type of consignment, unless they were fully protected against a fall in its value and certain that they would receive payment, was gambling on the fact that the war would last a further four to six months.

When these four things are taken together, it can be seen that all parts of the global cotton trade needed to operate what would today be called a just-in-time strategy. The holding of stock, unless as a deliberate act of speculation, carried an unacceptable risk. It was this fact, just as much as the inflated prices, that gave the worldwide cotton market its temporary nature throughout the war.

The primary sources for this chapter are principally the circulars of the Liverpool cotton brokers and of the Neill brothers, and the pages of the *Liverpool Mercury*. These sources are valuable to the study because they were written in the moment, and the moment changed with bewildering rapidity. They represent a series of snapshots over a five-year period by a group of well-informed people who were trying to make sense of a volatile scenario, but who were often wrong. A greater perspective is offered by secondary sources, but these are generally absent for the cotton trade. However, three works in particular illuminate the course of British public opinion during the war.[7] Four others discuss the political and diplomatic relationships between Britain and both protagonists, as well as the Confederacy's attempted use of cotton as an instrument of war.[8] A further study blends public and political opinion in a single work.[9]

It is not within the scope of this book to consider the causes of the American Civil War, but no one can deny that slavery was prominent amongst them. The *Mercury* greeted election day in 1860 with the headline "Slavery Doomed", while Congressman Alfred Iverson, Georgia, proclaimed that "it is the intention of the black Republican party to use the forms of government to extinguish the system of slavery, and we do not intend to wait till we are so weak that we cannot resist." But a war about slavery was necessarily also a war about cotton. Slavery and cotton were so inextricably linked that this could not fail to be the case. There was resentment in the South that about 40 per cent of its cotton income ended up in the hands of Northern banks and merchants. As one Southerner colourfully put it, "the South [feeds] from her own bosom a vast population of merchants, shipowners, capitalists, and others, who without the claims of her progeny, drink up the life-blood of her trade." The fact that this situation resulted largely from Southerners choosing to invest most of their capital in purchasing more slaves, rather than in developing the commercial infrastructure of their states, was ignored.[10]

The emotions and perceived grievances that created the clamour for secession needed a plausible strategy for it to be successful. Cotton was again the key. The phrase 'cotton is king' was first used in the title of an 1855 book by David Christy. Thereafter, the unchallengeable power of King Cotton was proclaimed throughout the South. The belief that a lack of cotton would force Britain and France to intervene in any civil war on its behalf, despite slavery, was an inviolable principle of Southern policy-making. After the war, Jefferson Davis's widow wrote that her husband had regarded foreign recognition as an assumed fact. "Why, sir," said a fellow diner to William Howard Russell of *The Times* at Charleston in April 1861, "we have only to shut off your supply of cotton for a few weeks and we can create a revolution in Great Britain. ... No sir, we know that England must recognize us." In June 1861, the *Charleston Mercury* declared that "the cards are in our hands, and we intend to play them out to the bankruptcy of every cotton factory in Great Britain and France, or the acknowledgment of our independence." Some Northerners shared that opinion. In June 1861, Alexander Schultz, Henry Neill's future father-in-law, bet William Seward that "[England] will knock every blockading craft at Charleston into kingdom come if the blockade is continued one hour beyond December next."[11]

Scott Marler has referred to the King Cotton strategy as "a sort of faith-based foreign policy". However, the faith did have a grounding in reality. The conviction of the South in the potency of its cotton was matched by a parallel conviction in Britain. Henry Ashworth told a meeting of the Society of Arts in 1858 that "the entire failure of a cotton crop, should it ever occur, would utterly destroy, and perhaps for ever, all the manufacturing prosperity we possess." What Southerners failed to notice was that pronouncements of this nature invariably came from British cotton manufacturers, and from the politicians connected to them, who were just as one-eyed about cotton as the Southerners were themselves. In 1861, W. H. Russell observed that "Liverpool and Manchester have obscured all Great Britain to the Southern eye." As a result, the South miscalculated. In Jay Sexton's words, "the singular economy of the Confederacy collapsed under the weight of its unexported cotton", whereas Britain's more diverse economy was able to cope with the consequences.[12]

The South therefore embarked on secession on the assumption that British support was a foregone conclusion. Meanwhile, the British cotton trade suffered from its own delusions: that there would be no war or that, if there was one, it would not last long. In the words of John Watts:

> Even the fall of Fort Sumpter [sic], great as was the result in America, caused very little emotion on this side of the Atlantic, for nobody believed in the possibility of war in North America. It seemed to be the universal opinion that either some agreement to continue the union would be arrived at, or that the Southern States would be allowed peacefully to set up a government of their own.[13]

As the Liverpool satirical magazine, the *Porcupine*, put it a few months later, "most Liverpool men appear to be under the impression that neither North nor South have the slightest right to go to war, because their going to war may possibly inconvenience Lancashire."[14] This was a creeping crisis. What began as unthinkable first became possible, then likely, and finally certain. So the first phase began.

The prevailing belief in the early months of the first phase (November 1860 to June 1862) was that any war would be short-lived and would have a minimal effect on trade, whoever won it. As late as January 1862, leading spinners such as Henry Ashworth, Hugh Mason and John Platt did not believe that there would be a crisis of supply. The general belief was that the North would be compelled to acquiesce in the independence of the South. *The Economist* declared that: "The secession is an accomplished, irrevocable, fact. ... Even if the North were sure of an easy and complete victory – short, of course, of actual subjugation of the South (which no one dreams of) – the war ... would still be ... an objectless and unprofitable folly." Smith wrote that, during March and April 1861, "the political situation of America still exerted little influence on the [raw cotton] market, the general opinion being that the Secession of the Southern States would be peaceably effected." In their annual circulars at the end of 1861, cotton brokers placed more emphasis

Figure 4 Collapse of cotton imports from America, 1861
(4-week moving lb totals; 1861 as percentage of 1860)

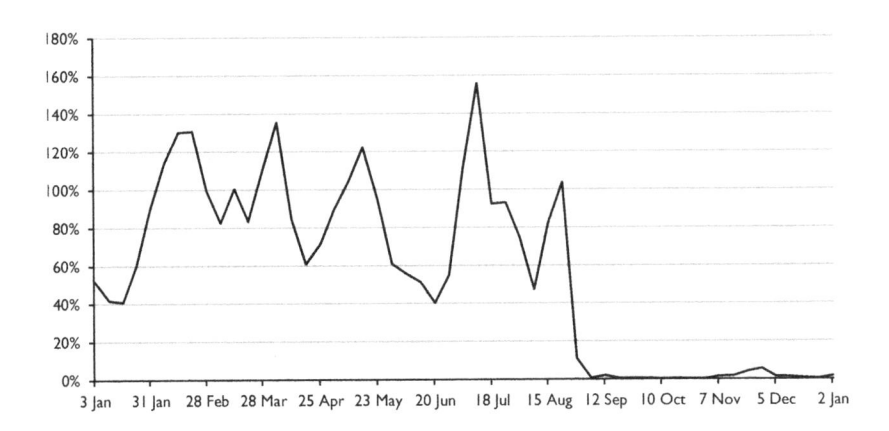

Source: Ezekiel Donnell, *The Chronological and Statistical History of Cotton*
(New York: James Sutton & Co., 1872).

on the alleged impossibility of the task the North had set itself than on the challenges faced by the South. Besides, the South needed only not to lose the war; the North needed to win it. "Hardly any foresaw that the greatest crisis in the cotton trade was at hand," wrote Smith later. "I remember as though it were yesterday the confident predictions that the war would be over in ninety days!" As a result, the trade was not unduly worried: cotton stocks would last longer than ninety days.[15]

The outbreak of hostilities in April 1861 thus made little immediate difference to the raw cotton market. American shipments through to the end of July were below the exceptionally high level of 1860, but not by very much. They then ceased, more or less overnight (Figure 4). America's share of the British raw cotton market plummeted from around 80 per cent to not much more than zero in a single month: August 1861. That share did not start to recover substantially until after the war had ended in April 1865.

Lincoln had announced the Union's blockade of Southern ports on 16 April, but it took several months to become effective. Although, by July, most of the American crop of 1860–61 had been shipped, not all of it had left the South: at least 16 million lb of cotton remained in Southern ports on 1 September 1861.[16] What caused the abrupt cessation of supply was neither the blockade nor the completed shipment of the old crop but the actions of New Orleans merchants through their concerted embargo on cotton exports. In July 1861, 130 of them wrote to the planters they represented as follows:

> The undersigned Cotton Factors* in the city of New Orleans ... recommend to their various customers and correspondents not to ship any portion of their crops of cotton to this city, or to remove it from their plantations, until the blockade is fully and entirely abandoned, of which due notice will be given.[17]

The Neill brothers, who printed this letter in their circular, attempted to warn the British trade what lay ahead:

> Strange and almost incredible as it may appear, it is nevertheless the fact that it is the deliberate intention of the American Governments – both North and South – to seal up the new cotton crop, so that not a bale of it ... shall leave the plantations during the continuance of the war. The North believes that the need of money will bring the South to terms; the South is just as firm in the faith that the need of cotton will bring the North to terms, or lead the European Governments to interfere.[18]

The embargo is sometimes referred to as if it was the policy of the Confederate Government, but it was not. Marler has demonstrated that it was the merchants of New Orleans who instigated it, followed soon after by those in Mobile, Savannah and Charleston. They acted against the wishes of Jefferson Davis's Government, which feared accusations of attempted blackmail and acknowledged the embargo only as a *fait accompli*. Next, in Marler's words, "with their deep-seated belief in King Cotton thus shaken but not yet abandoned, the merchants of New Orleans responded as do many religious groups when their devotion seems challenged by events: they took a more aggressive approach toward propagating their faith." When some of the city's merchants continued to receive cotton, a group of cotton factors persuaded the Governor of Louisiana to make the importation of cotton into New Orleans a criminal offence, while the Confederate Congress ordered the burning of thousands of bales of cotton at Southern ports.[19]

The embargo was lifted informally during 1862, by which time cotton was the only international currency the Confederacy possessed. Meanwhile, the Union had sealed the ports in the Gulf of Mexico and had captured New Orleans, although not before tons of raw cotton had been burnt on its quaysides. By that time, the North's blockade of the few Atlantic ports in the South with adequate harbours was sufficiently effective to ensure that little cotton left those ports for the duration of the war. In August 1861, the Neills again alerted the British trade to the dangers it faced:

---

* Cotton factors sold cotton on behalf of the American planters. Their role is explained in more detail in Chapter 6.

> The question ... portends ... not only individual ruin, but the national calamity of a great population being thrown out of employment without other means of existence, and yet this fearful emergency does not seem to be appreciated. ... The all but universal idea among merchants and spinners in this country ... is that the North is not in earnest in the idea of re-conquering the South. ... We beg to say, most unhesitatingly, that the sooner this idea is abandoned, the better it will be for the merchants, spinners and operatives of this country.[20]

From July 1861, the Neills were adamant that the war would last at least a year, that little American cotton would reach Britain while it lasted, and that manufacturers should move to short-time working immediately to eke out stocks and prevent a calamity. They also urged a substantial price rise to encourage supplies from other sources, especially India. In October 1861, they stated that "the North cannot give up the conflict till convinced of its utter hopelessness."[21] Writing from New York in December 1861, William Neill complained that:

> The letters from Liverpool show that very mistaken notions prevail there as to the probable receipts of cotton during the remainder of the present season. The presumption appears to be that the bulk of the crop would be shipped. Here, the opposite extreme of opinion prevails.[22]

The opposite extreme of opinion proved to be correct.

The early attitude of the British Government to the conflict was much the same as the attitude of the press and the cotton trade. Earl Russell, the Foreign Secretary, did not expect the war to last long, nor did he expect the North to win it. "The best thing now," he wrote to the British Ambassador in Washington, Lord Lyons, in January 1861, "would be that the right to secede should be acknowledged, & that there should be a separation." Twelve days later, he wrote to Lyons that "I suppose the break-up of the Union is now inevitable." Queen Victoria proclaimed Britain's neutrality on 13 May 1861: "We, being at peace with the Government of the United States, have declared our royal determination to maintain a strict and impartial neutrality in the contest between the said contending parties." There followed a long list of activities prohibited to British citizens, the more sensitive of which subsequently proved to be unenforceable at law.[23]

The Union made a calamitous start to the war as far as obtaining British sympathy was concerned. It denied that slavery had anything to do with the conflict. Many in Britain shared the sentiment of Giuseppe Garibaldi that, if the war was not about slavery, it was merely an "intestine war" over territory and sovereignty, "like any civil war in which the world at large could have little interest or sympathy". Then the North enacted the Morrill tariff, a protectionist measure that substantially raised the duties on British imports. This alarmed even Northern supporters in Britain, including the staunchly Unionist John Bright. The North had a press, especially in New York, that was vitriolically anti-British and a Secretary of State, William Seward, who was portrayed as scarcely less so. It suspended habeas corpus and introduced restrictions on civil liberties, which in Britain were evidence of a tyranny. At the same time, the Confederacy set out to obfuscate the issues. It played on Britain's attachment to free trade to claim that this, rather than slavery, was the cause for which it fought – an argument made more persuasive by the adoption of the Morrill tariff.[24] This claim was later ridiculed in a speech by Richard Cobden in November 1863:

> The Slave States were invited by the Free States [in January 1861] to say what it was they wanted, and from the beginning to the end of those 40 pages of a report of that council not one syllable was said about either the tariff or taxation. On the contrary, from the beginning to the end there was not a grievance that was alleged by the South which was not altogether connected with the maintenance of slavery.[25]

The issue of slavery, which should have been the North's trump card in a Britain that was almost unanimously abolitionist and in thrall to Harriet Beecher Stowe's account of slavery in *Uncle Tom's Cabin*, did not necessarily act in the North's favour. Apart from the fact that Lincoln's Government denied any intent to end slavery, it was believed by many, including Northern supporters such as John Stuart Mill, that an independent South would soon be obliged to emancipate its own slaves. Then, in November 1861, a Federal naval captain, acting on his own initiative, intercepted the British mail packet SS *Trent* and removed two Confederate diplomats. Feverish support for this action in America, and outraged opposition to it in Britain, nearly led to war with the Union.[26]

Much though Britain's lack of sympathy infuriated the North, it was the South that needed Britain's outright support, while the North – although it also wanted it – needed only Britain's abstention. Palmerston put it perfectly when he said that the two sides "sue us like rivals who sue a fair damsel – each party wanting us to take up her cause, and each feeling some little stinging resentment on account of that neutrality which they both of them in some degree characterise as unfriendliness".[27] A perspective on America's understanding of British attitudes was provided by an English merchant who toured the Confederate States in 1862. He summarised the Southern view of Britain's attitude to the conflict:

> We believe the *people* of England is with us; but your aristocracy, which hates a democracy; your capitalists, who hold United States and Northern Stocks; your Manchester men, who are making money out of their stocks of manufactured and raw cotton; your Sheffield men, who are selling steel to the Northern Government; your Birmingham men, who are selling rifles, swords, and bayonets; your Huddersfield, Leeds, &c. men, who are selling shoddy clothes; and your shipowners, into whose hands our Alabamas, &c. are throwing all the carrying-trade of the world – all these classes, who are all-powerful in England, are against us.[28]

Ironically, this was largely the Northern view of British attitudes too. In Britain, both sides had their partisans, but many did not like either side very much.

In October 1861, the cotton trade began to feel the first effects of the war, when production was cut by a third. As will be explored in Chapter 4, this was not the result of pre-war over-production, but neither was it the result of a shortage of cotton: stocks were still plentiful. Instead, it was the result of a paralysis of demand, caused by uncertainty. The war was still not expected to last much longer. As late as March 1862, Earl Russell was "expressing an expectation that the civil war may be concluded within three months". According to the Neill brothers, this sentiment was universal: "Differing on every point, the partizans of both sides in the contest agreed … that the war would be speedily over. Thirty to sixty days were generally assigned for its termination, and the longest term granted was ninety days."[29] In February 1862, the Neills had again disputed this viewpoint in a circular reprinted at length in *The Times*:

> It is pleasant to take a hopeful view – to believe that by foreign intervention, by a relaxation of the blockade, by a great victory on one side or the other, by financial pressure, or in some unforeseen way, peace may be restored and trade resume its former conditions. But what are the consequences of all this talk? They are simply a rapid acceleration of the ruin of the country's greatest manufacturing interest, and a prolongation of the suffering of the operatives. … As to the duration of the war … we have never had but one opinion – viz., that … the war would be a protracted one, and only be concluded when one or other of the combatants should be utterly exhausted. To determine when that point will be reached is the sole problem.[30]

The Times, in a sarcastic and patronising commentary on the Neills' circular, made clear its opinion that the North could not and would not sustain the war.[31]

It was not surprising, therefore, that during this first phase, the cotton trade was close to being petrified: manufacturers, wholesalers and the export trade waited for the war to end, for normal service to be resumed. Movement in any direction was fraught with danger, so all sectors of the global trade sold from stock. By late 1862, the world's pipeline of cotton goods was close to being drained. The supplies of American raw cotton in Liverpool had been used up. The stocks of both yarn and finished cotton goods, in Lancashire and abroad, were fast reducing. Most that had been produced at the old, pre-war price had been disposed of, although it took into the following year for this process to be completed.[32]

It is no coincidence that these circumstances should prompt the first huge spike in prices and usher in the second phase of the war (July 1862 to August 1864). Between June and October 1862 the price of raw cotton doubled. By June, it had become generally believed that "a very incorrect opinion had been entertained respecting the civil war in America", and that "too high an estimate had been formed of the ability of India to increase her supply of Cotton."[33] At last convinced of the impending scarcity, the cotton trade overreacted. Prices soared; speculation in the raw cotton market became rampant. In mid-July 1862, the Neills reported that "during the past few weeks the awakening of the cotton trade to a due sense, perhaps a somewhat exaggerated sense, of the situation has been sudden and extraordinary."[34] The realisation set in that the crisis would be protracted and that, while it lasted, a different trade would need to be constructed. Commentators did not see this clearly at the time. They related what they saw to what they were familiar with, but that relationship had been broken. As a result, their judgments – and sometimes those of later historians – often made little sense.

As the perceptions of the cotton trade changed, so there was a change in the world of politics. In both cases, the shift was due to a realisation that the war would not end soon. In the cotton trade, this led to an escalation in prices. In the British Government, it led to serious contemplation of an intervention in the war. This could have come in a variety of forms: direct military action through the breaking of the Union blockade by the Royal Navy, recognition of the Confederacy as an independent nation, an offer to mediate in the conflict or, without mediation, the proposal of an armistice. Although only the first of these options implied military action, any of the others might have led to war with the North. Lincoln's Government maintained that there was no war in America, merely an internal rebellion which needed to be suppressed. In that case, an offer of mediation was tantamount to recognition of the South and could be taken as an act of aggression towards the North.

Numerous historians have pored over the entrails of what individual members of the British Government thought about the merits of intervention.

The same minister could have contradictory opinions at different times, or even at the same time. Selective quotations can be used to advance almost any case. Yet the unassailable fact is that the Government did not intervene. Henry Adams, the son of the United States Minister to Britain, was told by Lord Granville that only three ministers certainly favoured recognition of the Confederacy. The problem was that the supposed three were the most powerful: Palmerston, the Prime Minister; Russell, the Foreign Secretary; Gladstone, the Chancellor of the Exchequer. If that had been true, between them they could probably have forced recognition through the Cabinet. It is perhaps this perception that led Howard Jones to assert that, in June 1862, "recognition of the Confederacy seemed a certainty." But little in his own evidence, and nothing in that of Duncan Campbell, who has also researched the matter extensively, could justify such an unqualified claim.[35]

It is true that Gladstone and Russell both held pro-Southern views. Gladstone expressed his publicly in his famous Newcastle speech of late 1862. He had already said that "the Northern States ... have undertaken a military enterprise of enormous difficulty. ... It is all but impossible that [their] military object should be effected." In the second half of 1862, both men supported intervention. This would have taken the form of an offer of mediation, based on an acknowledgment of the de facto existence of Southern independence. Russell was motivated by humanitarian concern rather than by a desire for Britain to become embroiled in the conflict. As Campbell has pointed out, both in the scale of its carnage and in the suppression of civil liberties, this war was more a precursor of the wars of the twentieth century, especially the First World War, than an exemplar of wars from the preceding decades. It is not surprising that a Liberal Foreign Secretary of the most powerful nation on earth should wish to intervene to end the bloodshed. He had believed that the war would be over in a few months. By mid-1862, it had continued for a full year, with no end in sight. There was surely a moral imperative to help bring it to an end.[36]

But Russell and Gladstone could not convince Palmerston, and they could not convince the Cabinet. The true feelings of Palmerston, as so often, were opaque. In September 1862, he wrote to Russell supporting recognition of the Confederacy as an independent nation. However, whenever a decision actually needed to be taken, he opposed it. Campbell and Max Beloff have both concluded that Palmerston was principally responsible for the decision not to intervene.[37]

It cannot be maintained that "recognition of the Confederacy seemed a certainty." At no critical time was it a course supported by the Prime Minister or by more than two of the Cabinet. Intervention was never a likely option, and British neutrality – as Britain understood it, which was not how either side in America understood it – was not in doubt either. Had Britain wanted to intervene, it had three specific excuses – the *Trent* affair, the inefficacy of the blockade, and the harassment of British ships at Nassau – and several more general ones for doing so. One cannot, therefore, sustain Karl Marx's case that only the pressure of the working class prevented the Government from going to war on behalf of the Confederacy.[38] Even if that pressure had existed in any substantial form, which it did not, it would merely have been urging what was already Government policy. It is surely significant that the Conservative Opposition did not dissent from the Government's approach or attempt in any way to undermine it.

Public opinion of the conflict was similarly obscure and multifaceted and has proved equally amenable to the prejudices of historians who have tried to unravel it. The historiography of the traditional interpretation of British opinion is ably summarised in the introduction to Campbell's study.[39] This tradition presents the Establishment and much of the middle class as almost uniformly pro-South, and the working class as almost uniformly pro-North. In both cases, these opinions were held to derive from class interests. Alternative opinions had existed for a long time but were largely ignored until the publication of Mary Ellison's book, *Support for Secession*, in 1973. Ellison argued that, far from supporting the Union, majority support in Lancashire was for the Confederacy, accentuated in the towns that suffered most from the famine. While she is now felt to have overstated her case and to have failed to establish her main conclusion, she cast sufficient doubt on the traditional view, epitomised by Philip Foner, to make any dogmatic return to it unsustainable. At the heart of her argument is the claim that the self-interest of the cotton operatives determined their reaction to the war. Yet nowhere does she examine what that self-interest was, simply assuming that it must have led to support for the South. She asserts that "to the impoverished spinning towns recognition [of the Confederacy] was a far more certain path to peace and cotton." Yet, as *The Economist* pointed out, "mere recognition would ... not shorten hostilities; it would get us no cotton; it would not relieve our manufacturing districts."[40] This was self-evidently true. The real self-interest of the cotton operatives lay in a speedy end to the war and the resumption of cotton imports from America. From that point of view, it was immaterial which side won.

While Mary Ellison took an axe to the traditional view of working-class opinion of the war, Campbell has taken an axe to the traditional view of Establishment opinion. Both axes had lain unsharpened in the woodshed for a long time and were in need of a grinding, but Campbell's conclusions are as problematic as Ellison's, especially in relation to the aristocracy. He attempts to find evidence of Southern sympathy in the printed words and speeches of aristocrats and finds almost none. From this he concludes that there can have been none, or very little. But, although he draws a number of important distinctions elsewhere, Campbell does not draw a distinction between what is said in public and what is thought in private. Private thoughts never present themselves as historical evidence, so no one can prove that, in this case, they were at odds with what was said in public, but there is enough circumstantial evidence to throw doubt on the matter.

The most convincing recent study of the issue is *Divided Hearts* by R. J. M. Blackett. The problem faced by historians of the subject is how to answer a quantitative question – how many people supported each side, both nationally and within sub-groups? – when there are no quantitative data available. Blackett manages to avoid this pitfall and to eschew dogmatic conclusions. The main points he establishes, none of which is easy to refute, are that the British public was well informed about the war and animated by it; that there was a deluge of meetings and pamphlets and petitions, few of them spontaneous, but organised by partisans of the two sides; that allegiances did not always follow class or religious ties, but that they mostly did; that the press was not as strongly anti-Union as has been portrayed; and that, while considerable support existed for both sides, the North enjoyed most of it (an opinion shared by Earl Russell), even in Lancashire, although opinion was more divided there. With the benefit of Blackett's work, there may now be a more nuanced understanding of the issues, and more of a consensus.[41]

There are, amidst the contradictions, two things that can be said with reasonable certainty about public opinion. The first is that Lincoln's Emancipation Proclamation, announced on 22 September 1862 and effective from the beginning of the following year, had a significant effect in Britain. The ending of slavery had now become a war aim. The favourable reaction to it was not unanimous: sections of the press saw it as a cynical manoeuvre and one that would have the effect, and perhaps had the intention, of fomenting a servile insurrection. The *Mercury* initially described the Proclamation as "a formal invitation of the Federal Government to the negroes to rise against their masters and their families. ... It is not an act of mercy and humanity to the negroes, but an act of hatred and vengeance against their masters." The next day it changed its mind: "This is ... a gain to humanity and freedom. ... This horrible war will not have been an unmixed evil. ... It is to be hoped that this tardy, hesitating, and imperfect act of homage to human rights may survive the political exigencies which have dictated it."[42]

In the end, the Proclamation did tilt public opinion decisively towards the North. It also cemented the second point. Few people in Britain, apart from a handful of pro-Southern zealots, could ever convince themselves that intervention in the war, whatever form it took, was in the national interest, or that there was any practical alternative to neutrality. After the Proclamation, intervention ceased to be a viable option for the Government, if it ever had been one. The *Mercury*'s correspondent on the Liverpool Exchange was not wrong in saying, in late 1862, that "England never will intervene, even if the war lasts for thirty years."[43]

But this view was not universal at the time, and there was no shortage of press rumours that made intervention seem credible.[44] Maurice Williams wanted to know:

> How is it possible, with the periodical panics that prevail ... that Merchants will undertake the serious responsibility of shipping Cotton from India, which entails a six months' operation, if at any moment, by an act of intervention on the part of our Government, their property may be depreciated fifty per cent. or more in value?[45]

Fellow broker Edmund Jardine concurred: "How was it to be expected that the merchant or planter would launch into extensive operations when the fickle action of those in power might suddenly cause him to suffer most serious loss?" Other brokers were beginning to appreciate that India and other countries were not, after all, going to come to the trade's rescue. Cruttenden & Oulton grumbled that "it is a matter of surprise to find so trifling an increase in the quantity received from other sources, to make up for the large deficiency from the United States." Kearsley & Cunningham bemoaned the fact that "from all new sources not enough Cotton has, we think, reached England in two years for one week's full consumption."[46]

The early months of phase two were therefore a time of profound change and disturbance. The British Government contemplated intervention. The American Government proclaimed emancipation. In the raw cotton market, the supply was pitiful, prices soared and there was an orgy of speculation. In cotton manufacturing, the situation for both mill-workers and their employers went from bad to worse. After short-time working began in October 1861, production continued to decline through to the end of 1862. The trough of the famine was in the winter of 1862–63. The numbers out of work (247,230) and the numbers claiming relief (485,434) both peaked in December 1862. By then, a quarter of Lancashire's inhabitants were receiving public assistance. Thereafter, matters improved slightly, but slowly. Liverpool raised a fund to help mitigate the distress. At a meeting called to discuss its distribution in August 1862, William Rathbone Sr said that Liverpool "had now an opportunity of showing to their manufacturing friends that they felt as members of one body ... and that there was no distinction ... between the Manchester men and the Liverpool men". His son was not having any of that: he did not trust Manchester to distribute funds properly and proposed that they should be handled by a small committee of Liverpool men.[47]

The second phase of the war (from the beginning of July 1862 to the end of August 1864) was characterised by low volumes, substantial price rises, great volatility and rampant speculation. Some hoped that – after the fall of New Orleans in April 1862, and then of Vicksburg in July 1863 – the Union's control of the Mississippi would enable cotton to flow to New Orleans and find its way to Britain. The *Mercury* was confident that millions of bales of cotton were in the vicinity of New Orleans. This illusion was reminiscent of those entertained about Indian cotton. A year earlier, the Neill brothers had noted that the owners and crews of most of the Mississippi cotton boats had been conscripted and the entire rail network given over to the war. Now, a broker reported that "planters or soldiers would destroy their crops rather than let them fall into the hands of the Northern army."[48]

Having tried and failed to use its possession of abundant cotton to entice British recognition, the Confederate Government now perversely tried to entice it by having nil cotton. Planters were directed not to sow cotton and, if necessary, to burn it. Owsley estimated that the Confederacy had destroyed over 1 billion lb of cotton by 1865, although that figure can have been little more than a guess. From start to finish of the war, the absence of American cotton from Britain was due as much to actions of the Confederacy as of the Union. Not that the North was disposed to start breaking its own blockade either. Britain's mills might have been starved of cotton, but so were the mills of New England. Where the Union was able to seize cotton, various means – many of them fraudulent – were used to transport it northwards.[49]

The year 1863 was when the financial consequences of the cotton scarcity began to be felt beyond the confines of the cotton market and to affect the money market. At the end of 1863, the Neill brothers warned what was likely to happen:

> Prices are now higher than justified by circumstances, and higher than can be maintained throughout the coming year. ... Nothing but a considerable abatement of the present speculative mania in cotton ... can prevent a financial crisis occurring sometime during the year. ... If speculators persist in the determination to pay £90,000,000 for a supply which ... they could as readily obtain for £60,000,000 or £70,000,000 except for over competition among themselves, they will be stopped short some day for want of money, and the speculative fabric they have erected will topple down on their heads.[50]

The *Mercury* thought that the Neills' estimate was absurdly high, but in the event the 1864 supply cost almost exactly £90 million.[51]

In retrospect, it can be seen that this middle phase of the war was building to a crescendo of recklessness in terms of speculation within the cotton trade and more widely in the economy. The fabulous prices paid for Indian cotton led to a depletion of Britain's gold reserves. At the end of 1864, the brokers

Robson & Eskrigge wrote that "in stocks of all descriptions, particularly in the shares of the new Joint Stock Companies ... enormous speculation was carried on, and just that blind confidence and security prevailed which nearly always herald a commercial crash." In mid-August 1864, the *Mercury* unwisely declared that "it is now generally assumed that monetary affairs will from this time gradually grow better." In September, the bubble burst.[52]

Many brokers blamed the crash on articles in *The Times* claiming that peace talks were about to commence in America and that the Democrats would choose a peace candidate for the forthcoming Presidential election. Both assertions turned out to be untrue. The articles may perhaps have lit the touchpaper but if they had never appeared there was no shortage of other tapers to do so. Speculation had caused the price of cotton to reach an unsustainable peak in July – nearly five times higher than its 1860 average. The bank rate rose to 9 per cent in September. Port arrivals of cotton in the first three weeks of September were more than double the weekly average for the year as a whole, creating the illusion of a sufficiency of cotton. All these ingredients, according to Maurice Williams, "culminated in a complete panic. This at once caused an entire stagnation in the trade of the manufacturing districts. ... The consequence was the greatest and the most rapid decline in the value of Cotton that ever took place in the previous history of the trade." Robson & Eskrigge reported that "business in Manchester was almost suspended, and a general feeling of alarm and insecurity took possession of the public mind."[53]

Thus began the third phase in September 1864. It ended whenever one conceives that the market returned to normality, which was not before 1867 at the earliest. It would be more realistic to say that it was in 1876: the first time since the war that the pre-war volume could be obtained at the pre-war price.

According to broker Paul Hemelryk, "failures came thick and fast in November, 1864. I remember one of my friends coming one morning down to his office and finding on his desk thirteen telegrams from Trieste, everyone of them announcing a separate failure."[54] Prices which, with a few corrections, had risen constantly through the war, began to oscillate violently. Looking at the 16 four-week periods from September 1864 to November 1865, comparing each period with its predecessor, average cotton prices rose by 10 per cent or more in three periods, and fell by 10 per cent or more in five of them. In both cases, it was sometimes much more than 10 per cent. No one who bought or sold raw cotton knew where they stood from one day to the next.

The overriding issue was the duration of the war and what would happen after it. Every military success and every reverse, every apparently informed commentary on the ability of each side to prolong and finance the war, fed into that calculation and constantly changed the balance of probabilities. The war's closing stages were not anticipated until the event arrived. At the end of

December 1864, Smith wrote that "at no time since the American war broke out did the hope of an early settlement appear fainter." At the beginning of February 1865, Henry Ashworth said that the duration of the strife seemed as interminable as ever. On 1 April 1865, the Neill brothers wrote that "the balance of probability appears largely in favour of such a protraction of the struggle as President Lincoln ... evidently anticipates." Eight days later, the war was over. In the preceding four years, so many decisive military campaigns had failed to prove decisive that, when truly decisive events did occur, they were not perceived as such. Attitudes in the closing months of the war mirrored those in the opening months: the war that was never going to begin was now never going to end.[55]

Through all those years, but especially in late 1862, there was the question of whether Britain would intervene in the conflict, either to recognise the Confederacy or to break the blockade, and whether as a deliberate policy or as the reaction to an unforeseeable event such as the *Trent* affair. This was complicated by the issue of whether France would intervene, unilaterally or as part of a joint Anglo-French initiative. At one time there were fears that Britain would be embroiled in a European war over Schleswig-Holstein; then those fears receded. All these uncertainties contributed to the confusion in the cotton market.

Then there were the questions over cotton imports: who, if anyone, would fill the void left by America and at what prices; wildly fluctuating assessments of the size of the Indian crop and its availability; debate as to what other cotton in the world might arrive in Britain. With all the supply issues, there was the question of the day-to-day effect on stocks and prices. In addition, the explosion in price and the degree of speculation had put strains on the financing of the trade. From 1861 to 1867, the Bank of England discount rate see-sawed between 2 per cent and 10 per cent.[56] On some occasions, it changed three or four times in the same month. It was not unusual for several events to hit the market at the same time, pointing in opposite directions. For four years and more, Britain's largest industry was the victim of an almost unimaginable instability. Even with hindsight, the period of the civil war is difficult to read; at the time, peering forward from one day to the next, it must have seemed illegible.

At the end of 1864, the brokers Cunningham & Hinshaw observed that the stock pipeline that had finally been emptied by early 1863 still showed no signs of being refilled, despite some increase in the volume of raw cotton available. Nor would it be refilled until prices and volumes attained a stable long-term level:

> At prices abnormally high the Market must necessarily be expected to be very sensitive. ... The rates now ruling are already too high and

risky to allow a trade at all in excess of the *bona-fide* requirements of the World to be carried on. Manufacturers will not produce Goods or Yarns at these high rates to stock them, nor yet to consign them for sale to foreign markets; neither will Merchants be disposed to come under unduly extensive or long protracted engagements.[57]

The temporary cotton market that had emerged in 1861, and which lasted well beyond the end of the war, was characterised not just by low volumes, the minimum stock cover and high prices, but also by an entrenched uncertainty. Long-term judgments were impossible to make with confidence. Cotton goods were produced, and they were sold, but no one was willing to risk replenishing the pipeline of stock, dissipated in the first months of the war. It remained a provisional market.

In the early stages of the war, almost the sole concern of the cotton trade was when it would end. As the war progressed, as the likelihood receded that slavery would survive it intact, or at all, and as the devastation caused by the war to the agricultural economy of the South was appreciated, it became clear that the close of the war would be the start of a process, not the end of one, and that its eventual outcome was as uncertain as the outcome of the war had been. No one knew whether or when large and regular supplies of American cotton might resume. No one knew whether cotton produced by free labour would be as cheap as cotton produced by slaves, or even whether sufficient free labour would be found in America to plant and harvest it. No one knew at what price American cotton would become available once the Southern economy had stabilised. No one knew what quantity of cotton might regularly be required from other countries to replace an American shortfall. No one knew what price would be required to attract that quantity on a long-term basis, and the experience during the war had been far from encouraging.

In the decades before the war, cotton goods had been produced in high volume at low prices. Cotton had become the pre-eminent fabric to clothe the expanding world population. It was now uncertain whether it could regain this former role, or whether it would become, if not a luxury fabric, then a substantially more expensive one. The war had given an indication of the price elasticity in the demand for cotton goods – previously unknowable – and it had turned out to be greater than might have been expected.[58] But unless prices could return to something close to their pre-war level, it was possible that cotton goods would permanently become a lower-volume market. This in turn made it uncertain whether the vast mill capacity in Lancashire, which had continued to grow despite the war, would now be filled or could be made profitable. Although none of these fears was in fact realised, they cannot be retrospectively dismissed.

The apprehensions of the trade, towards the end of the war and after it, were justified and they coloured its behaviour. When the dust settled, it became possible to see exactly what had been lost.

CHAPTER IV

Unfathomed Depths; Uncharted Mountains
Why the cotton famine was not caused by pre-war over-production

This chapter will show that the British cotton trade lost 54 per cent of its pre-war supply in the peak period of scarcity from 1862 to 1864, and 37 per cent over the period from 1862 to 1867. If lost market growth is taken into account, the figures are 64 per cent and 53 per cent respectively. Yet, to read the comments of most historians, this deficit was a mirage. They have claimed that the drastically reduced production of cotton goods in the war years was due mainly to their over-production before the war.

The historiography of this verdict can be traced back over time like accreted layers of silt upon a riverbed. Each succeeding historian seems to have assumed that some previous historian must have researched the claim when it would appear that – in Britain at least – not one of them has done so. There is no bedrock beneath the silt. References to this alleged over-production have been found in the works of no fewer than 16 historians over a period of a century and a half, and there must be many more besides.[1] This is an astonishing citation chain, especially since it lacks any credible foundation. The gist of the claim is that British manufacturers produced vastly too many cotton goods in 1859, 1860 and most of 1861, which they forced onto world markets, creating a glut of unsold goods, and that it was this surplus that forced the mill-owners to introduce short-time working in October 1861, which then developed into mass unemployment and the cotton famine.

This perspective has been described as 'revisionist', but it is not: it has been the mainstream view since it was first advanced in 1864. It has been argued most notably by Eugene Brady, who declared that "the so-called Cotton Famine was not predominantly due to a shortage of the raw cotton input, but was in large measure the result of an excess supply of cotton yarn and textiles", and by Douglas Farnie, the doyen of British cotton historians, who claimed that "there was no real shortage of cotton in Lancashire even during 1862."[2] But if there is one source that is responsible for this viewpoint taking root in historical literature it is Arthur Arnold's original book on *The Cotton Famine*, written in the winter of 1863–64. Arnold did not originate the claim, but he gave it a prominence it had not previously enjoyed. This was the heart of his argument:

> During the past two years [mid-1859 to mid-1861], the excess of production over consumption amounted to at least 300,000,000 lb. weight of manufactured goods. ... With this surplus stock in the hands of the trade, it cannot be a matter of surprise that manufacturers should have become anxious to work their mills "short time". ... They had in hand a stock of goods sufficient for the consumption of two-thirds of a year, therefore a rise in the price of the raw material and the partial closing of their establishments, with a curtailment of their working expenses, was obviously to their advantage.[3]

When Arnold asserted this figure of 300 million lb, he produced no evidence to justify a statement that has reverberated for a century and a half. He merely said that it had been 'estimated'. There is a strong indication, however, that the original source for the figure, and certainly the earliest so far discovered, was none other than Thomas Ellison, a fact hitherto unknown. In 1863, Ellison started his own brokerage firm of Ellison & Haywood. In their first annual circular, for the year 1863 and dated 19 January 1864, Ellison wrote that: "The aggregate *surplus* production of the years 1859–61 was at least 300,000,000 lbs. This reduced to Cotton would amount to 337,000,000 lbs, and represent 842,000 bales of 400 lbs each." In his book, to which the preface was dated six months later, Arnold wrote: "The excess of production over consumption amounted to at least 300,000,000 lb. weight of manufactured goods; which, in the raw material, would be equal to 842,000 bales of 400 lb. each." Ellison is not referenced in Arnold's work, but both the timing and the wording suggest that he was the direct source of Arnold's claim.[4]

Ellison did not justify the claim either. His circulars, and later his book, were festooned with meticulously compiled statistics, the accuracy of which there is no general reason to doubt. The figure of 300 million lb is mentioned casually in the text. It is placed next to a table which shows that, comparing the three years 1859–61 with the three years 1862–64 – itself a strange comparison, since Ellison was writing at the end of 1863 – the production of cotton yarn fell by 50 per cent. The relevance of the table to the statement is not explained. As will be shown, Ellison's own stock figures contradict his claim of an "aggregate *surplus* production" for 1859–61 of at least 300 million lb. And his own figures also contradict his allegation that, before the war, there was "a serious diminution in the profits of manufacturers". They show that the profits of British cotton manufacturers were 33 per cent higher between 1859 and 1861 than in the previous three-year period.[5]

Thomas Ellison:
cotton broker and historian
(LRO 380 COT/1/14/1, reproduced by permission of the International Cotton Association)

Ellison surely cannot have been suggesting that the true level of demand for cotton goods was only half that at which the trade had been producing for years: that would have been absurd. A more probable explanation, in fact the only plausible explanation, is that Ellison was reacting to the immediate present alone. At the end of 1863, when he was writing, the price of finished cotton goods had already more than doubled since the outbreak of war. This inflated price had drastically reduced the demand, and both that fact and the related scarcity of raw cotton had reduced the size of the market and the scale of production. Ellison was judging a normal period of past production in the light of an abnormal period of present sales. Measured solely by the market conditions when he was writing, too much had indeed been produced in the immediate pre-war years. A stock of finished goods that was not worthy of mention at the end of 1860 had become astronomical at the end of 1861. The stock had changed very little; circumstances had changed.

There is an urgent need for a revision of the so-called revisionism and there is no lack of detailed and reliable statistics to enable it. This chapter quantifies the supply of raw cotton to Britain during the war, Britain's manufacture of cotton goods, and its stocks of raw cotton and cotton goods, placed in the context of the years immediately before and afterwards. Weekly data have been taken from Ezekiel Donnell's verbatim reports of weekly cotton imports, sales, stocks and prices, and annual data from the compilations of George Holt and Thomas Ellison. Additional information has been taken from the annual cotton circulars of Ellison & Haywood for 1864, 1865 and 1866, and, for source of imports by country, from John Pender's handbook.[6] To ensure internal consistency, some raw statistics have been amended. None of the amendments is significant or contentious or affects the conclusions to be drawn from the data. Unless referenced separately, all data in this chapter are taken from these sources. More detail on the methodology is given in the Appendix.

* * *

In 1866, the year after the civil war ended, Britain imported 11 per cent more bales of cotton than it had in 1860, the year before it started. And 1860 had itself been a record year for imports. Yet appearances are deceptive. This simple statistic ignores three separate elements, all of which conspired to reduce the raw cotton available. Instead of the 1866 supply being 11 per cent higher than in 1860, it was 23 per cent lower. With a reasonable allowance made for lost market growth, this represented a mere 60 per cent of the market requirement. The years between were worse still by far. The three elements are unit of measurement, re-exports of raw cotton and wastage during manufacturing.

At the time, raw cotton was usually measured in bales. However, bales are a meaningless unit of measurement, since the weight of a bale differed from one producing country to another, and from one year to another. During the period under study, the weight of a bale varied from 160 lb (a Brazilian bale in 1865) to 500 lb (an Egyptian bale in 1864). A pre-war American bale weighed about 445 lb and an Indian bale, which was itself the average of three production sources on the sub-continent, about 370 lb. Through the war, the average bale weight declined by 18 per cent as heavier American bales were replaced by lighter Indian bales. Such an elementary fact should not have been overlooked. Yet Harnetty gave British consumption figures only in bales for the period 1855–72, and Farnie and Hall discussed changes to stock levels only in bales. Throughout his account of the civil war years, the Cotton Association's own historian based his analysis entirely on bales, resulting in some wildly inaccurate statements.[7]

The second element is the issue of re-exports. British imports of raw cotton are another misleading statistic. Cotton brought into British ports serviced not only British mills, but many of the mills of northern Europe. Much raw cotton was shipped directly to European ports, but some of the requirement of continental mills was imported to Britain, traded on the Liverpool market and then re-exported. The share of British imports that were re-exported varied over time, and especially during the civil war. Re-exports had already started to grow rapidly, more rapidly than domestic consumption, before the war began. This was partially because the manufacture of cotton goods was now rising more rapidly in continental Europe than in Britain. Re-exports barely fell in weight during the war, and they rose significantly as a proportion of imports. A minor reason for this was that American spinners in the Northern States were starved of raw cotton themselves: they too were acquiring supplies from Liverpool. Britain re-exported 19.9 million lb of raw cotton to the Union in 1862 (nearly as much as it received from the South), 13.3 million lb in 1863 and 14.3 million lb in 1864 – amounting to 7 per cent of all re-exports in those three years.[8] The farcical position was reached whereby cotton grown in the Southern States could be shipped to Britain under the nose of the Northern blockade, sold in Liverpool, and shipped back across the Atlantic to a Northern port, evading the Confederate cruisers built on Merseyside.

Farnie wrote that "Liverpool exalted the interests of the re-export trade over those of secondary industry and divorced its function from that of its manufacturing hinterland. ... It supplied the potential competitors of England with the sinews of production and tended to separate the interests of Liverpool from those of Lancashire." This was true and was central to Manchester's complaint: Liverpool sold whatever it could to whoever wanted to buy it, and always had done. Brady can have had no understanding of this fact when he wrote that "exports of raw cotton from the United Kingdom over the period of the famine supports the hypothesis [of] a textile glut." They do no such thing: to Liverpool merchants and brokers, continental spinners were as much their customers as British spinners.[9]

Hall argued that, if there had been no re-exports in 1862, British spinners would have had access to 40 per cent more cotton and the worst period of the cotton famine would have been relieved.[10] However enticing this conclusion may seem, it should be resisted. It is unlikely that a ban on re-exports would have had the effect on the British market that Hall suggests. Had the re-exported volume been retained for domestic consumption, the cotton scarcity would of course have been reduced. The question is whether – if re-exports had been banned – that entire volume of cotton would, in practice, have become available for British use. An alternative conclusion is that a ban would have made no difference. Continental spinners were permanently competing with British spinners for the same raw material, war or no war. Britain had no monopoly of the supply to Europe. It had no power to compel stocks from America or India or Egypt to be shipped to Britain. Continental spinners were at liberty to buy their own supplies at source and have them shipped directly to their own countries. They were already doing so.

Before the war, continental Europe imported 65 per cent of its supply directly from the producing countries. This percentage fell during the war years. However, the fact that continental Europe was still importing an average of 26 per cent of its supply directly between 1862 and 1864, a total of about 231 million lb, shows that the European trade had the means to ship from producers other than America in quantity. Much of the increased supply from Mediterranean countries during the war was shipped directly to southern Europe. But it made sense to continental spinners not to buy all their raw cotton directly. The British abolition of the import duty in 1845 meant that it was just as cheap for them to buy in Liverpool. Every conceivable type and grade of cotton was permanently available there, which it was not elsewhere. The provision of commercial services offered benefits. So they chose freely to buy a large proportion of their supplies in Liverpool.[11]

One must consider what would have happened had a ban on British re-exports been in place. (This may have been a hypothetical possibility in any case. *The Economist* maintained that a ban would be in violation of treaty engagements and would require an Act of Parliament.[12]) The need of the continental spinners for raw cotton was on a par with that of the British spinners. Their purchases in Liverpool prove that they were willing to offer at least as high a price. Faced with a re-export ban, the likelihood must be that they would have bought all their supplies from the producing countries, not just some of them. So the effect of a ban would surely have been to reduce the cotton supply that came to Britain, because the re-export component of that supply would have been diverted directly to continental Europe. No additional cotton would have become available to Britain. It is hard to see that much difference would have been made to the cotton famine either way.

The next step in quantifying the amount of raw cotton actually used by spinners each year is to allow for stock movement, both in Liverpool and at the mills. The stock of raw cotton in Liverpool warehouses was counted physically at the end of each year. However, although figures for mill stocks were also published annually, they are fictitious, having the undisclosed purpose of concealing the discrepancies that inevitably arose during each year between one verified stock count and the next. (The practice is explained in more detail in the Appendix.) This information therefore needs to be ignored, which means assuming that mill stocks did not change from one year end to the next, and that all the cotton purchased by spinners in a given year was spun in that year. In practice, this would not have been the case. The pattern of weekly purchases reveals considerable variations, meaning that raw cotton stocks held at mills could change dramatically from month to month and from week to week. The cumulative effect of these stock variations over several years would have been negligible, but the figures for the actual cotton spun in any one year include an unknown margin of error. It has been said that spinners held average stocks of about three weeks at their mills.[13] If this claim was based on the mill stock statistics, which indeed appear to support it, then it is suspect. Mill stocks would have varied from one mill to another, and from one period of time to another, but there is no means of measuring them.

The final element to consider when quantifying the cotton supply is the issue of cotton quality. There was wastage in all cotton manufacture and again it varied, both over time and according to the source of the cotton. American cotton was usually amongst the most reliable, which was one reason for its pre-eminence; Indian cotton the least. As the balance of imports shifted from the former to the latter, the level of wastage increased substantially. Since the statistics for British cotton consumption were derived from known sales to British spinners – in other words, at a point before manufacture – wastage is excluded from the consumption data. The loss on Indian cotton was more than double that on any other cotton. Its increased use raised the overall level of wastage by more than 60 per cent. More than one-sixth of the cotton that arrived at the mills in 1862 was unusable.[14]

Pre-war, India had accounted for about 15 per cent of cotton imports; in the three main years of the war that increased to 66 per cent (Table 2). The change was intensely unpopular with the trade. The reputation of Surat cotton (a specific type but used as the generic term for all Indian cotton) was so bad that the CSA went to the lengths of dummying up samples in every variety of end product to demonstrate its quality and versatility. It displayed the results at the International Exhibition of 1862, but the trade was unconvinced. A Lancashire brewing company thought itself so libelled by the epithet 'Surat brewers' that it brought an action for defamation.[15]

There was also a general deterioration in the raw material between the late 1850s and the early 1860s. The quality of American cotton sent to Britain had been declining for years but worsened substantially in 1859. At the end of that year, the broker John Wrigley & Sons declared that "a more fraudulently packed crop has never been exported." Francis Hollins alleged that "80,000,000 lbs of sand and dirt have been shipped to this country during this past year [1859] as a substitute for [American] cotton." This would have equated to more than 8 per cent of the year's American supply. The comments by several brokers a year later showed that the 1860 crop was little better. Some sand and dirt was shipped in any year: 4.7 per cent in 1856–57, according to the mill-owner John Baynes. He gave an American wastage for 1857 of 16.5 per cent. In which case, it must have been at least 20 per cent in 1859 and 1860. It seems likely that the 1861 wastage would have been just as high. If so, almost all the American cotton spun between mid-1859 and late 1862 would have been subject to an especially high level of wastage.[16]

This problem was nothing compared with the one presented by Indian imports. In 1857, Baynes estimated his losses on Surats at between 30 per cent and 40 per cent. In 1862, the position worsened. Smith wrote that "some of the lots that went home in the end of last season [1862] contained 50 per cent of extraneous matter." Early in 1863, *The Times* reported that "inferior pickings, which are not fit for the European market ... are being packed off, in the hope that under the present emergency they will take in the market." Nor was India the only exporting country to let standards slip in 1862. According to the brokers Thornely & Pownall, "we have received from Egypt the greatest apparent rubbish in the shape of cotton which that country ever exported."[17]

The increase in extraneous material was not the only issue affecting wastage during the war years. There were repercussions for quality as well as quantity. Indian cotton was of a shorter staple (length of fibre) than American. Most British cotton machinery was set up to run the American staple. Spinners struggled to make their machines run smoothly on an inferior raw material and one for which they were not designed. It is hard, however, to disentangle objective problems from prejudice on this issue. The Indian staple was about 15 per cent shorter than that of most American cotton. The Brazilian staple was between 15 per cent and 24 per cent longer; Egyptian 28 per cent longer. The machinery seemed to be able to cope with these other variances. It may be that the difficulty of spinning Indian cotton was exaggerated by some spinners, prepared to sit out the supply problem rather than have to use it. Maurice Williams claimed that many spinners "have closed their mills, rather than consent to spin Surat cotton." Nevertheless, it is easy to see why, apart from the increase in extraneous material, wastage might have been higher in 1862. Other anecdotal evidence suggests that the losses on Indian cotton gradually returned to more normal levels after 1862.[18]

The quality issues that affected raw cotton from several countries from 1859 onwards, together with the wastage implications of the temporary switch from an overwhelmingly American supply to a largely Indian supply, mean that this topic cannot be regarded as of marginal importance. If one wishes to quantify the effective supply of cotton during the war, one has somehow to quantify the increased levels of wastage. Precise figures for loss during manufacture were not collected on a formal basis: they were always estimates. Several sources other than Baynes provide information on the subject. Ellison estimated wastage figures for cotton spinning at "10½ per cent for the six years ending with 1861; 17 per cent for 1862; 15 per cent for 1863, and 14 per cent for 1864 and 1865". William Forwood, Vice-President of the Liverpool Chamber of Commerce, quoted the same figures later. Maurice Williams produced similar estimates. The figures produced by Baynes cannot be reconciled with those advanced by the others, yet they are all reliable witnesses. It is safer to use the figures quoted by Ellison and Forwood. They may appear low, but this is partly because Ellison estimated that the shortage of the raw material had forced spinners to find economies of usage of about 3 per cent.[19]

Table 4 combines the statistics for imports, re-exports and port stock movement, together with Ellison's wastage figures, to produce a column for the

Table 4 Yarn produced by British spinners, 1856–1867 (000 lb)

	Imports	Re-exports	Port stock movement	Calculated consumption	Wastage	Yarn produced	Indexed on 1860
1856	1,021,100	142,400	-47,400	926,100	10.50%	828,900	82
1857	976,100	134,100	47,500	794,500	10.50%	711,100	70
1858	1,025,500	141,800	-25,400	909,100	10.50%	813,600	80
1859	1,190,800	174,000	40,400	976,400	10.50%	873,900	86
1860	1,435,800	245,800	58,000	1,132,000	10.50%	1,013,100	100
1861	1,261,400	275,700	28,700	957,000	10.50%	856,500	85
1862	533,100	216,900	-114,700	430,900	17.00%	357,600	35
1863	691,800	260,900	-44,600	475,500	15.00%	404,200	40
1864	896,100	247,100	80,100	568,900	14.00%	489,300	48
1865	966,400	290,500	-50,200	726,100	14.00%	624,400	62
1866	1,353,800	393,700	60,000	900,100	13.00%	783,100	77
1867	1,273,800	354,100	-18,700	938,400	12.50%	821,100	81

Sources: George Holt & Co., annual cotton circulars (Liverpool Record Office, 380 COT/1/11/71); Thomas Ellison, *The Cotton Trade of Great Britain* (London: Effingham Wilson, 1886); Ellison & Haywood, annual cotton circulars for 1865 and 1866 (Liverpool Record Office, 380 COT/1/11/70–71).

production of yarn that is as close as one can get to quantifying the effective raw cotton supply to British spinners during the war. The data are indexed on 1860. For the three main years of the war, 1862–64, more than half the pre-war supply was denied to the market. The situation improved in 1865 only because American imports resumed in quantity towards the end of that year.

Now that reliable consumption figures have been established, it is possible to discuss the level of raw cotton stocks. As a preface to the discussion, a number of points should be made. The first is that Liverpool needed to maintain a permanently dependable level of cover for British spinners, thus enabling them to hold low supplies of cotton themselves. The second is that the stocks also existed for the benefit of the continental spinners who bought cotton in Liverpool: this was part of the port's role as the foremost cotton depot of Europe. The third point is that stocks were a necessary buffer against temporary import shortages. The fourth is that the theoretical availability of stocks was not the same as their practical availability. At all times, holders of cotton could and did withhold stocks from the market if they expected a rise in their value, and this – although it cannot be quantified – was widely believed to have happened constantly during the speculative mania of the civil war. The final point is that the end-of-year figures can offer only a snapshot at a particular moment. Shipments of raw cotton were irregular. Producing countries had different months of harvest and different shipping times, so arrivals, and therefore stock levels, always fluctuated greatly within any given year.

For this reason, end-of-year stock figures are misleading and are not reproduced here, except to calculate consumption. For the record, bearing in mind the emphasis that historians have placed on them, stock levels at the end of both 1860 and 1861 were unexceptional. The average end-of-year stock at ports for the period 1852–61 represented 11 weeks of trade sales. In 1860 it was 9 weeks, and in 1861 12 weeks. Without the cut-back in production in late 1861, the end-of-year stock cover would have been less than 6 weeks – the lowest for the entire ten years.

Brady, who managed to convince himself that there was no cotton scarcity in Britain during the war, based his argument largely on stock levels, and on the allegation that "the stocks of raw cotton in the United Kingdom did not fall significantly during the 'Cotton Famine'."[20] Brady chose to study the stock only at year-ends, despite the fact that weekly figures are available and would produce different conclusions. It could be pointed out that average port stocks in Britain in the 13 weeks ending 8 August 1861 were 405 million lb, whereas in the 13 weeks ending 19 November 1863 they were 58 million lb. That could be described as a significant fall. However, to emphasise this selective piece of data would be to obscure the more important points: that stock levels always needed to be reasonably high, and that they were always volatile, for the reasons given.

The weekly stock of raw cotton at ports averaged 402,000 lb in 1860–61 and 148,000 lb in 1862–64, before rising to 180,000 lb in 1865. Expressed in terms of the number of weeks of stock cover at the prevailing level of trade sales, cover averaged 21.5 weeks between 1860 and 1862, and 16 weeks between 1863 and 1865. (These figures include an estimate of mill stocks taken from the modelling used to construct Figure 5.) At several points during the war, total stock levels were very low indeed, even if all the cotton had been of usable quality and available for sale, which it was not. Throughout September 1862, the cover was less than 9 weeks. From July 1863 to April 1864, it was from 9 to 11 weeks; from September to December 1865, 8 to 10 weeks. This gave the trade little margin for error. The spinners were sailing close to the wind for almost the whole war. There were times when their mill stocks must have been close to non-existent.

However, the more important question is what the stock figures prove. There is no reason in principle that stock cover should have been lower during the famine than before or after it, relative to the level of production. Brady seems to have taken the presence of *any* stocks as proving a sufficiency of cotton. This suggests a fundamental lack of understanding both of the raw cotton market and of the requirements of a manufacturing industry. As already described, Liverpool conducted its business in its own way and with little regard to the interests of Manchester. Of itself, the stock level in Liverpool proves nothing. The criticism of Brady's argument is not so much that it is wrong about stock levels – although it is – but rather that these levels are largely irrelevant to the issue of a cotton scarcity. It is therefore not surprising that his conclusions were so breathtakingly mistaken.

No information exists for the weekly output of mills during the war, but it is possible to construct a model that shows probable levels of production. It is known how much cotton was bought by spinners on the Liverpool market each week. As explained earlier, the weekly purchases did not equate to weekly usage. However, by smoothing the purchase figures to remove extreme variations, while ensuring that the resultant mill stock figure is never negative and remains within plausible boundaries, one can produce estimated weekly production figures that are likely to be reasonably accurate. These are given in Figure 5, which shows that only after the end of the war did production start to climb back towards pre-war levels. In December 1864, the number of those out of work was still at half the level of two years earlier and would have been higher but for mill-workers finding alternative employment or emigrating. Altogether, 90,000 operatives left the industry during the war, about 14 per cent of the workforce.[21]

The situation for the weaving sector was as dire as it was for the spinning sector. The selling price for both sectors was unable to keep pace with the cost of the raw material, with the result that margins fell drastically on a

Figure 5 Calculated spinning volume, 1861–1866

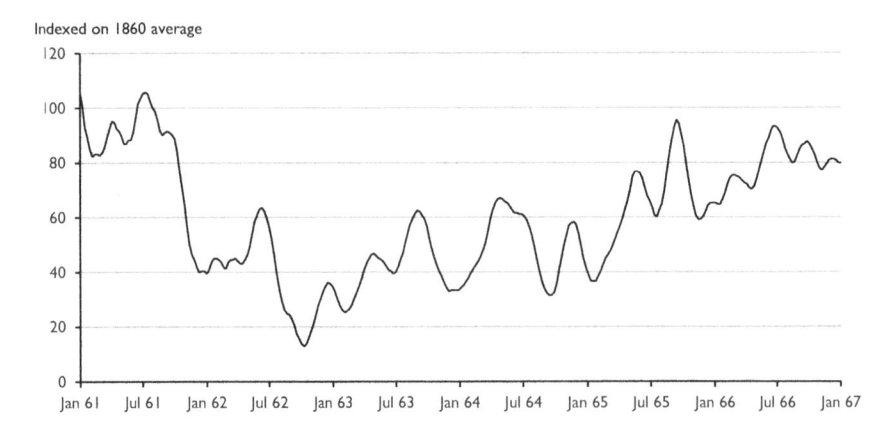

Sources: Ezekiel Donnell, *The Chronological and Statistical History of Cotton* (New York: James Sutton & Co., 1872); author.

volume that was also heavily reduced. The cost of the raw material, which was at roughly 36 per cent of sales value before the war, more than doubled to 75 per cent at its peak in 1864. Although the relative cost of wages fell, the balance left for capital costs and profit was not much above zero in the three main years of the war (Table 5). This may be contrasted with Arnold's assertion that "to the cotton trade there came in these days an unlooked-for accession of wealth, such as even it had never known before. ... In place of the hard times which had been anticipated, and perhaps deserved, there came a shower of riches."[22]

Rather like the *ryots* and merchants in India, manufacturers improved their margins by adulterating their product. The *Mercury* complained that "certain samples of goods have been analysed, and found to contain only about 60 per cent of cotton fibre. The proportion of fermented flour was 14 per cent, and mineral matter 13 per cent."[23] Smith elaborated:

> The practice of sizing cloth with flour and other ingredients ... had always prevailed to a moderate and allowable extent. ... But when the price of Cotton per lb. actually overshot that of Cotton cloth, as it did many times in the last three years, manufacturers were driven to size their cloth excessively to make a livelihood. It was woven from the coarsest yarn they could make use of, and saturated with cheap and worthless ingredients. ... From all parts of the world complaints were received of the worthlessness of these adulterated goods. Great quantities of them

Table 5 Manufacturing costs and margins, 1856–1866

	Cotton purchased (000 lb)	Average pence (p.) per lb	Cost of raw cotton (£000)	Cost of wages etc. (£000)	Sales value (£ 000)	Raw cotton (percentage)	Wages etc. (percentage)	Capital costs and profit (percentage)
1856	926,100	2.54	23,523	27,565	62,748	37%	44%	19%
1857	794,500	2.84	22,564	25,445	59,838	38%	43%	20%
1858	909,100	2.53	23,000	27,910	63,084	36%	44%	19%
1859	976,400	2.58	25,191	30,330	72,223	35%	42%	23%
1860	1,132,000	2.54	28,753	33,600	80,588	36%	42%	23%
1861	957,000	3.40	32,538	31,360	74,331	44%	42%	14%
1862	430,900	5.80	24,992	14,520	42,726	58%	34%	8%
1863	475,500	8.63	41,036	15,690	59,795	69%	26%	5%
1864	568,900	10.07	57,288	18,680	76,307	75%	24%	0%
1865	726,100	7.07	51,335	23,850	83,266	62%	29%	10%
1866	900,100	5.85	52,656	31,288	102,763	51%	30%	18%

Sources: George Holt & Co., annual cotton circular for 1866 (Liverpool Record Office, 380 COT/1/11/71); Ellison & Haywood, annual cotton circulars for 1865 and 1866 (Liverpool Record Office, 380 COT/1/11/70-71).

arrived abroad mildewed and rotten, and those that were sound had no durability.[24]

It is true, as Arnold and others have alleged, that manufacturers did profit from a windfall early in the war, when they were able to sell accumulated stocks, produced at a pre-war cost, at the higher price then obtaining. That was hardly their fault, and the prices at which the stock was sold showed nothing like the advance attained by the raw material. A contrarian argument would be that, had the manufacturers not held those stocks and been able to sell them at a higher price, more mills would have needed to close and more people would have been thrown out of work. Ellison put it fairly when he wrote that "many millowners ... regained a portion of their losses, in the shape of profits on stocks held at the commencement of the famine; but a large number lost nearly everything they were worth, while many were reduced to bankruptcy."[25]

Despite all the evidence of a scarcity of raw cotton, Brady wrote that "contemporary data and literature ... suggest that the so-called Cotton Famine was not predominantly due to a shortage of the raw cotton input."[26] As has been shown, contemporary data suggest no such thing. But, if Brady's starting point was contemporary literature, it is perhaps not surprising that he reached the conclusions he did. Because the reach of the British cotton trade was global, it is easy to underestimate its frequent insularity and myopia. The international element was the mercantile arm. The manufacturing arm, despite the fact that it sold throughout the world, albeit mainly to end customers it barely knew except through their burgeoning orders, was firmly rooted in Britain, in Lancashire, and in the present. The cotton brokers in Liverpool were similarly insulated from a wider perspective. The mentality of the cotton trade was to forget what had happened ten years ago, five years ago, five minutes ago, and to concentrate on the immediate present, and on how five minutes' time might differ from now. This attitude is evident throughout Maurice Williams's compilation of his end-of-year circulars for the years 1861–67. Each year's report starts from the present reality. Almost nowhere is there a sense of what has been lost since 1860. This outlook is not helpful to historical analysis. If taken at face value, many of the brokers' comments make little retrospective sense.

"We can now congratulate ourselves," wrote Williams – never averse to a little self-congratulation – in December 1863, "that even should the American war still continue for years, the dangers of a Cotton Famine [scarcity] are passed by and overcome." At the time he wrote those words, British production of cotton yarn was at less than 40 per cent of its pre-war level and the cotton famine was still raging. How can such a statement be explained? The report of the brokers Colin Campbell & Son at the end of 1860 offers a clue. They wrote that any "advance in the value of the raw material, would ... cause a system of economy to be adopted, and in that case, the Consumption would readily adapt itself to the Supply, and ... do away with the probability of scarcity, which has frequently been predicted, but never experienced." By this logic, a scarcity could never be experienced: its *reductio ad absurdum* would be that, in the absence of any cotton, consumption would 'readily adapt' itself to zero. At the end of 1863, the same brokers wrote that "it is a remarkable fact that ... our supplies from that quarter [America] have nearly doubled", without mentioning that this doubled quantity still constituted a 97 per cent reduction in the American supply of two years earlier.[27]

Williams and Campbell may have been extreme examples, but they were not untypical. Many brokers lost all sense of the historical continuum of their market. They described only how things seemed to them at that particular moment in Liverpool, which is not how they seemed anywhere else, notably in Manchester, nor how they should seem to any subsequent historian.

The scarcity affected both cotton communities, but it did not affect them equally. When a commentator such as Williams expresses the view that "we shall, ere very long, be receiving more Cotton than we require", he is referring to cotton at the price it is currently obtaining.[28] At that inflated price, demand is suppressed and available supplies will be sufficient. Williams's comments were typical of those whose livelihoods depended on raw cotton, now selling in small quantity but at exorbitant prices; they did not reflect the views of those whose livelihoods depended on manufacturing it in bulk, who had invested in extra machinery to do so, and who were now receiving less than half the supply that they and their machines needed. Without the war, prices would have been nowhere near their wartime level; demand would have been much greater; supply would have been available. The assorted remarks of many cotton brokers make sense only in light of the fact that their observation point was fixed in Liverpool and in the immediate present. There is little sense of Manchester, little sense of what used to be, and no sense at all of what might have been, but for the war.

Into this hall of mirrors stepped Eugene Brady. He concluded that "rather than causing a significant physical shortage of raw cotton, the American Civil War induced expectations *which were never realized* [emphasis added] of a future shortage."[29] Everything in this analysis contradicts that conclusion. Even if one maintains that a market that had grown consistently for years, decades in fact, would suddenly have stopped growing for no apparent reason, one cannot contend that there was no scarcity. The British cotton trade lost 54 per cent of its pre-war supply in the peak period of scarcity from 1862 to 1864, and 37 per cent over the period from 1862 to 1867. The question is whether it was this scarcity, or a pre-war over-production of cotton goods, that was the principal cause of the famine.

The fact that the over-production claim has never been scrutinised is not for want of data. As with raw cotton, there are full statistics on Britain's cotton manufactures, exports and stocks in the years before the civil war and every means of assessing whether the immediate pre-war years were anomalous or not. There are also the reports of the brokers, who might have been expected to comment with concern upon what, in retrospect, Ellison called a "gigantic amount of over-trading". These varied sources are now examined in detail. Not one of them supports the claim of substantial pre-war over-production.

The first discovered reference to a possible over-stocking of export markets dates from May 1860, in the annual report of the CSA.[30] It would appear that the issue lay fallow until late 1861, when the introduction of short-time working invited discussion as to its causes. From then until the publication of Arnold's book in 1864 and beyond, it was the subject of an intense debate. However, almost all the references to over-production, and to glutted markets, date from late 1861 onwards, by which time the civil war had started and a different, temporary cotton market had emerged. In November 1862, *The Economist* went to war on the issue:

> One of the most astonishing of the doctrines gravely propounded is that there is in reality no cotton famine at all, and that the prevailing distress is the result simply of over-production. ... These strange stories are set afloat by persons who evidently know nothing about the cotton manufacture; nor, it would seem, about any kind of trade whatever.[31]

This view did not impress Henry Reeve, the author of an anonymous article in the *Edinburgh Review* in January 1863:

> Why, then, are so many mills closed? The reason is obvious. About eighteen months ago, at the commencement of this crisis, the markets of the world were literally encumbered with Manchester goods. Had a sale been forced, they would not have fetched a tenth of their value, perhaps not of their cost. So large was the stock on hand that it has sufficed to supply the whole demand of the world for nearly two years with no very great augmentation of price.[32]

The Economist was apoplectic at this claim. It demolished "a rambling article in a once eminent ... periodical [containing] ... views and statements ... marked by an inaccuracy so startling and an ignorance so profound that they cannot be passed over in silence." The paper then advanced a contrary version of events:

> The statement that the stock then on hand [at the end of 1860] has sufficed to supply the wants of the world for two years is equally

extravagant and ignorant, – and the reference drawn from it, that for some time back the production of cotton goods has exceeded the demand, is utterly unwarranted, and indeed is contradicted, by well-ascertained facts. That up to the close of 1860 there was no "glut" or "over-production" is clear from the circumstance that 1858, 1859, and 1860 were the most profitable years cotton manufacturers and cotton exporters have ever known.[33]

Historians have chosen to ignore the opinion of the most eminent economic paper in the country to the extent of not even mentioning *The Economist's* arguments, let alone engaging with them. They have also chosen to prefer Arnold's interpretation of events to that of John Watts, who wrote the more authoritative of the two contemporary books on the famine.

Arnold did not mention *The Economist's* arguments either, although he must surely have been aware of them. They were known to Otto Henderson, author of the best-known subsequent work on the famine, who referred to them in a footnote without saying what they were. Although Henderson gave more weight to the cotton scarcity than other commentators, he also wrote that "at the time, many believed that the American War was the sole cause of the crisis and cotton manufacturers naturally did nothing to dispel this impression. ... Contemporary economists (Karl Marx), historians (J. Watts, R.A. Arnold) ... and well-informed persons generally, recognised the truth." But they did not: they recognised what they wanted to recognise, and it was not the truth. It is, moreover, discreditable to recruit Watts to their ranks. Watts wrote that "if there had been no war in America, the large profits of 1859–60 would have been brought down to average by a heavy fall of prices on accumulated stocks in 1861." This is a very different claim, and one that might have proved true, although even that is doubtful.[34]

Yet Arnold's book has come to be regarded as the main primary source on the famine. Henderson confirmed this anointment in the 1930s, and everyone since has assumed it. But Arnold's claims have never been examined, not even by himself. Over-production is a term that demands to be defined if it is to be blamed for the famine. If manufacturers produced too much in those years, what should they have produced? If stocks of cotton goods were too high, what was the correct level of stocks? These issues are not addressed. Not by Arnold; not by Henderson; not by anyone since. *The Economist* addressed them at the time. "The truth is this," it said, "'over-production,' and 'over-supply,' are purely relative terms, and are so vague and inaccurate that it would be well if we could forego their use. In one sense, over-production and glutted markets must be matters of periodical recurrence." Arnold, on the other hand, did not seem even to understand the need for stocks, or the part they played in the global cotton trade. "[The trade] had in hand a stock of goods sufficient for the consumption of two-thirds of a year," he wrote in amazement. In reaching this figure, he has conflated the stocks of the raw material with the stocks of finished goods, despite the fact that these played two quite different roles within the market and had no inherent connection with each other.[35]

Perhaps it was inevitable that the plutocrats of the cotton trade would become scapegoats for the famine in the eyes of those who knew little about business, but who started with a prejudice against the mill-owners. In a situation that was so confused that it was possible to sustain, with some credibility, any number of viewpoints, it must have been tempting to many to choose the one that temperamentally suited them. When Arnold, a future Radical MP, wrote that, during the famine, "to the cotton trade there came ... a shower of riches", he was making an absurd claim. As has been shown, manufacturers processed, on average, less than half the raw cotton their mills needed for at least three years. The rise in price of cotton goods lagged a long way behind the rise in price of the raw material. The fixed costs of the mills were spread over less than half their normal volume base. As with any recession, different companies were affected to differing degrees, but most – although not all – manufacturers had a torrid time throughout the civil war, as Table 5 demonstrates. Even Henderson felt obliged to distance himself from his mentor on this issue: "While some manufacturers and agents made considerable profits, others made none of the exceptional gains that have been described but suffered severely throughout the Cotton Famine and the subsequent financial crises."[36]

In Britain, the insistence on over-production may principally have had the political purpose of blaming mill-owners for the famine or have reflected anger at the failure of many of them to do more to mitigate the effects of the famine on their employees. In America, there has been a parallel debate. There, the issue translates to a supposed over-abundance of supply. And the political edge to the debate is that, because of this alleged over-supply, the South chose the least favourable moment to implement the King Cotton strategy. In addition to Brady's comments, Howard Jones declared that "bumper crops in the two years previous to the war had allowed the two chief benefactors of that trade, Britain and France, to stock huge surpluses that freed them from economic pressure throughout this pivotal period." Gavin Wright was of the opinion that, "between 1860 and the late 1870s [worldwide] cotton demand plunged and then stagnated", without appearing to relate this reduced demand either to the reduction in the availability of cotton or to the rise in its price. David Surdam has considered these implausibilities from the point of view of the worldwide, not purely the British, demand for raw cotton. His conclusions mirror those reached here: the world market was strong at the beginning of 1861; demand did not significantly weaken for most of that year; stocks of raw cotton were not inordinately large; raw cotton prices showed little, if any, weakening; and the period 1861–62 should have been an effective time for the Confederacy to use its power in the market.[37]

It is disappointing that Farnie should have been more vituperative than anyone in ridiculing the idea that the civil war was responsible for the famine, referring to it as "a stupefying misconception". The pages in which Farnie discusses these issues are laced with an extreme animus towards the cotton trade in particular and free traders in general. He refers to a "shortage of cotton which had not in fact existed" and endorses Brady's placing of the blame for the famine "almost wholly upon the preceding period of production which had expanded far in excess of any existing demand". The most misleading, slender, and selective evidence is produced to justify these extreme statements. Farnie reports that stocks of cotton goods were at 23.5 per cent of annual production at the end of 1860, and at 33.6 per cent at the end of 1861. This statement is not contextualised by a discussion of the level of such stocks at other times, nor qualified by recognition that the 1861 figure might have been affected by the outbreak of the civil war. As part of the evidence for a crisis in the export trade, Farnie reports that "the export ... to the U.S.A. sank by 64.5 per cent ... after the outbreak of war", without mentioning that the introduction of the Morrill tariff in America, which had the effect of raising the duty on British processed cotton imports by 71 per cent, was responsible for this. He claims that there was a "heaping up of stocks" of raw cotton in Liverpool, but goes on to discuss their level in bales, which results in conclusions that are categorically wrong. He states that "supplies of American cotton ... continued to flow across the Atlantic and furnished in 1861 ... 65 per cent of [the cotton] imported by Britain", without mentioning that 99.7 per cent of this import arrived before the Confederate embargo was imposed in July, which he does not mention either. Nor does he say that very little American cotton arrived in Britain for the following four years. He alleges that the price of raw cotton "remained low for six months after the bombardment of Fort Sumter", whereas in fact it rose by 56 per cent. He borrows Arnold's phrase, "a shower of riches in place of the anticipated hard times", without acknowledging a source, and despite the fact that elsewhere he catalogues the heavy decline in mill profits.[38]

Farnie wrote that "if those [re-]exports [of raw cotton] had not doubled, then the consumption of cotton by the mills of Lancashire might have been maintained in 1862–65 at an average level ... only one-seventh less than in 1850–9."[39] Yet his argument up to this point is that consumption did not need to be maintained at that level, or to be any higher than it was. He ignores the fact that the raw cotton did not physically exist in 1862–65 to have produced more goods: maintenance of anything close to pre-war production levels was an impossibility. And to imply that consumption from 1850 to 1859 was static and could be treated as a single entity, when it had in fact increased by 66 per cent over the period, is entirely misleading and invalidates the conclusion — even supposing that those re-exports could ever have been available to Britain.

The contention of both Brady and Farnie is that the heavily reduced production levels during the cotton famine were a necessary correction of the over-production of the previous period, that stocks of finished goods were excessively high in 1861, and that stocks of the raw material were also high and — even with the reduced supply — sufficient for consumption. Price is barely mentioned in this context. A glut of a commodity almost invariably results in a fall in its price. The average price of yarn rose by 2 per cent in 1861, by 48 per cent in 1862, by 54 per cent in 1863 and by 6 per cent in 1864. The average price of cloth fell by less than 1 per cent in 1861 and rose by 45 per cent in 1862, by 38 per cent in 1863 and by 13 per cent in 1864.[40] The average price of raw cotton rose by 27 per cent in 1861, by 105 per cent in 1862, by 39 per cent in 1863 and by 11 per cent in 1864. None of this is mentioned by Farnie. The over-productionists need to explain how these price movements evidence a sufficiency of raw cotton and a surfeit of cotton goods.

There is an alternative narrative. All aspects of the British cotton trade grew strongly through the 1850s. The large American crop of 1859–60, coupled with a resultant fall in price of the raw material and the trade's habit of manufacturing what was available when it was available, led to production somewhat exceeding demand in 1860 and the first part of 1861. Without the intervention of the war, the level of stocks would not have excited much comment. Nor is it likely that the stocks would have had much effect on prices, or on margins that were already abnormally high, in view of the small forthcoming American crop of 1860–61. As it was, the outbreak of the civil war paralysed the global market. A prolonged war, and the efficacy of the Confederate embargo and the Union blockade, would lead to a worldwide cotton scarcity and inflated prices. But no one expected a prolonged war. Augmented by continued arrivals of cotton from elsewhere and by production at a reduced level, stocks of both raw cotton and cotton goods in Britain would last longer than the maximum of 90 days anticipated, and almost certainly — although the evidence is anecdotal — stocks of cotton goods throughout the world as well.

The global trade needed a pipeline of goods and in 1861 the pipeline was well-stocked. With the uncertainty over America, the safest course of action for the trade was to sell from stock. The demand for new supplies fell immediately, which led to the introduction of short-time working. When the war failed to end, or American supplies to resume, the price of raw cotton rose rapidly. Even though the price of cotton goods failed to keep pace with this increase, it also rose substantially and continuously. The global trade was reluctant to pay an increased price while it held stocks at a lower price, bearing in mind that the war could end at any moment.

The pipeline drained throughout 1862. Until the war was over, the global trade bought only for immediate requirements, at an inflated price. The pipeline was not refilled until after the war had ended and the market had stabilised. There was a temporary, provisional worldwide cotton market throughout the war. As the Neill brothers explained it:

> If we reflect upon the volume of stock in transit between the grower ... and the merchant in Liverpool; then from him through the hands of brokers, speculators, and perhaps exporters, to the spinner; and from him to the manufacturer, and thence in the form of goods to the wholesale warehouseman, and on to the shopkeeper or the exporting merchant, with, perhaps, another ten or fifteen thousand miles to travel, and foreign merchants, brokers, wholesale dealers, and retail dealers to hold it for a time before the goods finally reach the hands of the actual consumer, it is impossible to believe that this transit stock of cotton, and the productions thereof, can at any time be less than the equivalent of one year's consumption. It was formerly estimated at as much as three years' consumption. But whatever it may really amount to, it will, when duly considered, account for many seeming anomalies in the trade – such, for example, as the impossibility of moving the stocks of goods held in most markets, at any considerable advance in price, for the first twelve or eighteen months of the war.[41]

The Economist referred to 'well-ascertained facts' and they indeed exist. There is statistical evidence to support the view that there was nothing untoward about British cotton manufacture or exports in the period 1859–61. In Figure 6, Britain's production of cotton goods is shown for the period 1853–61. The dotted line on the graph shows the same data as the solid line, but with the growth rate equalised over the period. In other words, the sum total of goods represented by the solid line is equal to the sum total of goods represented by the dotted line. The same technique has been used in Figure 7. The effect is to make it easier to see anomalous years within the period. Figure 6 shows that production grew by a compound 4.4 per cent p.a. over the period. The rate of growth was consistent, other than in 1857, a year in which less raw cotton was available, and in 1860, when manufacturers took advantage of a large supply and a reasonable price to produce at somewhat above the level of immediate requirements.

Figure 7 shows the exports of cotton goods over the same period. The years 1859 and 1860 indeed showed strong sales, but so did the period as a whole. Compound growth was 6.4 per cent p.a. over the eight years. In 1859, it was 6.2 per cent, and in 1860, 6.8 per cent. Exports then fell by 8.9 per cent in 1861. Over-productionists would say that this fall was caused by the glutting

Figure 6 British production of cotton yarn and cloth, 1853–1861

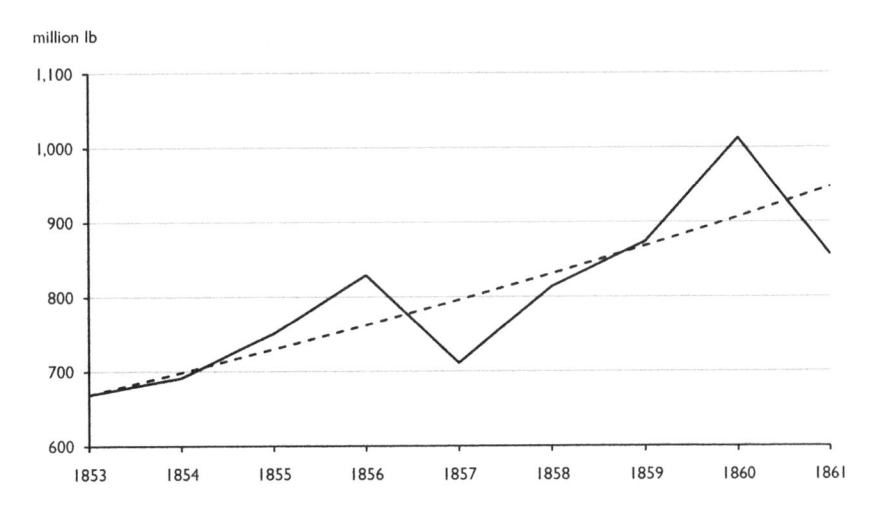

Source: Ellison & Haywood, annual cotton circulars for 1865 and 1866 (Liverpool Record Office, 380 COT/1/11/70-71).

Figure 7 British exports of cotton yarn and cloth, 1853–1861

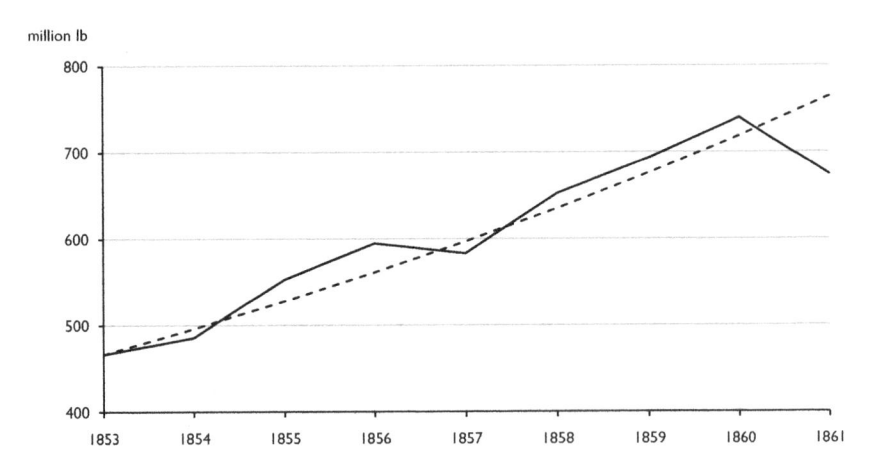

Source: Ellison & Haywood, annual cotton circulars for 1865 and 1866 (Liverpool Record Office, 380 COT/1/11/70-71).

of markets, but it seems altogether more plausible that it was caused by the paralysis of demand following the outbreak of the civil war. If the retrospective comments on glutting during 1859 and 1860 had been true, the consequence should have been either a complete collapse in 1861 exports, or a collapse in export prices, or both. There was neither. Exports were still 3 per cent greater than in 1858. Exports of cotton cloth to China actually increased.[42] Exports of cloth to India, supposedly a saturated market by the end of 1860, fell by only 3 per cent in 1861.[43] None of this would have been possible if all markets were sated. The export prices obtained in 1861 were much the same as in 1860. The average price of cloth fell by 3.0 per cent, while the average price of yarn increased by 4.3 per cent. Total cotton exports to India and China, both supposedly saturated markets by the end of 1860, fell by only 8 per cent and 5 per cent respectively in 1861.[44] None of this justifies the belief that markets were glutted.

Henderson argued that the export boom of the late 1850s was a short-term anomaly. He wrote of "a big temporary demand for cotton goods from the Far East (now that the Indian Mutiny and the war in China were over)" in his damnation of 1860 exports in particular. Yet the facts belie the idea of any 'temporary demand'. Exports of cotton cloth to India and China already stood at 388 million yards in 1850, and they reached 1,340 million yards in 1873 – a compound growth rate of 5.3 per cent p.a. over a quarter of a century, despite including the war years. This demand cannot sensibly be described as 'temporary'.[45]

The incontrovertible fact is that the 1850s were a period of rapid international growth for British cotton goods. At certain times, there were certain problems with certain markets. That was, and is, in the nature of international trade. But there was no general problem with British cotton exports in the pre-war years. Further confirmation of the true situation is provided by the issue that is supposed to prove the opposite: the stocks of cotton goods. Table 6 shows the end-of-year level of manufacturers' stocks for the years 1856 to 1866 (earlier data have not been found). The figures show that the stocks of finished goods were reasonably consistent from 1856 to 1860, with some increase in the latter year. There was then a further increase in 1861. However, if the argument made here is accepted, that increase should be regarded as the consequence of the market paralysis from about mid-year. It would be helpful to have monthly figures for 1861, but they do not appear to exist. The suspicion must be that the fall in orders began in the third quarter of the year, leading to curtailed production in the fourth quarter. In that case, additional stocks amounting to about five or six weeks of sales at their then level had been created between the end of 1859 and mid-1861. This is a significant increase, but not large enough to justify the hysterical remarks that have been made. It may be that the stocks at the end of 1861, which were about 3 million lb, were responsible for the currency of that figure. If so, they had not been accumulated over two or three years, as Ellison and Arnold claimed. Stocks were not equivalent to "the consumption of two-thirds of a year", let alone "the whole demand of the world for nearly two years".

Table 6 Stocks of cotton goods, 1856–1866 (000 lb)

	Opening stock	Manufactured	Sales	Closing stock	Weeks' stock
1856	130,000	828,900	749,700	209,200	14.5
1857	209,200	711,100	739,300	181,000	12.7
1858	181,000	813,600	810,600	184,000	11.8
1859	184,000	873,900	865,100	192,800	11.6
1860	192,800	1,013,100	913,100	292,800	16.7
1861	292,800	856,500	848,100	301,200	18.5
1862	301,200	357,600	519,300	139,500	14.0
1863	139,500	404,200	489,000	54,700	5.8
1864	54,700	489,300	517,700	26,300	2.6
1865	26,300	624,400	630,900	19,800	1.6
1866	19,800	783,100	774,500	28,400	1.9

Sources: George Holt & Co., annual cotton circular for 1866 (Liverpool Record Office, 380 COT/1/11/71); Ellison & Haywood, annual cotton circulars for 1865 and 1866 (Liverpool Record Office, 380 COT/1/11/70-71).

The other important point revealed by Table 6 is the degree of destocking that took place during the war. By 1865, stocks of cotton goods in Britain were close to non-existent. This is compelling evidence for the draining of the stock pipeline in the early years of the war and for the insufficiency of the raw cotton supply.

If there was a problem with stocks, one would have expected mounting concern as it was unfolding. The cotton brokers' circulars are a valuable source of information. What were the brokers saying about the issue at the time? At the end of 1859, they were not saying anything. On the contrary: according to Hollinshead, Tetley & Co., "the demand for textiles is greater than can be supplied." As for stocks, T. & H. Littledale & Co. were pleased to say that "[they] are moderate". Maurice Williams was delighted to report "a demand for the manufactured article in excess of the power to produce." The Manchester firm of J. C. Ollerenshaw concurred: "There are no heavy stocks of goods and yarns in the world, and the trade is in as sound and healthy a position as possible." Isaac Cooke & Sons felt that "the 3,850,000 bales just disposed of have not been equal to the supply of the world's present wants." As for the future, Hall & Mellor were convinced that "the present large Consumption will not only be maintained but go on increasing, and we may therefore need a larger supply to meet the demand."[46]

It might be thought that concern about stock levels would take time to trickle back to Lancashire from distant countries, that December 1859 was too soon to expect an appreciation of the problem, and that the reports for 1860 would rectify this. They did not. In December 1860, two years into this 'gigantic' amount of over-trading, Liverpool seemed unaware of its existence. Robson & Eskrigge declared that "the striking fact illustrated by this review is the ease with which the consuming power of the world has appropriated the immense supplies of the year, without leaving at its close excessive stocks in the hands of merchants." John Wrigley & Sons were confident that "the hopes for the future are bright enough for even the most sanguine." Thornely & Pownall reported that "our remarks cannot be closed, without noticing the expectation of enlarged commerce with China, the magnitude of our transactions with India, and the unparalleled prosperity of the manufacturing districts." Hollinshead & Tetley wrote that: "Owing to the vast number of new mills brought into operation the increase [in consumption] is unprecedented; and this too without creating any surplus stocks of the manufactured article, either at home or abroad." Cunningham & Hinshaw believed that the problem was with supply and not demand: "We shall certainly not receive [in 1861] that supply which will be requisite to meet our rapidly increasing ... demands." Samuel Smith acknowledged some reduction in demand from India, but reported that "the elasticity of trade elsewhere fully made amends for it."[47]

At the end of 1860, therefore, most of the way through a three-year period of allegedly vast over-production, the consensus amongst the brokers was that there was no problem with exports or with glutted markets, that stock levels were reasonable, that production was struggling to keep pace with demand and that the problem, if there was one, was with the supply. Yet, a year later, some of those same brokers had not only changed their minds but had convinced themselves they had been wrong for the previous two years. Isaac Cooke, last heard at the end of 1860 calling for "a still greater quantity" to be manufactured, had now decided that "the extraordinary amount of goods and yarn exported during the previous two years, had, at the commencement of 1861, completely overstocked all ... Markets."[48]

At the close of 1861, when those words were written, the cotton trade was engulfed in such a maelstrom that a calm appreciation of its component parts must have been impossible. In November and December, when the annual reports were compiled, the country was in the grip of the *Trent* affair, when it looked as if Britain might declare war on the Union. The cotton trade had little idea where it stood throughout the year. The fact that, by the end of 1861, Liverpool had come to the announced view that Manchester had over-produced, and had then over-stocked its markets, cannot be taken as proof that it had. Some problems may become apparent only in retrospect, but it is hard to believe that this was one of them, not least because there was unarguably a major new element that entered the equation in 1861. The positive comments, and the lack of negative ones, in the brokers' reports for 1859 and 1860 should not be disregarded, even if one makes generous allowance for the time it might have taken for news to have percolated back from overseas markets. While cotton men were frequently wrong in their prognostications, Liverpool brokers were not ill-informed about the current state of their market. If export markets had been overstocked to the degree that was later asserted, it would have been noticed well before the end of 1860.

The issue of pre-war over-production has now been examined from three perspectives: the statistics of Britain's cotton production and its export trade in cotton goods from 1853 to 1861; the statistics of cotton stocks from 1856 to 1861; and the anecdotal evidence of the Liverpool brokers in their annual reports for the relevant years. Not one of these perspectives supports the over-production argument. Not one of them supports the notion that export markets were glutted. All three perspectives tend to the same conclusion: that, prior to the civil war, the British cotton trade was enjoying a strong and consistent growth in the global demand for its goods, that it was manufacturing at a level broadly consistent with that demand, and that the most pressing problem was a growing insufficiency of supply.

In addition, there is the evidence of new investment. For more than four years, the cotton trade was in turmoil. Well-financed mills could make for stock and wait for the price of yarn or goods to catch up with the price of the raw material, but smaller mills had to close. Some spinners and weavers went out of business; many struggled to stay afloat. Until the war ended, and until its consequences became apparent, no one could say for certain what the future held with regard to the cotton supply and its price. On top of this, if the over-productionists are to be believed, the earlier level of demand had been an illusion, and Lancashire's pre-war capacity had been substantially in excess of the market requirement.[49]

Yet, although much of its existing machinery for processing cotton lay underused or idle for most of the war, and although its commercial outlook was at best precarious, the industry continued to invest in new mills and equipment. "There is at least ten to fifteen per cent more spinning machinery in existence than before the war," wrote Williams in 1868. He added that "owing to the number of new mills built during the American war ... there is a great scarcity of skilled work people." The total number of mills nevertheless declined but, as Forwood wrote, "the decrease ... was due to many mills with old-fashioned machinery, and in out-of-the-way places, being closed, while the increase in the number of spindles is accounted for by the modern mills, completed during the American war, being of a large size." Cotton manufacturers and investors clearly believed they were still in a growth market, temporarily undergoing a reversal, and they were surely right.[50]

It is a mistake to believe that the initial move to short-time working must have been caused either by a cotton scarcity or by excessive stocks, and that – since there was no scarcity in 1861 – it must have been the latter. It was neither. The cause was the uncertainty occasioned by the outbreak of war, leading to a paralysis of demand. The reason that short-time working developed into the famine is that there was, by 1862, a scarcity of raw cotton, and its inflated price suppressed worldwide demand throughout the war. In both cases, the war was the direct cause of the distress.

The fundamental failing has been to have misunderstood the role of stocks within the market, and thus to have misinterpreted the stagnation in demand in the early months of the war. A reasonable level of stocks, in every country and in every branch of the trade, was essential. By the end of 1861, raw cotton prices had more than doubled from their level of mid-1860 and were higher than at any time since the mid-1830s. No one in the trade, anywhere in the world, could predict the future course of prices, whether of the raw material, or of yarn or cloth, even one month hence. In those circumstances, the safest course was to reduce inventories and to sell from stock. That was true at all levels of the trade, in all parts of the world.

Shipping times between Britain and Asia were from four to six months. At no stage of the civil war could there be a sure opinion that it would continue for that length of time. There was no reason to buy new supplies at higher prices when the war might end, the rise in price would be reversed, and the trader would be left holding over-valued stock. As one broker explained, "goods made from high priced Cotton will not be exported with much freedom to distant markets, as for instance to India and China, when advices may be sent that these will be shortly followed by shipments the produce of low priced cotton."[51] The consequence of this perfectly rational approach was to paralyse the market. The normal intercourse of the cotton trade, the constant topping up of its supply line, became too dangerous. What Arnold and subsequent historians have described as a process of excessive stocks being sold off over time was in fact the process of an essential pipeline emptying itself because the financial risk of keeping it topped up had become too great. That process seems to have taken about 18 months.

Before the war started, there was nothing to suggest anything other than the normal ebb and flow of a healthy trade. It is impossible to say with certainty what the exact course of the market would have been without the war, but there is no reason to believe that the growth of the preceding years and decades would suddenly have come to a halt. By late 1860, it was already known that the forthcoming American crop of 1860–61 would be a great deal smaller than its record predecessor. In the event, it was 22 per cent smaller – a major shortfall, the effects of which were camouflaged by later events, causing it to be ignored subsequently. However, it is fundamental to an understanding of what might have happened to the British market had the war not intervened. Both imports and stocks would have fallen anyway from late 1861, the price would have risen anyway, the level of production would have needed to fall, and the stocks of finished goods – which, as with the raw material, existed partly as a precaution against a short crop – would also have reduced and would have been sold without undue difficulty. The chance of any scenario remotely resembling the cotton famine was zero.

If one considers the six-year period 1856–61 and advances the extraordinary proposition that the cotton trade over-produced throughout those years, that demand was in reality flat, and that everything produced at above the 1856 level was surplus to requirements, the cumulative over-production at the end of 1861 would have amounted to 124 million lb of yarn. The shortfall in 1862 alone, compared with 1856, was 471 million lb. And demand was not flat: it grew constantly during the 1850s without, until after the war had started, exciting any comment except admiration. This growth resumed, albeit weaker, as soon as the supply problem caused by the war was over.

By the end of 1862, the fog was beginning to clear for some of the more perceptive brokers. James Howell reported that "the reserves of the world are now probably at length exhausted."[52] Newall & Clayton declared that:

> At low prices we might never have heard of the overproduction of which so much is now said. ... So long as the war continues, nothing but high prices can keep consumption in check, as there is every reason to believe that the goods made from cheap Cotton are now well nigh exhausted in all quarters of the world, and a new range of prices must rule for some time to come.[53]

Robson & Eskrigge reported:

> We see the enormous vacuum of Cotton goods that must have resulted from the famine. The exhaustion of stocks must sooner or later induce a demand, which our resources will be quite inadequate to supply, and which only a very high range of prices, both for the raw material and the manufactured article, can reduce within practicable limits.[54]

This is exactly what happened. The market slowly recovered from its paralysis and global trade began to flow again, albeit more sluggishly than before and at greatly inflated prices. But it was a different market.

This chapter has quantified the raw cotton available to Britain during the civil war. The one question left unexamined is what the market growth might

Table 7 Estimated consumption deficit of British cotton, 1861–1867 (000 lb)

	Demand for yarn @ + 4.3% per annum	Yarn produced	Percentage of demand produced	Annual deficiency	Cumulative yarn deficiency	Cumulative cotton deficiency (waste 10.5%)
1860	1,013,100	1,013,100	100%	0	0	0
1861	1,056,700	856,500	81%	200,200	200,200	223,700
1862	1,102,100	357,600	32%	744,500	944,700	1,055,500
1863	1,149,500	404,200	35%	745,300	1,690,000	1,888,300
1864	1,198,900	489,300	41%	709,600	2,399,600	2,681,100
1865	1,250,500	624,400	50%	626,100	3,025,700	3,380,700
1866	1,304,300	783,100	60%	521,200	3,546,900	3,963,000
1867	1,360,400	821,100	60%	539,300	4,086,200	4,565,600

Sources: George Holt & Co., annual cotton circulars (Liverpool Record Office, 380 COT/1/11/71); Thomas Ellison, *The Cotton Trade of Great Britain* (London: Effingham Wilson, 1886); author.

have been without the war. Although any quantification of that growth will be speculative, Figure 1 surely leaves no doubt that substantial growth was indeed lost. Now that the myth of over-production has been refuted, it is time to return to the issue of lost growth.

British production of cotton goods grew by a compound 6.3 per cent p.a. in the decade from 1851 to 1860. In the decade from 1871 to 1880, and still suffering to some extent from the effects of the war, it grew at a compound rate of 2.4 per cent.[55] Given that any estimate of the lost growth during the war decade will be guesswork, it seems reasonable to take an average of these two figures, a compound growth rate of 4.3 per cent, to give an example of the probable effect of the war on British cotton. Table 7 provides this information. As late as 1867, the country was receiving only 60 per cent of the supply it could have used at peacetime prices. In total, more than 4.5 billion lb of raw cotton was probably denied to British manufacturers in the seven years to the end of 1867. By the time re-exports are added to the equation, the figure is closer to an import deficiency of about 6 billion lb, or a supply of about four years. Farnie wrote that "the new monarch of the world of textiles, 'King Cotton', was ... dethroned during the Cotton Famine of the 1860s and regained its prewar eminence only during the early 1890s."[56] How this statement squares with what he had previously written is far from clear.

It is now time to consider another unexamined aspect of the civil war mythology: that Liverpool was a rabidly Confederate town.

CHAPTER V

Liverpool, Louisiana?
The town's contradictory response to the civil war

"More than any British city, Liverpool stood by and sided with the pro-slavery Confederate states during the Civil War." "The world's largest cotton port was the most pro-Confederate place in the world outside the Confederacy itself." "No other city in Britain could with so much cause be accused of unofficially fighting on the side of the South during the Civil War." "Liverpool became a bastion of pro-Confederate sympathy and business during the war." "Liverpool had become a stronghold of Confederate sympathisers ... swarming with Confederate agents." It was "a pro-Confederate hotspot."[1]

Like the myth of pre-war over-production, Liverpool's Confederate credentials have been presented as a self-evident fact, requiring no substantiation. As with that other 'fact', it has not been investigated, but repeated as an unsupported assertion by one historian after another. Unlike the over-production 'fact', this 'fact' contains more than a grain of truth. However, the reality was a great deal more complex than those headline quotes suggest. It is undeniable that Liverpool was a hotspot during the war, but the heat was experienced in different and conflicting ways. The port was indeed swarming with Confederate agents, but it swarmed with Union agents too.

As discussed in Chapter 3, recent scholarship has undermined the notion that opinion in Britain during the civil war – whether of the Government, the press, or sectional interests such as cotton operatives and the working class in general – can be reduced to a one-line summary. Many considerations, often conflicting, fed into the perceptions of individuals and groups, making their attitudes to both the war and their own self-interest in it, which were not necessarily the same thing, complicated and sometimes contradictory. This is also true of Liverpool, where generalisations must equally be avoided.

What was done in the town to assist the South was more obvious, and more newsworthy, than what was done to assist the North.[2] The building of warships for the Confederacy became a national scandal. The activity of blockade-running had all the allure of a *Boy's Own* adventure, and has prompted a vast literature ever since. Liverpool's historical association with the slave trade may also have played its part in public perception of a sympathy with the South, both in the 1860s and since. Amongst some sections of the town, there was vigorous support for the Confederacy, expressed noisily and often reported nationally. Because of its location, Liverpool was the centre for Confederate operations in Britain. This has all helped to create the illusion of a town that was monolithically pro-South. However, a less noisy support for the North co-existed with these other sympathies and, most of all, a strong support for British neutrality and non-intervention. Liverpool should not be presented as an overwhelmingly pro-Southern town, but rather as one that had considerable vested interests in the conflict and was determined to protect those interests.

More than any other place in Britain, Liverpool was the first point of contact between the country and the Southern States of America. That was true before the war, during it, and after it. There were many merchants and others in Liverpool who had close relationships with what became the Confederacy and who supported it vociferously. However, Liverpool was equally the first point of contact between the country and the Northern States of America, and that was also true before the war, during it, and after it. The same could be said of many other parts of the world. Liverpool was Europe's largest port. The town was multi-cultural before the word was invented. B. Guinness Orchard reported that "Scotchmen jostled Germans, and Irishmen Frenchmen. Italians and Dutchmen, Yankees and Parsees, Spaniards and Canadians, Greeks and Swiss abounded." Liverpool was the final footing for emigrants to America, most of them bound for the Northern States, where many Liverpudlians had relatives. It was also the conduit, before the transatlantic cable, through which all American news entered the country, and all domestic news for America left it. The information that Britain received about the civil war was received first in Liverpool, unless the ship had already docked in Ireland. Ellison tells the story of how news was brought ashore, runners for the London papers scrambling to be first to the town's only cable office.[3]

No comprehensive study has been made of Liverpool's role in the American Civil War. There is a substantial literature on both blockade-running and the Confederate warships, some of which will be mentioned where relevant, but of which the detail is unimportant to the intentions of this chapter.[4] As with so much in this book, a lot depends on anecdotal primary sources, and again on the coverage by the *Liverpool Mercury*. Other material should have been available from the Foreign Office files in the National Archives, but both pieces of relevant information are absent. Some secondary sources throw valuable light on unseen corners, and in particular Graeme Milne's commercial history of Liverpool, Jay Sexton's detail on Union arms purchases in Britain and the PhD theses of Neil Ashcroft and Francis Hughes.[5] All this information has been used to create a picture that is more subtle than the familiar caricature.

The conclusion reached in Chapter 3 was that the sympathy of most Britons, and most Lancastrians, lay with the North, especially after Lincoln's Emancipation Proclamation. There is no proof that Liverpool either conformed to this general pattern or departed from it. Several historians have trawled the Lancashire press for evidence of political activity during the war. In Liverpool, they have found next to nothing. There was a meeting in January 1863 at the Clarendon Hotel, which endorsed Lincoln's Emancipation Proclamation. There was an anti-slavery meeting at the Royal Court Theatre in February 1863, which was disrupted by a strong Southern contingent. The abolitionist Henry Ward Beecher spoke at the Philharmonic Hall in October 1863, "greeted with enthusiastic cheers ... not ... unmingled by ... hisses". No evidence of a public pro-Confederate meeting has been found. No evidence of any political meeting that could be characterised as working class has been found. This suggests that public agitation over the war did not run high in Liverpool. Nor is that surprising, given Liverpool's continued prosperity. It had no cotton mills, so there were negligible effects from the famine. The only people in the working population of Liverpool who appear to have suffered significantly from the war were the cotton porters at the docks.[6]

When the ship *George Griswold* arrived in Liverpool from New York with food supplies for starving cotton workers, all the men employed at the docks, from customs officials to porters and stevedores, refused payment for their services. The ceremony at St George's Hall, sponsored by the Chamber of Commerce, was filled with both "the merchants and other inhabitants of this town".[7] This suggests at least some fellow feeling for their compatriots in the rest of Lancashire. But neither this, nor anything else, suggests that strong political opinions on the war, let alone agitation for a particular outcome, held any significant attraction for the working men and women of Liverpool. In the absence of any evidence to the contrary, the probability must be that public opinion in the town mirrored that in the country.

The Liverpool press, like the national press, represented a range of opinion. The *Mercury* – which had a higher circulation than the rest of the town's newspapers put together – was strongly Liberal in domestic politics. At first glance, it was equally strong in support of the Confederacy, and its readers could have been forgiven for thinking that the paper did support the South. However, it is more accurate to say that the *Mercury* was vitriolically anti-Union. It published ceaseless tirades against Lincoln's Government and systematically misreported the Union's motives and its military progress. But, while this translated into a vicarious sympathy for the Confederacy, it never became an endorsement. The *Mercury*'s coverage of the war mirrored that of *The Times*. It once described *The Times*'s views on the war as 'rabid', but it was equally rabid itself.

From time to time, and perhaps to correct the general impression it was giving, the *Mercury* printed diatribes – the paper was fond of diatribes – against the evils of slavery, and it was this issue, as for so many other newspapers and individuals, that prevented it from championing the South. However, its conviction that the North could not conceivably be victorious led it to demand constantly that the Union should end a pointless war and recognise the Confederacy's de facto existence, trusting that time and necessity would soon force the South to abolish slavery of its own accord. "Disunion is an accomplished and irreversible fact," it said in August 1862. Two months later, the war had become a "useless struggle, in which [the North has] not the remotest chance of success". By April 1863, "the independence of the South is now merely a question of time" and, at the end of that year, "the conquest of the South still appears to us to be impossible." In June 1864, "[Grant] has very little chance of taking Richmond and none whatever of conquering the Southern Confederacy." Even as late as September 1864, the paper thought that "the war can only end in one way, namely, in the establishment of the independence of the Confederate States."[8]

As shown in Chapter 3, this opinion was almost universal in Britain. Francis Hamilton, a partner of Brown, Shipley & Co. in Liverpool and a strong Northern sympathiser, wrote to its associated company in New York in August 1861 that "the writer believes as strongly as he believes anything that the conquering of a country like the Southern States ... is an utter impossibility." For the *Mercury*, just as anti-Union vitriol did not translate into support for the South, a belief that the war should end forthwith did not translate into support for British intervention. The paper declared that Britain should "give the most favourable construction possible to any doctrine of international law which will permit us to stand aloof from the American struggle". In the wake of Gladstone's Newcastle speech in October 1862, the *Mercury* uncharacteristically supported recognition of the Confederacy. At all other times, it was resolutely opposed to recognition, or to intervention in any form, and was acutely aware of the likely consequences for relations with the North, on which the livelihoods of so many of its readers depended.[9]

The *Mercury*'s coverage of the cotton famine was negligible, and always carried an air of distance. Its short pieces were headed 'Distress in Lancashire', despite the fact that Liverpool was in Lancashire. In contrast, the headlines in the *Manchester Examiner and Times* referred to 'Distress in the manufacturing districts'. This hints at a truth suggested by much other reading about Liverpool at this time: in its own estimation, the town was something close to an independent state, more concerned with the wider world than with what lay on its own doorstep. This may help to explain Liverpool's apparent sense of detachment from the county, and from the country, of which it was a part. It shared many of the attitudes held elsewhere but does not appear to have participated widely in their expression.

The town's politicians did not support intervention either. During the war, Liverpool was represented by one Conservative and one Liberal MP. Marginally, however, it was a Conservative town at this time, discounting the limitations of the franchise. No Liberal topped a parliamentary poll in Liverpool between an atypical 1855 by-election and 1882, when Samuel Smith was elected. The Conservatives also kept control of the town council during this period. As one might expect of a port immersed in commerce, it elected representatives of both parties who would look after merchant interests and who were not known for their political dogmatism. The two MPs who represented Liverpool were Thomas Berry Horsfall (Conservative) and Joseph Ewart (Liberal). Both men came from families steeped in the mercantile history of the town. Horsfall, like his father, had served as Mayor of Liverpool. According to one obituary of him, "like his father, he stood in the front rank amongst the merchant princes of Liverpool." He had been elected President of the Liverpool Chamber of Commerce on its refoundation in 1850. Ewart was related to the Gladstone family and was an "American, East India and general merchant" in Liverpool; his father had been a cotton broker and founding partner of the firm of Ewart, Myers & Co.[10]

Both men had family links to Liverpool's slave trade, Ewart more closely than Horsfall, although it is Horsfall who is listed in the records of compensation paid when slavery was abolished. Neither was prominent during the civil war, although both were said to be simultaneously pro-emancipation and pro-South, a feat of moral gymnastics that was by no means uncommon in Britain. In February 1862, at a meeting of the Liverpool Chamber of Commerce, Ewart made a speech strongly in favour of British neutrality and of taking care not to give offence to the Union. He questioned whether the blockade was effective and said that Britain might be justified in disregarding it but doubted whether this would be "wise or politic". In May 1864, Horsfall presented a petition from Liverpool ship-owners asking for the Foreign Enlistment Act, the antiquated legislation of 1819 which the Government relied upon to enforce neutrality, to be amended so as to prevent warships for belligerent nations being built in Britain. As will be seen, these standpoints reflected precisely the interests of Liverpool merchants. Apart from these instances, the *Mercury* reported no comment on the war by either MP.[11]

There is nothing to be found in public, newspaper or political opinion in Liverpool that marks the town out as being substantially different from the rest of the country. However, it is not opinions but rather the activities of its commercial sector that account for Liverpool's reputation. Before addressing that subject in the round, it is necessary to dispose of the issue of blockade-running, which has over-dominated and distorted Liverpool's role in the civil war. Mary Ellison's lengthy chapter on the blockade implies, as do other sources, that the blockade-runners ran between Liverpool and the Southern ports. This, however, was seldom the case, at least once the practicalities of the activity had become apparent early in the war.[12]

There were many Southern ports, but most of those on the Atlantic coast were unusable, which is why, once it had sealed the ports in the Gulf of Mexico, the Union was able to enforce the blockade with tolerable success. Even the usable Atlantic ports had shallow approaches that required ships with shallow drafts. The vessels also needed to be small, and thus with limited cargo space, fast and nimble. In every way they were unsuited to ocean-going voyages. So, in practice, there were two parts to the trade in blockaded goods, only one of which involved running the blockade. This part featured voyages, through the blockade, between a depot port (usually Nassau in the Bahamas) and a Southern port (usually Charleston or Wilmington). The other part featured voyages between Liverpool and the depot port. As William Forwood, himself involved in blockade-running, recalled, "the *modus operandi* was to send out a depot ship to Nassau or Bermuda and employ in connection with this swift steamers to run the blockade and bring back cargoes of cotton."[13]

Sometimes the same companies were involved in both parts of the trade, but much of the real blockade-running was undertaken by American firms, especially by John Fraser & Co. of Charleston, the parent company of Fraser, Trenholm & Co. in Liverpool. The other part of the trade, between Liverpool and the depot port was, technically, not blockade-running, but normal commercial shipping. This distinction is what enabled 40 Liverpool ship-owners, in their memorial to Earl Russell complaining about Federal harassment of British vessels at Nassau, to declare truthfully, if misleadingly, that "such vessels are perfectly innocent of any attempt to run the blockade." *The Times* reproduced this letter, but did not publish the list of signatories, which would have given a good idea of which Liverpool ship-owners were engaged in trading blockaded goods. Despite a comprehensive volume of Foreign Office correspondence concerning complaints about interference with shipping in the Bahamas during the civil war, this memorial is missing.[14]

A great deal less cotton was grown in the South during the war, partly on the instructions of the Confederate Government, partly because of conscription, and partly because land had been turned over to growing food. Most Southern cotton went to the Union. Of the cotton grown in 1862–64, only about 14 per cent came to Britain. Yet, according to Mary Ellison, "on the British side of the Atlantic ... [blockade-runners] shipped 8,250 cargoes, worth $2,000,000, and 1,250,000 bales of cotton were run out from the South to pay for them." Even if these figures were correct – which they are not: only about 400,000 bales came from America in 1862–64, and nearly half of these were run out across the Mexican border, not through the blockade – blockade-running, romantic though it may have been, accounted for only a small part of Liverpool's trade during the war. The port had 96 per cent of the incoming blockade trade and 60 per cent of the outgoing, but the cargoes involved were negligible. Raw cotton imports from the Southern States accounted for about 12 per cent of Liverpool's dock revenues before the war. The volume of cotton imported from America was reduced by about 94 per cent during the three main years of the war. If the Mexican imports are ignored, the incoming element of the blockade trade, more than half the total, accounted for less than 0.5 per cent of the port's revenues during the war.[15]

It is true that, without the arms and supplies that the trade provided, the South could not have sustained the war. Blockade-running was far more important to the Confederacy than it ever was to Liverpool, however profitable it was to a handful of individuals. Virtually the entire trade of the port during the war was with countries other than the South, much of it with the North. Liverpool's role in the blockade trade has therefore been exaggerated and glamorised. So has its role in building the ships. Although Merseyside shipyards did build some of the blockade-runners, most of those built in Britain were built on the Clyde (53 per cent) or in London (21 per cent).[16] It is altogether more relevant to study the 99 per cent of Liverpool's trade during the civil war that had nothing to do with blockade-running.

At this time, Liverpool was hugely prosperous. Property and income tax returns laid before Parliament in 1857 showed that the town paid more such taxes than anywhere in Britain except London. Liverpool was bigger than Manchester and its population increased more rapidly between 1821 and 1871, when it was the largest mercantile community in Europe. In 1847, it had appointed the first British medical officer of health, and by 1860 it was already building working-class dwellings from corporation funds.[17]

Despite the assumption that Liverpool must have suffered greatly during the war, this was not the case. Before the war, tonnage through the port had been rising, on average, at the rate of 3 per cent p.a., and dock revenue at 8 per cent, although the progress of both was erratic. Comparing the three years 1862–64 with the three years 1858–60, total tonnage grew by 7 per cent and dock revenue by 5 per cent.[18] Considering the vast reduction in incoming cotton, this was a remarkable achievement. The town's merchants were able, and very quickly, to replace their lost business. In 1863, when one might have expected the effects of the war on Liverpool to be at their worst, William Forwood was arguing for substantial dock extension.[19]

The American share of Liverpool's commerce inevitably declined. In the years 1858–60, dock revenue from the American trade had accounted for 41 per cent of the port's total; in the years 1862–64, it was 30 per cent. Some of the shortfall was balanced by an increase of 27 per cent in revenues from the Indian trade. It is possible, from the port revenue statistics, to make a rough calculation of the relative pre-war revenues from the Northern and Southern parts of the American trade. Virtually all the trade in 1862–64 was with the

Engraving of the Princes' Dock, Liverpool, 1830, with bales of cotton on the quayside (reproduced by permission of the International Cotton Association)

North. The American revenues for those years were at 78 per cent of their total for the years 1858–60. The conclusion to be drawn is that, before the war, only about a quarter of Liverpool's American trade was with the Southern States, while three-quarters was with the Northern States.

The magnitude of this trade with the Union, accounting for 30 per cent of the port's revenues, is vital to understanding the attitudes of Liverpool's merchant community during the war. Even before the war, Liverpool earned far more from other parts of its trade with America than from its trade in raw cotton. Farnie has estimated that Liverpool docks had a more valuable trade in the export of cotton cloth than in the import of raw cotton.[20] Despite the vast quantities of Southern cotton piled up on its docks and in its warehouses, raw cotton was always less important to the port of Liverpool than it might appear.

Much of the trade with the Union during the war came from grain imports. Britain was not self-sufficient in wheat. When harvests were poor, as they were in the early years of the war, considerable imports were required to cover the deficiency. These had mostly come from European nations, but the usual sources diminished during the war. B. Schmidt's study has shown that, from 1861 to 1863, America supplied nearly 41 per cent of Britain's wheat and flour imports. They rose from under 22,000 tons in 1859 to over a million tons in

1862. These two years were exceptional, but they dramatise both the scale and the volatility of the trade. All this wheat and flour came from the Northern States, and most of it came into Liverpool. The *Mercury* commented that a war with the North would cause huge problems for the supply of wheat and other foodstuffs. Schmidt's conclusion that this was critical to the attitude of the British Government has been disputed by subsequent historians, who have emphasised that imported wheat would have been available from other sources, and also that there was little or no Cabinet discussion about it. However, the issue must surely have been present at the back of the mind when British politicians were contemplating intervention. It should also be mentioned that, according to US Treasury reports, nearly half the American national debt was held overseas and that, in 1861, 90 per cent of it was held in Britain. It is unlikely that this played no part in political calculations.[21]

The essential facts are that, at all times, the greater portion of the commerce of Liverpool involved countries other than America and, of its American trade, most was with the North. During the war, this situation became even more marked. *The Times* reported that "where one cargo goes forth to the South, 50 at least go to the North." The collapse of American cotton imports led to a greatly expanded trade with the Far East, South America and the Mediterranean, from which most of the cotton now came. When Mary Ellison says that Liverpool "trade[d] with the South as an independent nation", she gives both a political and an economic slant that is misleading. Liverpool simply traded. As it always had. With anyone. But not very much with the South, independent or not.[22]

In his study of Liverpool shipping agents who handled the Southern trade before and after the civil war, Neil Ashcroft found that, of the 127 firms involved in the trade in 1860, 100 were still trading in 1867. The rate of attrition was therefore low. However, the fact that most survived until 1867 says nothing about changes to the scale of their businesses. A significant number – albeit still a small minority – of Liverpool merchants would have been catastrophically affected by the collapse of American raw cotton imports, and many of these sought to recoup their losses through speculation or blockade-running. Most firms specialised by commodity and/or by country. From 1855 to 1870, about 70 per cent of all traders are said to have specialised by region, and over 60 per cent by commodity. However, as Ashcroft has established, "beyond them was a pool of work, shared amongst a shifting population of occasional participants – emphasised by the fact that over half of the total firms (53 per cent) have been identified as handling only one vessel [in the American cotton trade] in all the antebellum samples." This suggests that there were a number of large firms that dominated key trades, surrounded by a plethora of jobbing firms that had no single mainstay and were used to adapting to circumstances. Other research confirms this view.[23]

There is a further point to make about the import of American raw cotton to Liverpool. While most of it came directly from the ports of the Southern States – before the war, New Orleans supplied about 58 per cent of the Southern import; Mobile, Savannah and Charleston 10–15 per cent each – 14 per cent of total imports came via New York and a great deal of the 86 per cent that did not was consigned by Northern merchants. This point was even more relevant to the outgoing trade. The *Morning Post* reported that, before the war, "upwards of three-fourths of the European goods consumed by the South have been shipped to Northern ports, for transmission thence to the South." As far as business relationships between Liverpool and America were concerned, therefore, there was a lot less contact with the South, even before the war, than might be thought.[24]

As Graeme Milne has noted, "Liverpool traders are assumed to have been pro-Confederate because of their investments in the cotton trade, and the port as a whole is assumed to have suffered when that trade was curtailed, but little systematic work has been done to determine the reality of the situation." Milne's own research has largely addressed the second assumption, but the first assumption has not been challenged and the absence of concrete data has already confused others. Mary Ellison's remark about Liverpool "unofficially fighting on the side of the South" was given at the top of the chapter, and she made similarly dramatic points elsewhere. However, at other places in her narrative, she contradicted herself: "The reaction of Liverpool was far more complex than that of any other town or region in Lancashire. ... There was a greater degree of backing for the North there than has been realized." Blackett also struggled in vain to find evidence of Liverpool's true sympathies.[25]

The chief manifestations of Confederate support in Liverpool are easy to describe. The town was the headquarters of Fraser, Trenholm & Co., the Charleston-based company that had been the largest importer of cotton into Britain before the war and became the Confederacy's unofficial bank in Europe during the war. Charles K. Prioleau, its managing director, masterminded the blockade trade, and his house in Abercromby Square was said to have been the unofficial 'Embassy' of the Confederacy. Commander James Bulloch, the South's chief naval procurement officer, was based in Liverpool, from where he sourced the *Florida* and the *Alabama*, as well as the notorious Laird 'rams', all built on Merseyside. James Spence, the most effective British propagandist for the South, lived and traded in Liverpool. Many of the merchants involved in trade with the Southern States championed the Confederacy. Some of them formed the Southern Club, with a membership of about 200, most of whom had a connection with blockade-running. The Forwood family flew the Confederate flag at their offices and on their ships, when in port. For all these reasons, it was and remains easy to portray Liverpool as a predominantly Southern town. The question is how far these activities, which were high-profile but involved comparatively small numbers of people, were representative of Liverpool as a whole.[26]

The attitudes of the mercantile community of Liverpool will be considered under the umbrella term 'merchants' – a word which embraces a wide range of activities, most of them connected with the port. The noisiest merchants were, as usual, supporters of the Confederacy. At the commencement of the *Trent* crisis, Mary Ellison reported a meeting of "enraged cotton brokers and merchants" in the saleroom of Liverpool's Exchange, demanding a war with the North: "This normally cautious body of men passed a violently anti-Northern motion." Most of those attending – Spence, Forwood, Cowie, Fernie, Bushby, Longrigg, Prioleau, amongst others – were merchants with substantial interests in the American cotton trade, together with a few cotton brokers. Referring to the same meeting, Marler reported that "Spence easily secured the support of Liverpool's cotton merchants for an angry resolution."[27] The *Mercury* interpreted the meeting differently:

> The frothy excitement which the less judicious and less experienced of our merchants and brokers evinced yesterday has a good deal subsided. The appearance in the *Times* and other papers of the account of the indignation meeting ... has rather tarnished the reputation which Liverpool merchants possessed for good breeding and good sense. ... That it indicated the public feeling in this town is as untrue as to say that the meeting was convened by the most influential of the mercantile body. ... We do not hesitate to say that Tom, Dick, and Harry [*a snide reference to the Littledale family: merchants and cotton brokers, and prominent supporters of the Confederacy*] had the almost entire management of the affair, and that they appear to have enjoyed it amazingly.[28]

Given the sympathies of the *Mercury* during the war, this represents a significant statement.

Many members of Liverpool's merchant community were less partisan and more pragmatic than their 'less experienced' colleagues. Their main concern was anything that constrained free trade. For that reason, the North had angered them with the Morrill tariff and the imposition of the blockade, and the South with the embargo. The South's methods of prosecuting the war angered them just as much, none more so than the activities of the *Florida* and *Alabama*. These armed cruisers, both built on Merseyside, roamed the Atlantic and other oceans, and sank or captured any Union vessel they found. To many Liverpool ship-owners, this was piracy. Furthermore, much of this Northern merchant shipping was insured in Britain, which prompted the Chamber of Commerce to write a letter of protest to Earl Russell. However, Liverpool also gained from the depredations of these cruisers. Their success in sinking merchant ships flying the Federal flag prompted many Northern ship-owners to transfer the registration of their vessels to Britain. Richard Cobden complained that "we had rendered the mercantile marine of America practically valueless". In 1860, 11,000 tons of US shipping had been sold to British buyers; in 1863, it was 329,000 tons. Many vessels were acquired by firms that had previously acted as the Liverpool agents of American owners. By the end of the war, the size of Britain's merchant marine fleet had overtaken that of America and accounted for 37 per cent of the world's shipping tonnage. As with so many issues during the civil war, this one cut both ways.[29]

It is difficult to assess the private views of Liverpool merchants towards the war. The American Consul in Liverpool, Thomas Dudley, compiled a list of those known or suspected to be trading with the Confederacy, which he sent to the State Department in June 1862. Out of 255 companies or individuals named – not a very great number, considering Dudley's diligence and the size of the town's merchant community – 19 were cotton brokers and 43 had been substantial recipients of American cotton in 1860. But these names were not necessarily representative of Liverpool's mercantile community as a whole. Other historians have emphasised Liverpool's ties with the North and its awareness of the dangers of alienating these relationships. John Crosby Brown, in his history of the family business which included the firm of Brown, Shipley & Co. in Liverpool, may have reported that "it was a source of profound grief to Mr Shipley that at the outbreak of the Civil War the sympathies of the English aristocratic and mercantile classes, and among them his old Liverpool friends, were in great measure with the Southern cause", but most members of these classes throughout Britain were sympathetic to the South, so his statement does not suggest anything unique about Liverpool.[30]

As with public opinion in the country as a whole, one cannot quantify support for each side amongst Liverpool's merchants. Many of them, probably a majority, had an emotional sympathy for the Confederacy. However, emotional sympathy is not the same as a perception of self-interest, or a rational appreciation of wise policy, and here Liverpool's attitudes were a great deal clearer. It is not hard to say where the self-interest of Liverpool merchants lay. Like the cotton operatives, their first interest was a speedy end to the war, irrespective of who won it. Their second interest was a policy of British neutrality and non-intervention, as their principal newspaper urged. Having lost, for the time being, their trade with the Southern States, the last thing the merchants needed was a disruption to their trade with the North, let alone a war with the Union. Intervention would have produced the former and might have produced the latter.

These attitudes were reflected in the Liverpool Chamber of Commerce, despite the presence there of the leading Southern propagandist, James Spence. At a meeting in August 1862, the Government's policy of neutrality was endorsed by several speakers and opposed by none. In late October 1862, Spence failed to persuade the Chamber to memorialise the government for recognition of the Confederacy. Altogether, as Blackett observed, "Spence had little success generating public support in what many considered the most pro-Confederate city in the nation."[31]

On 8 November 1862, the Chamber wrote to Earl Russell, protesting at the ravages to merchant shipping caused by the *Alabama*. A special meeting of the Chamber in April 1863 considered the issues raised by the building of that ship and agreed to petition the Government to prevent systematic evasion of the Foreign Enlistment Act. This led to a memorial to the Foreign Secretary from 31 Liverpool ship-owners, suggesting changes to the Act by giving greater power to prevent the construction in British ports of ships destined for belligerents. It complained that: "Your Memorialists share in the regret with which a law-regarding community must naturally look on successful attempts to evade the provisions of an Act of Parliament passed for a single and simple purpose, but which has been found not to give the Executive all the powers needed." Twelve of the ship-owners were substantial importers of cotton, and 10 of them of pre-war American cotton. They were motivated partly by a fear of what would happen if Britain was subjected to the same treatment as the Union in any future war: much of its merchant marine would be liable to be sunk, and much of the rest would choose to sail under a different flag. It is clear from the minutes that one aim of the memorial was to stay on good terms with the North. The *Mercury* reported that "a copy of the report of the special committee was transmitted to the New York Chamber of Commerce, whose acknowledgement, lately received, is couched in friendly terms."[32]

The Chamber of Commerce was not unanimous in its opinions. However, the reports of its proceedings suggest that the principal Liverpool merchant interests, as defined earlier, had majority support throughout the war. This contradicts Mary Ellison's assertion that it tended to support the South. And when she refers to "pockets of sympathy for neutrality" existing in Liverpool, all one can say is that they were very deep pockets.[33]

In addition to its Chamber of Commerce, Liverpool had an American Chamber of Commerce, composed of Liverpool merchants who traded with America, some British and some American. In 1859, it had 29 members and met twice a year to consider grievances, the regulation of fees, and other trading issues. Liverpool was home to the largest American community in Britain at the time, many of them cotton traders or financial men from the North, whose social life in the port revolved around the US consulate and the American Chamber of Commerce. Given their origins, one would think that most of these Americans supported the Union, although that cannot be assumed either. The minute book of the American Chamber at this period does not survive, and its meetings were not reported in the *Mercury*, so its precise views are unknown. Its presidents during the civil war were George Melly (1861), S. B. Guion (1862), Thomas Stolterfoht (1863), Charles Melluish (1864) and W. Maxwell (1865). Guion shipped coal and other goods to the Union free of charge. All except Melluish were recipients of American cotton in 1860. In 1865, the membership included known Southern partisans from the firms of Richardson, Spence & Co. and C. & D. MacIver, and known Northern partisans from the firms of Brown, Shipley & Co., Guion & Co., Rathbone Brothers & Co. and Melly, Forget & Co.[34]

This, in as far as it can be ascertained, was the political and mercantile climate in which the cotton brokers of Liverpool operated. Their own sympathies are equally hard to decipher. In their annual circulars, political opinions are seldom ventured. There is a certain amount of political analysis, especially in the circulars at the end of 1860 following Lincoln's election, but it is expressed in terms of the likely impact upon the cotton trade rather than with any sense of a desired outcome. At the end of 1863, Samuel Smith declared that it is "past doubt that the institution of slavery must perish", a conviction repeated by Robson & Eskrigge. But such comments do not necessarily imply approval, although in these cases they probably do. The most overt opinion was expressed by Maurice Williams who, with typical understatement, declared the South's war of secession to be "the most gigantic and wicked of all rebellions in the history of the World". But no one reading their printed commentaries could identify brokers collectively as being partisans of either side. As with other commercial elements in the town, politics seem to have been merely politics, but business was business.[35]

In addition to the bulk export of merchandise such as cotton goods, Liverpool docks handled a more specialised commodity during the war: arms and ammunition. These cargoes were sourced outside Liverpool, but the port was the agent of their transmission. They may have formed a tiny proportion of the port's trade, but they were of vital importance to the consignees. When the civil war commenced, neither side possessed enough of the armaments and clothing that were needed to fight it, and both sides looked to Britain to supply the shortfall. It is hyperbolic to claim, as one newspaper did, that "the Northern armies are clothed by Bradford and armed by Birmingham", but, especially in the early part of the war, the claim did contain a great deal of truth. One of the anomalies of the Foreign Enlistment Act was that it ignored small arms purchases. There was nothing illegal in both North and South sourcing armaments in Britain. It may have violated the Queen's proclamation of neutrality, but that proclamation was not law.[36]

Historical comment has focused on what Britain did to arm the South but, in terms of weaponry, it did more to arm the North. Because there was no blockade to run, this has attracted less attention. Most of these arms shipments went through Liverpool and must have been forwarded by merchants and ship-owners who were content to consign them. In March 1863, Russell wrote to the American Minister, Charles Adams: "[The] Government are entitled to complain of both parties ... and their complaint applies most to the [Federal] Government, because it is by [them] that by far the greatest amount of such supplies have been ordered and procured." Arms exports were not recorded as such but were listed under euphemisms such as 'sundries' or 'hardware'. John Laird MP, under fire in the House of Commons for his firm's building of the *Alabama*, provided detailed figures. He examined the bills of entry for London and Liverpool and found vast shipments of weaponry to the Union, transported by – amongst others – Barings Bros and Brown, Shipley & Co. Laird claimed to have found evidence that between May 1861 and December 1862, 41,500 muskets, 341,000 rifles, 26,500 gun-flints and nearly 50 million percussion-caps had been sent to the North. He alleged further substantial quantities for the first quarter of 1863 and said he believed that these figures understated the actual shipments. "The Northern States," Laird declared, "have been well supplied with the most efficient means of warfare from this country, through the agency of some most influential persons."[37]

One of the 'influential persons' Laird may have had in mind was his fellow Conservative MP Thomas Baring, who ostentatiously walked out of the chamber during Laird's speech. Laird had correctly named Barings Bros as a facilitator of Federal procurement. Jay Sexton has described how, in 1862, the bank trebled its advance to the Union's purchasing agent George Schuyler. In total, Britain and other European countries supplied the North with more than a million small arms in the first two years of the war, whilst its manufacturers converted to arms production. A record in the Parliamentary Papers for 1864, reporting arms shipments from Liverpool to America, shows that in 1862 Liverpool sent almost 200,000 firearms and nearly 12 million percussion caps to New York. Laird's figures do not seem to have been an overestimate.[38]

The Confederacy was equally engaged in buying arms in Britain, and this activity continued throughout the war, when resources permitted. In the second half of 1862, its limited funds abroad were so overdrawn that purchasing operations were put on hold. However, by early 1863, Caleb Huse, its chief procurement agent, had purchased more than 130,000 long arms. It has been said that the Confederate army fought the battle of Shiloh with weapons and ammunition entirely smuggled in from Nassau on the blockade-runner *Fingal*. Another source estimates that the South imported more than half a million small arms in total, most of them from Britain.[39]

The most notorious contribution made by Merseyside to the Confederacy was to its navy, non-existent at the start of the war and the scourge of the Union by its end. The ravages wrought by the *Florida*, built by William

C. Miller & Sons in Liverpool, and the *Alabama*, built by Laird Brothers in Birkenhead, and the unsuccessful attempts of the British Government to prevent them from leaving port, have been well documented and need no repetition. Whatever it appeared to say, the Foreign Enlistment Act, never tested in a court until the civil war, was not held to disallow the construction of warships for another country in a war in which Britain was neutral, unless the armaments were flagrant and the destination certain. The courts did not uphold the Government's attempts to use the Act to stop the *Florida*, and it also failed to stop the *Alexandra*, a Confederate cruiser built on Clydeside. Earl Russell said of the failure to prevent the escape of the *Alabama*: "In a single instance, we fell into error." It was a big error given the reparations claimed by the Federal Government, later agreed at $15.5 million.[40]

Whatever the legalities, the Government was determined not to fail again when confronted by the Laird 'rams', two formidable warships with armoured under-water beaks under construction by Laird Brothers. The 'rams' and all other suspected Confederate vessels were detained. Commercial opinion in Liverpool was divided: many ship-owners were relieved, while Thomas Horsfall represented the contrary view that the Government's "course of conduct ... amounted to oppressing the commercial interests of the country." The Solicitor General admitted that detention was an act of policy though not of strict law. When a legal challenge followed, Palmerston simply purchased the 'rams' for the Royal Navy. Laird Brothers were among the contractors to the Navy. They were already building one ship for the Government, HMS *Agincourt*, and were no doubt in hope of further contracts, which they later obtained. This may have influenced the company's decision to let the 'rams' go quietly. Two letters from John Laird relating to the detention are listed among the Foreign Office papers transferred to the National Archives but are marked there as 'missing at transfer'.[41]

Far less well-known are the attempts made by the Union to purchase warships in Britain. In fact, before the Laird 'rams' reached the Royal Navy, they might have been diverted to the Union rather than to the Confederacy. In April 1863, at the instigation of US Treasury Secretary Salmon P. Chase, and with the involvement of US Navy Secretary Gideon Welles, two American businessmen, John Forbes and William Aspinwall, were sent to Britain to purchase warships already under construction for the Confederates and to outbid the South for them. The targets included the 'rams'. Forbes and Aspinwall were given $10 million in bonds with which to negotiate a $5 million loan from Barings. However, the bank was not enthusiastic about the project and gave the Americans scarcely half what they requested. Even that proved impossible to spend. Despite the bribes offered to shipyard workers to disclose information, little progress was made, and the secret mission was aborted when a pro-Southern New Yorker disclosed its existence to *The Times*.

Forbes and Aspinwall returned home empty-handed, apart from $6 million in unconverted bonds.[42]

This was not the first time that the Union had attempted to purchase warships in Britain, nor the first time that Navy Secretary Welles was involved. In the same House of Commons speech by John Laird reported earlier, he claimed that "in 1861, just after the war broke out, a friend of mine ... came to me with a view of getting iron-plated vessels of war built in this country for the American Government – the Northern Government."[43] Laird then gave some details of this approach, but was otherwise circumspect. However, when Richard Cobden publicised a letter he had received throwing doubt on Laird's claim, Laird responded vigorously and in detail. He may also have heard that Welles had described him in the US Senate as "a mercenary hypocrite without principle or honesty".[44] The letter sent to Cobden had been written by Welles to Charles Sumner, chairman of the Senate Committee on Foreign Relations, saying that Welles "has an indistinct remembrance that his department was importuned by more than one person on behalf of Messrs. Laird".[45] This may not be thought to be among the more convincing of political denials.

Laird then released for publication a series of four letters from his unnamed contact, all written between 30 July and 25 October 1861. These extracts, culled from various letters, reveal the immense detail of the approach made to him:

> I have had frequent interviews with our "Department of Naval Affairs", and am happy to say that the Minister of the Navy is inclined to have an iron-plated ship built out of the country. I send you herewith a memorandum ... from the department. I have assured my Government that you will keep this matter entirely and strictly to yourselves. This ship is designed for a specific purpose, to accomplish a definite object ... to force an entrance into Charleston harbour. The floating battery or iron-plated ship [is] to be so constructed as to be able to pass the forts comparatively unharmed. She is not required to have a speed exceeding six knots. She must not draw over fourteen feet. She must have no masts. There should be a rudder at each end to avoid turning. She must carry eight guns (rifled), weighing each about 10,000 lbs.[46]

In the same correspondence, Laird was asked to quote and provide designs for a six-wheel gunboat, with similar detail provided. It would appear that Laird was prepared to entertain building gunboats for the Union, because he was later thanked for sending drawings, which his contact had "laid ... before the Secretary of the Navy" and who hoped "to send you an order for the construction of one or more gunboats". However, "the Secretary was rather disappointed that you have not sent any response to the memorandum in reference to a shell and shot battery." It is possible that, by this time, Laird had been approached by Bulloch to build vessels for the Confederacy. It is also possible that taking the responsibility for shelling Charleston was a step too far for this Southern diehard.[47]

Presumably, this correspondence in the *Mercury* was relayed to Washington by the American consul in Liverpool, Thomas Dudley, if by no one else. Further denials were now required. On 24 August, the *Mercury* published a letter from Charles Sedgewick, a New York congressman and former chairman of the House Committee on Naval Affairs. He identified the go-between as a Mr Howard of Brooklyn. Howard was said to have possessed plans for vessels, produced by Laird, and Sedgewick assumed him to be an agent of Laird's. He directed Howard to Welles, who turned the proposal down.[48] This claim is even less convincing than the previous attempt at a denial. The relevant Laird correspondence dates from the second half of 1861, whereas Sedgewick claimed that the approach from Howard was made in July 1862. In that same month, the *Alabama* was completed and Welles would have been fully briefed about the vessel and its constructor by Dudley. It seems inconceivable that Laird would have been interested in building ships for the Union at that point, particularly as his firm had also signed the contract to build the Laird 'rams' in the same month.[49] The lameness of Sedgewick's case suggests that Laird was truthful in his account of the Federal approach, while the detail of Laird's briefing suggests a project inconsistent with someone hoping to broker a vague deal. Finally, it seems unlikely that Welles would have used the precise phrase 'mercenary hypocrite' unless Laird had previously appeared willing to build gunboats for the North: no other aspect of Laird's behaviour could be described as hypocritical, however mercenary it was.

The vast activity that took place in Liverpool during the war years – the building of ships for the Confederacy; the approach to build ships for the Union; the formidable supply of armaments to both sides; the efforts to replace the lost American cotton trade; the urgent arrivals of cotton from elsewhere; the bravado of blockade-running; and political and mercantile partisanship on both sides – took place in a port where the activities of all were under constant surveillance by both combatants. Thomas Dudley for the Union, and James Bulloch for the Confederacy, wanted to know everything that happened. The *Mercury* deplored the way that both sides had made Liverpool "a kind of supplemental fighting ground", each with its own headquarters and spies, where respective agents promoted their cause and attempted to thwart the plans of their opponents. Nor were the two belligerents the only ones involved in espionage. According to the *Mercury*, "it is currently reported that the head constable of Liverpool, acting under instructions from the Government, is employing Detectives Cousin, Skaife, Smith, and Horne to go about incog. and obtain information respecting suspicious vessels, and also to watch the movements of the leading Confederates."[50]

So Liverpool was certainly a hotspot during the war, but it was far from being a Confederate hotspot alone. The *Mercury*'s correspondent on the town's Exchange referred to "the mercantile community here, the majority of whom are strongly in favour of the Confederates", but – even if he was right – most of them did not urge the Government to act upon their opinion: in fact, the reverse.[51] As for public opinion in the town, there is no evidence that it differed from what is now felt to have been the mostly pro-Union sentiment in Britain generally. In the same way that it is impossible to speak of the varied and conflicting experiences of the cotton trade during the war in the same breath, it is impossible to do so with the opinions and attitudes of Liverpool's citizens and merchants. The interests of specific sub-groups need to be teased out from the generalisations. For every Spence or Forwood or Littledale in Liverpool, there was a Brown, a Rathbone and a Melly.

It is indisputable that a large number of the most prominent Confederate supporters in Britain were based in Liverpool, but that is not surprising in view of Liverpool's geographical significance. To proceed from that fact to assert that Liverpool as a whole was overwhelmingly pro-Confederate is a *non sequitur*, and plenty of contrary evidence exists to dispute such a viewpoint. It is possible that there was greater support for the Confederacy in the town than elsewhere, but such a claim is unproven and unprovable.

Liverpool's permanent and intimate connection with both parts of America meant that many people there had an intense personal interest in the civil war, and also a strong vested interest in it. From a financial and mercantile point of view, those interests and connections had more to do with the North than with the South. For most merchants, a quick end to the war was the priority. However, for some of them – many cotton brokers and speculators; the more successful of the blockade-runners – nothing was more devoutly wished than a continuation of the conflict that had so enriched them. In fact, self-interest always seemed to take precedence over opinion, no matter how strongly held. Maurice Williams, despite his vehement views on the war, was happy to profit greatly from the speculation it induced, as he had been to profit from slavery before it. The convinced Southerner John Laird was prepared to entertain the thought of building gunboats for the Union. The cotton commentator Henry Neill came from a staunch anti-slavery family and was nearly expelled from Louisiana on the eve of the war for his abolitionist views, yet he was arrested on a captured blockade-runner outside Charleston harbour.[52]

During the war, as always, Liverpool went about its business of trading. It was not Liverpool, Louisiana, nor was it Liverpool anywhere else. It was simply Liverpool. And being simply Liverpool during the civil war meant an immersion in "huge commercial imposthumes ... [which ripened] into horrible rankness," as the *Porcupine* so colourfully put it, and as will be explored in the next chapter.[53]

CHAPTER VI

A Toll Booth on the Mersey
How Liverpool enriched itself at Manchester's expense

Despite famine conditions in Lancashire and financial despair in Manchester, for much of the war Liverpool was a boom town. The broker Paul Hemelryk remembered that "the excitement during the American war was very great, and the profits sometimes beyond conception. ... Yes, those were great times, times of prosperity, when cotton brokers came down to business in their carriages, and on horseback." The *Mercury* gave it as "the opinion of some persons that the year 1863 has been the most profitable year ever known in Liverpool. The cotton trade ... has never been more profitable."[1] Another broker, Edward Braddyll, celebrated the prosperity in verse:

> Our Cotton Exchange was a busy sight, – the busiest in the town;
> For the price of Cotton was running up, whilst the Stock was running down.
> And every Broker in all the lot, old, young, or great or small,
> Full many an order had he got, and he quickly filled them all. ...
> They bought themselves new traps and drags, they smoked the best cigars,
> And as they walked the Exchange Flags* they thanked their lucky stars![2]

These verses were written specifically about the year 1863, the height of the cotton famine, a year during which much of Lancashire was starving. Nothing could better illustrate the degree to which the cotton trade in Liverpool was disconnected from its hinterland.

Chapter 4 followed the volume of raw cotton through the war years; this and the next chapter will follow the money, and consider who competed, and with what success, for a share of the spoils. This chapter begins by providing the financial context for the Liverpool raw cotton market: how the

---

* 'The Flags' refer to the flagstones outside the Liverpool Exchange, where all raw cotton was traded.

transatlantic trade had been organised before the war, and how everything changed from August 1861. It will then attempt to quantify the value of the raw cotton traded during the war, in the same way that Chapter 4 quantified the volume. The issue of speculation – which Liverpool always hoped could be left blushing in the wings – will be dragged reluctantly to centre stage. Throughout these years, Manchester became progressively enraged at the way that Liverpool made its already desperate situation worse. For most of the time, it had no choice but to suffer in silence: it needed cotton, and it needed to pay what Liverpool demanded for it. Towards the end of the war, Manchester broke its silence. The chapter concludes with the story of the explosive argument between the spinners and the LCBA.

There is no single source, primary or secondary, that sheds comprehensive light on these issues. The financing of the pre-war American trade has been described in two major secondary sources[3] and mentioned in others, although never with much, or sometimes any, reference to Liverpool. The quantification of market value relies on the same sources as that of volume: Holt and Donnell. The section on speculation is based largely on contemporary anecdotal sources, although Chapter 7 will bring some structure and concrete information to the issue, especially as it affected the brokers. The dispute between the LCBA and the spinners is based on the surviving minute books of the LCBA.[4]

Before the war, with 80 per cent of Britain's cotton coming from America, the first link in the financial chain was between the Southern planter and his representative, the cotton factor. In theory, the factor was the planter's agent for selling the crop; in practice, he was many other things as well. The similarities between Southern factors and Liverpool brokers are striking: both were bankers to their clients; both produced market circulars; both simultaneously bought and sold cotton, with the consequent conflicts of interest; both could choose to withhold stocks from the market if the price was not right; both speculated in cotton; and the factor was sometimes a planter as well, just as the broker was sometimes a merchant. The planter frequently pre-sold at least one year's crop to his factor. These mortgages were arranged by the factors and provided by banks, mainly in the North, with the advances often used to purchase more slaves. Most planters were in permanent hock to their factor. According to one contemporary writer, "not one in fifteen is free of debt". The less scrupulous mortgaged their crops several years ahead and several times over or borrowed from a second factor to pay the first. Alfred Stone claimed that "millions of dollars have been advanced by Southern factors upon the mere personal word of the planter, with no formal security at all. ... If cotton was king, the cotton factor was the power behind the throne." Another historian has written that "default and suspension of payments were common. Planters frequently leveraged themselves to the hilt, incurring debts of such magnitude that repayment was simply impossible."[5]

The cotton factors, mostly based in the Southern ports, charged a commission of 2.5 per cent for selling the cotton. It was sometimes sold directly to British spinners, although this was not a frequent occurrence, or to local agents of British merchants, or to Southern banks, but mostly to New York merchants, who often had their own representatives in the South. The New York merchant then sold on the consignment. British sales were made directly to a merchant house in Liverpool, or in London, or through that merchant's corresponding firm in America, if one existed. Sometimes the cotton was sold outright, and sometimes on commission, at a normal rate of 5 per cent. The cotton was then shipped to Liverpool. The British merchant imported the cotton, warehoused it and arranged for its sale on the Liverpool market through a broker. In this typical chain of events, there were five intermediaries between the planter and the spinner – cotton factor, New York and Liverpool merchants and two Liverpool brokers. There could be more. Occasionally there were fewer.[6]

At every stage, money for the consignment was advanced from the acquiring party to the disposing party. As Woodman noted, "anyone with cotton on hand could easily get an advance from the merchant to whom he chose to consign it ... in cash – immediately, even if he planned to consign his cotton to a merchant a long way off." The norm for these advances was 67 per cent to 75 per cent of the expected value of the consignment. The balance was usually paid at 90 days. These advances were effected by bills of exchange, discounted on receipt to provide ready cash for the disposer. The transatlantic cotton trade operated on the basis of extended credit, governed by Anglo-American finance houses in New York, London and Liverpool.[7]

The slowness of communication and transport meant that, even at 90 days, the consignment needed to be paid for by the recipient soon after, and sometimes before, he had physically acquired the cotton. The recipient needed an advance himself. Importing merchants were not always well capitalised; many were ship-owners, with their money tied up in ships; most were content to let their brokers become the bankers for their cargoes. That is how, in Britain, the selling broker came to make advances to the importing merchant, which gave him leverage over his client and influence over the timing of the sale of the cotton. One source has said that, as early as 1800, the broker was giving financial support to the importer "on a scale and with a purpose which suggests that its provision was much more than an ancillary function. The increasing profitability of the broker's practice ... provides a realistic explanation of why the broker became the central figure in the market."[8]

Liverpool brokers, via their bankers, financed most consignments between their arrival in Liverpool – or before it – and the spinner's settlement of his purchase. Brokers did not need to be highly capitalised, but they did need substantial access to credit. In practice, there must have been a diffuse system of rolling credit, only notionally related to individual consignments. Under this system, it was possible for the same cotton to be mortgaged more than once simultaneously. This is what happened during the speculative mania of the civil war, which is why a sudden fall in the price could cause not just one advance on that consignment to unravel, but many.

By the end of the 1850s, Anglo-American financial institutions had become the real powerhouse of the trade, with the result that the North effectively controlled the South's crop. Southern States belatedly tried to create their own commercial infrastructure, but they were too late. In 1860, 85 per cent of America's chartered banks were in the North, as well as 90 per cent of its industrial output. By then, New York was effectively the economic capital of the South, and it achieved its wider commercial pre-eminence principally because of cotton. Woodman concluded that "the power behind King Cotton's rickety throne was located in New York and Liverpool rather than in New Orleans, Mobile, Savannah, and Charleston." The *New York Times* put it more succinctly: "The proceeds of the Southern crops comes [sic] North simply to pay Southern debts."[9]

New Orleans and the other Southern cotton markets had long been uncertain places for those with a stake in raw cotton that was dependent on its price, as Liverpool was to become with a vengeance during the civil war. Cotton was a risky business: new operators could come in with little experience and little capital, undercut the market and speculate on price; it was not a securely profitable long-term business. Taking a cut as a banker, or as a broker, was a great deal safer, which is why these two groups became the most powerful forces in the transatlantic trade. Barings Bros and Brown & Co., previously large shippers of cotton, led the way in the migration to financial services. Brown & Co. controlled the letter of credit business and became the largest provider of foreign exchange in America. New Orleans, the financial centre of the South, was to a large extent an outpost of New York and was thus regarded with grave suspicion by many Southerners before and during the war.[10]

This system, with its elaborate ritual of financial pass-the-parcel, raises the question of what happened when the music stopped in August 1861. At that point, what should have become the Southern cotton crops of 1860–61 and 1861–62 would have been largely mortgaged. The cotton factors would have had debts to the banks they could not repay, and the planters to the factors. Some of this debt would have remained in the South, but most was held in the North. At the outset of the war, State legislatures in the South passed 'stay' laws, forbidding the repayment of any debt to Northern or foreign creditors while the war lasted. Estimates of Southern debt at that point range from $30 million to $100 million in New Orleans, and $150 million to $300 million overall (up to $9 billion today).[11]

Whatever the true amount, Anglo-American banks must have been the first losers from the crisis. Which merchants suffered, and to what extent, would have depended on the degree of forward contracting. British merchants were helped by a difficulty in negotiating bills of exchange from late 1860, following Lincoln's election. At that time, the brokers Cowie, Smith & Co. reported that "the commercial distrust and political excitement having created a financial convulsion in the United States ... all the avenues of business have been almost closed, and the wheels of the machinery by which Cotton is ordinarily forwarded to Europe, have been much impeded", a hiatus which the Neill brothers confirmed.[12] In the event, this was just as well. From early 1861, any forward contract for the purchase of American cotton would have been reckless in the extreme. But earlier forward contracts had almost certainly been agreed, for which a majority advance would have been paid, on cotton that would never be delivered. Some of these contracts would have been entered into by British merchants and underwritten by British banks. Much of this money was presumably never recovered. Yet the losses, which can have occurred only early in the war, did not result in any substantial bank, broker or merchant failures in Britain at that time. So either the losses were bearable, or they were recouped through the copious profit opportunities that the war afforded.[13]

In August 1861, therefore, it was not just American cotton that was suspended, but the financial infrastructure of a vast trade. Connections that had been formed and nurtured over decades, trust that had been built up, became irrelevant in an instant. Networks that had supported an annual trade of about £3 billion at today's prices, giving confidence to all engaged in it, dissolved overnight. There must have been similar networks, on a smaller scale, that had supported the pre-war import of cotton from India, Brazil, and Egypt, and these no doubt expanded to handle the greater wartime volumes. But many of those who dealt in cotton during the war, both in Britain and in other countries, were new entrants to the market, tempted by the prices and profits on offer. None of this is quantified or documented, but it must have had a destabilising effect on the market, on its financial operations, and on the level of trust that existed between its participants. The American trade, in terms of its shape and dominance, had not fundamentally altered for decades. Suddenly, in August 1861, that trade ended, and with it the structures within which Liverpool operated. Over the following years, it was not so much a case of new structures being put in place as of an unstructured free-for-all.

To place this period of time in context, Figure 8 shows the approximate value of British raw cotton imports over the course of the nineteenth century. Because the price of cotton fell during the century, the value of imports rose more slowly (about eight- to tenfold) than their volume (about thirtyfold).

Figure 8 Rough value of British raw cotton imports, 1800–1900

Source: B. Mitchell with P. Deane, *Abstract of British Historical Statistics* (Cambridge: Cambridge University Press, 1962)

Table 8 Value of British raw cotton imports, 1858–1867

	Import (000 lb)	Weighted pence (p.) per lb	Value (£ 000)
1858	1,025,500	2.53	25,945
1859	1,190,800	2.58	30,723
1860	1,435,800	2.54	36,469
1861	1,261,400	3.40	42,888
1862	533,100	5.80	30,920
1863	691,800	8.63	59,702
1864	896,100	10.07	90,237
1865	966,400	7.07	68,324
1866	1,353,800	5.85	79,197
1867	1,273,800	4.17	53,117

Source: George Holt & Co., annual cotton circulars (Liverpool Record Office, 380 COT/1/11/71).

Nevertheless, the financial ascent of the market is clear. Having considered in Chapter 4 the dramatic fall in the volume of raw cotton received during the war, it is sobering to note the dramatic rise in its value. The value of imports attained a monetary peak in 1864 that would not be repeated until the similarly extreme circumstances of the First World War.[14] Table 8 gives the detailed figures for the years 1858–67. It can be seen that, at the height of the war and despite a huge reduction in volume, the value of raw cotton imports was two and a half times greater than it had been even in the boom year of 1860. Over the years 1861–66, their value was about £150 million greater (£15 billion today) than it would otherwise have been.

It is difficult to quantify how much the Liverpool market was distorted by speculation during the war. The scale of the reported activity was breathtaking. Through 1862, at the height of the frenzy, speculative sales were running at 72 per cent of the level of genuine sales; at their peak in late August, they were nearly double genuine sales. However, there is every reason to believe that the actual level of speculation was much higher than the reported level. To understand the issue, it is necessary to know how the official figure for speculative sales was compiled. As Ellison explained:

> The sellers [selling brokers] furnished an account of all cotton sold, but the buyers [buying brokers] returned only the purchases for [re-]export or on speculation; the balance of the sales, after deducting the two items named, being put down as deliveries to consumers [spinners], which item, along with the [re-] export, was deducted from the import and previously existing stock to ascertain the quantity still in the warehouses.[15]

In other words, sales to speculators fed through into the column of stocks held in Liverpool and were excluded from the domestic consumption column.

Cotton sales were logged only when the cotton passed through the hands of an LCBA broker. If a speculator wished to sell his or her cotton on the open market, the transaction would, in theory, have needed to make this passage. But that would not necessarily happen if one speculator wished to sell directly to another. Nothing compelled such a transaction to be conducted by a broker, and there would have been every incentive for the two parties to avoid the commissions involved. Ellison anonymously confirmed the practice: "Prior to [1876], any merchant might have sold to any other merchant 'futures' without the intervention of a broker."[16] As will be shown in Chapter 7, there was a large unregulated broking market in Liverpool during the war, unconnected with the LCBA, which dealt in speculative trading. But even if an LCBA broker was involved, the transaction would not necessarily have been recorded. Ellison's explanation of how the statistics were compiled begs the question of what would happen if the same broker bought cotton from one speculator and sold it to another within the same week. Many transactions could have been netted off against each other without appearing in the weekly statistics.

A flavour of the times, and of the way in which the same cotton was sold on multiple occasions, is provided by Ellison:

> The same parcel of cotton was sold over and over again by the same broker, and occasionally two, or even three, brokerages would be made on the same lot of cotton in the course of the same day. ... "I am sorry to part with that lot of cotton," a leading broker said to me one day, "because I have already earned fifteen brokerages out of it."[17]

This was no doubt an extreme example, and may even have been a joke, but it would seem to confirm a widespread practice. The first transaction was always a sale on behalf of an importer, and the last a purchase on behalf of a spinner. But an importer could sell his cotton only once, and a spinner buy it only once, assuming neither was also speculating. All the transactions in between must have involved speculators. This suggests that the speculative sales recorded in Liverpool during the civil war, and perhaps at other times too, may have been the tip of a very large iceberg. This in turn raises questions as to the value of the trade in raw cotton. Table 8 shows the value of raw cotton imports, which is effectively the same as the value of the raw cotton sold to spinners, whether in Britain or on the continent. But, by definition, this assumes that each parcel of cotton was sold only once. The value of all the raw cotton traded is therefore another matter altogether. Because the true level of speculation will never be known, it is not possible to quantify it. What must be certain, though, is that the value of transactions during the civil war far exceeded the value of imports. It is possible that their value in 1864 reached its highest level, not just until the First World War, but ever. Amongst the biggest losers in this giant casino, in their not unreasonable opinion, were the spinners.

The speculators were doing what all speculators do – betting on price movements in the market or, to give it a more neutral tone, buying and selling futures. To a limited extent, cotton futures had been traded before the war. The short period of history before the transatlantic telegraph, when cotton was still transported in sailing ships, but steamships were available to bring samples of the shipment and market intelligence in advance of the main cargo's arrival, created the opportunity for trading to arrive. The futures market, as it was to become, could not properly exist before the transatlantic cable was put into service in July 1866. Technically, the establishment of the Liverpool futures market dates from 1873; in practice, something very close to it had existed for some time. Nevertheless, the war period saw the proliferation of futures trading on a massive scale, from almost a standing start. There was no regulation of the activity. Anyone could trade cotton on speculation, even if they had no capital behind them. The hedging and other mechanisms that would later offer protection to the participants did not exist. This type of futures trading brought endemic instability to the market: it was a form of gambling that conferred no benefit on anyone trying to make a legitimate living from the trade.[18]

Speculation in Liverpool escalated after the start of the war, and its nature changed. Initially, it had involved cotton that was already in the town. From there it was a short step to trading cotton that was not in Liverpool, but was, or was about to be, on the water. And from there it proved to be a short step to selling cotton that might never be in Liverpool and was not even known for certain to exist.[19] Smith offered a description of the practice:

> Most of the Indian Cotton shipped in the latter half of the year [1863] changed hands repeatedly on the way, and the confidence of Speculators became so strong that ... shipments not due for three months were readily saleable at nearly the prices current on the spot. ... Many persons ventured on the novel practice of contracting to provide or deliver Cotton at distant dates without having the article in possession. ... Having once taken root it appears to have established itself as a permanent element of the Trade.[20]

Many of the buyers of this non-existent cotton had no use for it and were buying it solely for the purpose of selling it again. In the words of broker Jules Bertois, "they are busy selling what they have not got to people who don't want it."[21]

For the spinners, who were the victims of this speculative mania, the main culprits were the cotton brokers. Not only did the brokers sell freely to speculators and encourage the distortion of the market, but they were frequently speculators themselves. Manchester believed that the brokers held the cotton import hostage, allowing it to leave only when its price had been artificially inflated and a ransom of 1 per cent had been paid. Liverpool was little more than a toll booth on the Mersey. Its traders seemed not to understand, let alone share, Manchester's distress. To read the contemporary market reports of the cotton brokers is to enter a parallel universe to the one inhabited in Manchester. 'Good news' and 'bad news' are the reverse of what one would assume. High prices are good news for Liverpool, but dreadful news for Manchester. The expectation of a prolonged war is good news for Liverpool, because it means a continued scarcity and continued rising prices. An imminent end to the war is bad news because it presages an end to the supply crisis, with falling prices. Ellison referred to "a peace 'scare' or ... some other ... adverse influence". At the end of 1863, another broker announced that "the determination shown by both parties [in America] to continue the struggle in face of every difficulty, gave confidence to the Trade." These statements could only have been made in Liverpool.[22]

The first allegation of the spinners was that brokers frequently acted for both the seller and the buyer in a transaction, trying simultaneously to achieve the highest price for one client and the lowest price for another. "There were," conceded Ellison, "brokers who both bought and sold, but they were an exception to the rule, and comparatively few in number." As ever, Ellison tried to protect the reputation of his profession and to gloss over its irregularities. In 1841, a spinner had declared that "with few exceptions every broker is at once a buyer and a seller of cotton. He is in the pay of two parties, whose interests and objects are diametrically opposed, and whose interests therefore he cannot equally and simultaneously serve." An anonymous letter to the *Mercury* claimed that "the brokers will, whenever they can, both buy and sell the same lot [which] is allowed by the loose morality of the 'flags'." The LCBA admitted to the practice itself. Having investigated a complaint into one of its members, its minutes reported that "the history of the transaction deeply impressed the Committee with a sense of the caution and candour incumbent upon a Broker in dealings in which both buyer and seller are his own clients." The practice itself received no criticism.[23]

The second allegation was that brokers were themselves traders and speculators, buying and selling on their own account and ramping prices. It was not a new charge, and the brokers were again guilty. In 1817, John Slack, a broker himself, had deplored the fact that "a great evil exists both in London and Liverpool, by brokers being both merchants and dealers; the duty, and only duty, of a broker is to be a middle-man between the buyer and seller, and not to buy and sell on his own account." Ellison wrote that the broker John Newall "was closely watched by other operators, and the statement that 'Newall was buying,' or that 'Newall was selling,' had a marked influence on the course of the market", which must surely suggest he was an active trader. He also wrote of two other brokers that "Sam Gaskell was at times a large operator in cotton" and that "one would suppose ... that Mr Reede [of J. S. M. Reede & Co.] was a very extensive operator." In the Bank of Liverpool Reference Books, the broker James Thorburn was described as 'very speculative' and the firm of Finlay & Lance as 'adventurous'. A scurrilous verse sheet named the Littledales as speculators: "L means the great cotton spec house, renowned of yore, where are Harold and Johnny, and two or three more."[24]

Brokers were not usually well-known figures and attracted neither biographers nor press comment. In addition, speculation was not an activity many would have been inclined to vaunt. However, some information has survived. Even Ellison could not evade the issue, admitting that his mentor, Maurice Williams, had gone heavily into cotton speculation during the civil war, amassing a fortune of over £100,000 (£10 million today). Samuel Smith was said to have possessed "phenomenal talent as a financier and ingenuity as a speculator". By his own account, he stuck scrupulously to broking during the early years of the war, "nor did I take any interest in cotton on my own account till I became a member of a merchant's house, James Finlay & Co., in 1864." He remained a broker, however, and this statement suggests that he traded cotton on his own account thereafter. This portrait of an anonymous 'Methodist broker' does nothing to dispel the feeling that the dealings of Smith and Williams were far from atypical: "Being both a selling and a buying broker, with large capital and extensive connexions, he was a power in the market. ... Commissions on sales, commissions on purchases, thirds on joint speculative operations, profits on his independent ventures, all swelled the heap."[25]

The broad charges laid by the spinners against the brokers were justified: they had frequent conflicts of interest. Undoubtedly, raw cotton prices in Liverpool during the war would have been substantially lower but for speculation. In early 1864, the Neills had referred to "speculators persist[ing] in the determination to pay £90,000,000 for a supply which ... they could as readily obtain for £60,000,000 or £70,000,000 except for over competition among themselves", which suggests that the Neills believed that the market was overvalued by about 40 per cent. Ellison acknowledged that "a better scheme for inflating prices could not be invented."[26]

Whatever the inflation of price, the brokers were certainly guilty of failing to control their own market in the way that they had largely done before the war. The established Liverpool cotton trade proved unable to maintain discipline during the fever of wartime speculation and unregulated gamblers were rife in the market. Ellison conceded that the war had "brought into the cotton market and on to the 'Flags' a large number of operators who had no respect for the traditional customs of the place". He looked back fondly on a time "when the word of every merchant and broker ... was his bond ... and when the perpetration of the contemptible practices now either virtually sanctioned, or passed over without adequate condemnation, would have secured for the guilty a rapid journey to Coventry". As usual, Ellison did not describe those 'contemptible practices', nor say who had perpetrated them. Hemelryk said that he did not think "that the American war did the community much good, except that it attracted a great many men to Liverpool, who have remained here ever since." Forwood agreed that "the American war considerably disturbed Liverpool society, and brought to the front many new people." These remarks do not suggest that the old people found the new people congenial.[27]

However, the spinners were not innocent bystanders to these events. As early as 1833, a witness to a parliamentary enquiry "mentioned having heard of certain spinners with stocks which would serve them for six months; others with supplies sufficient for twelve months. This he considered not the business of the manufacturer or spinner, but speculation." Immediately before the war, some spinners had attempted to bypass Liverpool merchants and brokers and import directly from America. One broker sniffed that "it is to be hoped that the experience which the [spinners] have had during the past twelve months, in importing cotton direct, will induce them to confine their operations to the Liverpool market." At the end of 1862, one broker reported: "Spinners have throughout the year, been largely engaged in speculative operations." Another stated that "during the whole year Spinners have themselves been amongst the most active of Speculators." Farnie reported that Oldham spinners made large wartime profits through speculation. At the end of 1863, the brokers Daniel C. Buchanan & Co. reported that "another powerful interest was brought to bear against Cotton; certain parties in Manchester bearing the Market to an extent never before known, and selling Cotton, which had no existence whatever (for distant arrival)." It is not known who these 'certain parties in Manchester' were, nor how widespread or concerted their activities, but they appeared to be trying to beat Liverpool at its own game.[28] Later in the war, the Neill brothers, neither brokers nor spinners and with no known interest in the matter, criticised an anonymous Mancunian who had attacked them in *The Times*:

> Strenuous efforts have been made by some anonymous writer or writers in pamphlets, circulars, &c., to exaggerate the effect of the large stock, and to give currency to preposterously large estimates of future supplies. ... We have alluded above to circulars and pamphlets which have been issued, apparently all from the same hand, and freely circulated, with the manifest purpose of depressing the market.[29]

There is no doubt that Mancunians were complicit in the attempt to rig cotton prices during the war. While speculators in Liverpool offered inflated prices for non-existent future cotton, hoping to prompt a further rise in the market, speculators in Manchester offered deflated prices for non-existent future cotton, hoping to prompt a fall. Hemelryk shed further light on the practice:

> People sold cotton without having it, believing in a fall of the market, and as they had to declare the ship's name at a moment's notice, they simply looked at the shipping list, chose out the biggest ship, and finding out what cotton was being offered by that ship, they risked it, declared

the name and marks, and trusted that on arrival of the ship, they would find a seller of this cotton and tender it. ... I believe a firm in Manchester was the first to discover that it would be sometimes profitable to sell what one has not got, and what eventually might not be wanted.[30]

This was not the only dubious practice on which Hemelryk commented. He related how a cheaper type of cotton was frequently substituted for a more expensive one in Liverpool, especially when it was to be re-exported: "I do not say that this was right; I simply tell you how it was done." He told the story of a merchant who accepted an order for a certain number of bales, the weight unstipulated, at a fixed price per bale. By the time the cotton arrived, the merchant's buying price had doubled, so he divided each bale in half. Commenting on the wartime speculation, Hemelryk admitted that "the business was overdone, and there was no regular system. ... Some even sacrificed their conscience in order to get out of their difficulties." He then added that "I know that I can speak with confident pride and satisfaction as to the high character and moral tone of men in my particular line of business."[31]

Even though much of the foregoing is anecdotal, a picture begins to emerge of the dealings in the raw cotton market in Liverpool at all times, but especially during the civil war. According to Smith, "soon after I commenced business there arose the wildest speculation that any living man has seen. ... Gigantic fortunes were made by speculation. Almost every one plunged into cotton speculation: a single lucky *coup* made a fortune."[32] Not all the speculators were professional gamblers, or even professional cotton men. In fact, they were not all men:

> Speculative operators, including a not unimportant sprinkling of the fair sex, flocked into the market. ... Every section of society ... was represented. ... The Church, the law, the medical profession, the Army and Navy, the country gentry, and the local tradesmen were all in evidence; while buying orders came in from Bath, Cheltenham, Leamington, and other centres of retired nabobs.[33]

Ellison's words were echoed in doggerel by Edward Braddyll, who suggested that these amateur speculators were not content to gamble merely on spot cotton, but would dabble in cotton futures and be investors in the Confederate Loan:

> I listened, – it's not my usual way, – and as sure as I'm alive
> I heard the smiling Parson say – "Those Dholleras to arrive!" ...
> And all next Sunday, in the church, he thought of North and South,
> And when he had to pray for peace the words stuck in his mouth. ...

> On every stair, I do declare, a jolly old lady pants;
> And at many a door is half a score of wealthy maiden aunts!
> That lady there, so neatly dressed, to em-bon-point inclined, –
> Let us follow her in, she has lots of tin, and hear a bit of her mind.
> Having seated herself by the Broker, at the subject she went with a dash, –
> "I have come for a fresh spec in Cotton, I'm expecting a little spare cash.
> "I shall want an advance for a time, – well, perhaps, I may candidly own,
> "Besides specs in Cotton that I'm – rather deep – in Confederate Loan!"[34]

Yet the fact is that some brokers were ruined by the war, as Chapter 7 will show. To a large extent, but not entirely, this was due to the failure of their speculative ventures. As a generalisation, an informed speculator would have found it difficult not to make money by betting on a continued rise in price through to the end of 1863. "It needed not a little self-denial to abstain from what seemed so easy a way to fortune," reflected Smith. In vain did one or two brokers urge restraint. Francis Hollins summarised 1862 as "a year that has enabled the rash or the reckless without means to amass large fortunes, whilst many of the prudent and the wise, with means, have looked on, and still look on, with fear and trembling for the future". At the same time, Edgar Musgrove urged that "utmost caution should be used in trading in the article, and so avoid, as much as possible, the troubles that must sooner or later fall upon the Trade, by a return to the natural level of prices when this most unfortunate War is brought to a close".[35]

It is, however, necessary to stand back and ask exactly what is meant by 'speculation'. The *Porcupine*, never slow to reveal the worst of Liverpool's excesses, wrote – perhaps with tongue in cheek – that "we should be sorry to convey the impression that the Cotton market is nothing else but a medium for speculation."[36] The Cotton Association's historian considered the position of the importing merchants:

> Ostensibly they were not speculating, and would have been highly indignant if their activities had been so described. They only conducted their normal and highly essential legitimate business of importing and merchanting cotton. Nevertheless, they were forced to speculate on every bale of cotton they brought into the country, as there was, of course, no cover against price fluctuation and so, because of the phenomenal rise in prices, many fabulous fortunes were made.[37]

It would be similarly harsh to condemn either merchants for withholding stocks in the hope of a rise after prices had fallen or spinners for buying advance stocks in quantity when they feared a rise. The reality was that everyone who bought and sold raw cotton, unless they were on a fixed commission, like the brokers, or already knew the selling price when they agreed the buying price was, in one sense, speculating. It was unavoidable.

"But all commerce is speculation," wrote John Lalor in 1852. "Where is the line to be drawn? ... Amongst the manufacturing districts of England, the tendency to gambling speculation is probably more constantly ready to start into life than elsewhere, and when in movement to go to greater lengths." Geoffrey Searle has suggested that the Limited Liability Act of 1855 further fuelled a change in the moral climate of commerce: "The facilities for speculation named and unashamed enormously increased. ... Investors ... ceased to be entrepreneurs of the old kind, but more closely resembled a social group to which severe moral opprobrium still attached, *gamblers*." The problem, as both Lalor and Searle acknowledged, is that it was difficult to say where commerce ended and gambling began. The Liverpool cotton market never did resolve that conundrum.[38]

Nor did it help that cotton trading during the civil war, and not only in Britain, represented the first occasion that the futures of a commodity had been traded in volume. It was unknown territory, and the checks and balances that would later make futures trading tolerable, and eventually an essential component of all commodity trading, had yet to be considered, let alone put in place. As late as 1905, by which time the most egregious faults of the practice had long been removed, a firm of cotton brokers felt the need to assure its clients that futures trading was a respectable activity and that "it has been repeatedly decided in law that the Liverpool Cotton Contract is a genuine trade contract, and not a gambling or speculative medium."[39] No one could say the same of the LCBA's contract during the war. An anonymous cotton broker sent a copy of it to *The Times*, together with this commentary:

> By this contract an absolute sale is made, but provision for payment is totally deferred until the arrival of the cotton. ... The buyer has to find neither cash nor deposit ... loses no interest, and has time to choose when to sell – in fact, everything is in his favour. ... Now for a sanguine speculator what better terms could be invented. Whether he is worth £50 or £50,000, if he can only make a purchase "to arrive" he may, without one sixpence outlay, realise a handsome profit on a quantity of cotton for which he could not have provided had he purchased it on the spot.[40]

Ellison commented that "so long as prices continue to advance, all is smooth enough, but with a contrary movement of any importance there would be a general financial upturning, in which the strong and the weak, the legitimate trader, and the reckless speculator, would come down together."[41] It was this system, and principally the speculation in cotton yet to arrive in Liverpool, that enticed reckless gamblers to the market, suffusing it with false trade throughout the war. When the market turned sour after 1864, the innocent were ruined along with the guilty. And all of it was enabled by the LCBA, perhaps unwittingly to start with, but not thereafter, because it enriched the brokers nearly as much as the speculators. This, more than anything, is the bomb beneath the goody-two-shoes world that Ellison would have us believe.

Liverpool had not been entirely trusted before the war by the wider business community, which struggled to observe any firm evidence of principle. *The Times* complained that the port's traders repelled questions about financial matters "with a zeal which shows a greater sensitiveness for the reckless speculator than for the legitimate trader".[42] Not surprisingly, these accusations mounted during the war until the Exchange correspondent of the *Mercury* felt compelled to respond:

> The attempt ... to make out that downright undisguised "gambling" is rampant on our Exchange flags, will ... be regarded with the contempt it merits by the mercantile community of Liverpool. It is a libel on the character of our merchants and brokers alike, and a mendacious charge against the mode in which they conduct their business. It has long been the fashion in commercial circles in the metropolis to indulge in disparaging remarks respecting the condition of commercial morality in Liverpool. Every opportunity is seized to declare that Liverpool is the hotbed of speculation, and ... Liverpool is made a scapegoat for the sins of others. The epithet "gambling", however, has not until now been applied to us.[43]

The columnist then somewhat spoils his case. "Admitting, for the sake of argument," he goes on, "that the alleged evil does exist ... does this London 'Merchant' mean to maintain that there is a dangerously numerous body of mere worthless speculators infesting the Liverpool cotton market to whom respectable brokers sell their principals' cotton, and yet that these unprincipled speculators are ... well known to the brokers?" The evidence suggests that this was precisely the state of affairs.

The volume of speculation causes another chunk of masonry to fall from Ellison's pristine edifice: the theoretical fact that brokers took a 0.5 per cent commission on cotton transactions. If, to take what might now seem a modest example, a broker bought and sold the same parcel of cotton three times, he would be taking a commission of about 3 per cent of the eventual selling price. With the inflated price, he could have been earning twenty times the amount of commission on the same weight of cotton as he had before the war. The brokers' commission earnings on trade sales alone would have trebled in the peak year of 1864. When one adds speculative sales, both recorded and

Figure 9 Sales of raw cotton to British spinners, 1858–1867
volume (solid line); price (dotted line); value (dashed line)

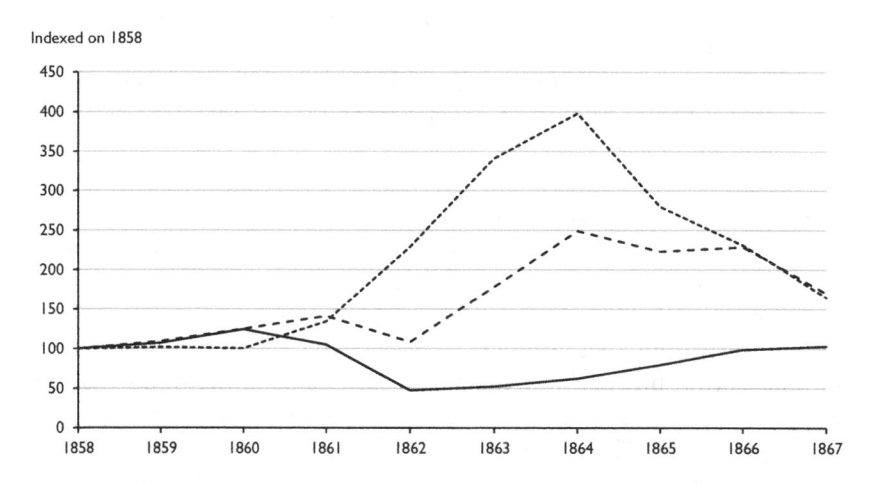

Sources: George Holt & Co., annual cotton circulars (Liverpool Record Office, 380 COT/1/11/71); Thomas Ellison, *The Cotton Trade of Great Britain* (London: Effingham Wilson, 1886).

unrecorded, the multiplier would have been many times greater. Were it to be claimed that the level of brokers' commissions was in fact double, treble, or more, their theoretical level, it would take a brave historian to gainsay it. Even at the minimum level of earnings, this is a full and sufficient illustration of how Manchester's disaster was a bonanza for the brokers of Liverpool.

When surveying this whirlwind of speculative activity, of fabulous fortunes won and lost, of the integral role played by the cotton brokers, of the enormous personal rewards some of them gained as a result, it is easy to forget that the country's greatest industry was still in crisis. By 1864, the worst of the cotton famine might be over, and the spinners and weavers that remained in business might have found a viable way of coping with the altered landscape, but the manufacturing industry remained a shadow of its pre-war self. If one now brings together the volume information from Chapter 4 and the price information from this chapter, the overall effect of the civil war on the British raw cotton trade can be seen more clearly. Figure 9 ignores sales for re-export and to speculators and reflects sales to British spinners only. It is indexed on 1858 to place the disruption of the war years in context. It shows, in broad terms, that the volume of sales halved while their value doubled. This was the result of the explosion in prices, fuelled by speculation. It is no wonder that the impecunious spinners should have felt aggrieved, as Braddyll again confirmed:

> At last, however, the cotton was bought, but the flames of wrath were kindled,
> And a Spinner was rare who hadn't thought he was being robbed or swindled!
> The Buying Brokers were very polite, and their Clients they did assuage;
> They stood them drinks – it was not quite right, but the Spinners were blue with rage![44]

Not at all, said Ellison: the spinners were perfectly content with the "happy-family condition of things".[45] It must have slipped his mind that he had previously, and anonymously, written: "The cotton spinner has always regarded the Liverpool speculator as his natural enemy. ... It is not surprising that [spinners] occasionally say hard things about Liverpool cotton brokers."[46] It must also have slipped his mind that, by 1864, a large group of spinners no longer considered themselves part of this happy family. They formed the Spinners' Association, with Hugh Mason as President and Maurice Fitzgerald as Secretary. It must be said that, if you wanted a leader to carry the fight to the enemy with all guns blazing, Hugh Mason was your man. Fresh from his demands for the impeachment of the Secretary of State for India and the dismissal of the Prime Minister, described in Chapter 2, Mason turned his firepower on the brokers. The first annual meeting of the Spinners' Association took place at the Clarence Hotel, Manchester on 19 July 1864. Mason started by regretting the small attendance:

> The brokers of Liverpool taught them a lesson, and they (the Lancashire spinners) would be dunces if they did not profit by it, and take a leaf out of their book. The Liverpool brokers were a small body, but united. The consumers were a numerous body, but disunited. ... He could not see why the gentlemen of Liverpool should fatten upon the distress of the cotton spinners of Manchester.[47]

There were 283 members of the Cotton Spinners' Association. Numerically, they represented about a quarter of all spinners, although probably a greater proportion of spinning capacity.[48] There were a number of influential names on the committee, which suggests that the Association was a body of some substance and rather more than Mason's personal hobby horse. The fact that the LCBA felt obliged to engage with the Association, despite its initial refusal to recognise it, also suggests that it carried some weight within the trade, enough to inconvenience Liverpool. In 1882, it was this Association which represented the spinners at the discussions that led to the formation of the Cotton Association.[49]

Hugh Mason: mill-owner, politician and scourge of the brokers (from Wikipedia; in the public domain)

The first annual meeting was the opening salvo in a war that continued furiously if intermittently for more than three years. The emotional nuances of the communications between the two groups are arguably as significant as the issues themselves. In the passages below, all quotations and statements, unless separately referenced, can be found in the minute books of the LCBA.[50] On 28 October 1864, the Spinners' Association escalated the conflict and wrote directly to the brokers. Its letter consisted of three resolutions concerning the process of arbitrating disputes, the tare allowance, and the time limit for the return of sub-standard cotton. It is significant that, while the Association mounted furious public assaults on the integrity of the brokers and the evils of the commission system, its specific proposals were usually concerned with more mundane issues. This suggests that, whatever the bluster, it knew it would not make headway on issues of substance.

The brokers replied on 11 October, refusing to recognise the Spinners' Association, and stating that as the LCBA "has hitherto communicated with the Manchester Chamber of Commerce, as the recognised organ of the Trade in this District, should further correspondence be thought desirable, it had perhaps better come through that channel." However, the LCBA could not resist defending the arbitration system, by which the selling and buying brokers in a disputed transaction each appointed a proxy broker to resolve the matter, keeping the process firmly within the family. "A Cotton Broker," it declared, "is best qualified from his knowledge of the Custom of the Trade to give a satisfactory decision, and it is generally regarded by Buyer and Seller equally, as most likely to be partial [*sic: a revealing slip of the pen*] and disinterested."

On 18 November, the spinners responded. They regretted that "the reply ... should have been so very unsatisfactory" and wanted to know if the LCBA intended to communicate with them. They received the answer to this question by default. The LCBA did not reply. On 15 December, Fitzgerald wrote again: "As you have not honoured me with either a reply to or acknowledgment of having received my letter of the 18th ultimo ... I am now to request you to inform me if I may expect any answer to the communication referred to." This time, Studley Martin, secretary of the LCBA, did reply. Briefly. He referred the spinners to the LCBA's previous reply. On 21 January 1865, the spinners went public. They placed an advertisement in a Manchester newspaper, which was cut out and pasted in the LCBA's minute book. It included this onslaught on the brokers:

> It is plain that the Liverpool brokers, employed by the spinners, decline to hold communication with the committee. ... The position ... now assumed by the associated brokers would show that ... they are diametrically opposed to the spinning interest; and it becomes a question whether it would not be better for the trade to employ brokers unconnected with the association, and who would pledge themselves to act strictly for the buyers' interest.
>
> There can be no doubt but that very many of the associated brokers act for the advantage for both sellers as well as purchasers of cotton, and at the same time are speculators on their own account, thereby fostering high prices of cotton, and at the same time encouraging gambling and speculative operations, which, for the last two years, has kept cotton at a price totally inconsistent with that which would have ruled, had the Liverpool market been governed simply by supply and demand. [*This grievance mirrored that of American planters: "Many cotton Factors are also cotton Speculators, having an interest directly opposed to the interests of the planters"* (Phalen, *Consequences*, p. 98, quoting an 1858 issue of *Farmer & Planter*).]
>
> The question of commission paid for brokerage is also one that deserves serious attention. ... On the same [amount] of cotton purchased this year the broker's commission would be ... exactly five times as much as formerly, for doing precisely the same work; and so increased at a time too when spinners are least able to bear fresh imposts.
>
> It would be well for the spinners to consider whether ... it would not be possible to adopt a mode of remuneration that would do away with the broker being so deeply interested in the maintenance of high prices.[51]

The spinners demanded that brokerage fees be calculated on the volume of raw cotton, not its value.

At an LCBA meeting on 27 January 1865, a response to this broadside was debated and agreed. The brokers claimed to have known nothing of the Spinners' Association, apart from its title and the name of the Secretary. It "begs most distinctly to disclaim any intentional discourtesy on its part" and "cheerfully recognises the great respectability of the names forming the Committee". It goes on to maintain that the LCBA did not exist to protect the interests of cotton brokers, but wholly for the purpose of gathering statistics for the benefit of the trade, and for "protecting and fostering with perfect impartiality the interests of buyer and seller. ... It would be surely better not to inaugurate ... discussions under a mistaken feeling of hostility, or in retaliation for a fancied discourtesy which we again assure you has no foundation in fact."

Between this letter on 27 January and 10 March 1865, only one 'weekly' meeting of the LCBA was minuted. By 17 March, a meeting had taken place between representatives of the two associations. On that date, Edgar Musgrove, the current LCBA President, wrote a long and waffling letter to Mason, who would be pleased to know that "nothing exists in the rules of the CBA, to interfere with the Buyers rights to appoint any arbitrator whom he may prefer." This was hardly surprising, since the LCBA barely had any rules at the time. Also, "it is not within the power of the CBA to organise a change [to the commission system] of the kind suggested." Musgrove ignored the overriding question – massive conflicts of interest – altogether.

The issue then appears to have lain dormant for a while, but it was reignited in early 1867. Mason wrote again to the LCBA on 14 March. Again, he published his letter in a newspaper, and again it was cut out and pasted in the LCBA minute book, the source and date unmentioned. The spinners' grievances now focused on the mis-reporting of cotton stocks and on the fact that the LCBA officially recorded speculative sales: "Speculation is not legitimate trade; you[r] circular should not notice what is unsound and injurious." Mason's letter concluded with the words:

> We are not disposed longer to submit to have our claims disregarded by our brokers. ... We are ... addressing an association comprising agents for cotton sellers as well as agents for cotton buyers, and also persons who act in the double capacity of attempting to serve both buyer and seller. We confess the difficulty of our position in this respect.

When this letter was read to a meeting of the LCBA the following day, James Macrae, President in 1860, proposed that discussion be postponed "for some of us to cool down". Mason never lost the ability to get under the skin of his enemies. When his letter was debated on 22 March, one member grumbled that "no good would come from any correspondence. Mr Mason's letter ought not to have been sent – there is self respect due to ourselves." The LCBA's reply was sent on 27 March. "Without entering upon any argument as to the legitimacy of speculation," it said, "it is proper for us to say that it is a mode of investment to which spinners frequently resort."

In December 1867, *The Times* quoted from a pamphlet which may have been written, or at least inspired, by Mason. The LCBA's response the following day complained of "words ... which convey the imputation that it is the interest of a section of the Cotton Brokers' association at Liverpool to make the buying and selling of cotton both a monopoly and a mystery".[52] Perish the thought.

It is impossible to refute a single major accusation the spinners made in this dispute. They were all demonstrably true. And yet they did not win the argument. But, as Mason pointed out, the spinners employed and paid the buying brokers. They were the clients. It is hard to think of another line of business where the service providers are more powerful than their clients or feel so safe in patronising them. Some of the statements made by the brokers must have been untrue, and in particular the claim that it was not within the power of the LCBA to effect a change to the commission system. It must have been within their power. If the Liverpool brokers had felt a responsibility for the wider interests of the cotton trade, they would have made the change themselves. However, fault lay with the spinners as well. The story of the Spinners' Association has parallels with the CSA: a worthy cause enjoying lukewarm support from the manufacturers. In a speech in October 1866, reported in the Manchester press but not in Liverpool, Mason rounded on his own side: "He was sorry to say that after issuing 500 circulars for a meeting of the Spinners' Association, only three men could be got to attend. Therefore they had only themselves to blame for their grievances."[53] Yet the financial clout of Manchester should have exceeded that of Liverpool. It appears that it did not, and that most spinners regarded an attempt to take on Liverpool as a futile contest.

The conclusion must be that those who traded raw cotton had no empathy with those who manufactured it. Raw cotton was controlled by the Liverpool brokers, especially the selling brokers, to a degree that the theoretical structure of the trade would not suggest. Most brokers had no interest in what happened to the cotton once it left Liverpool, or in its price. They were not concerned with "protecting and fostering with perfect impartiality the interests of buyer and seller". They were concerned solely with protecting and fostering their own interests.

CHAPTER VII

The Brokers and the Broken
The nearest truth about Liverpool's cotton brokers

It is now time to put some flesh on the decaying skeleton of Liverpool's cotton-broking fraternity, disinterred in the previous chapter. The best place to start is with the theoretical model offered by Ellison as to how the raw cotton trade in Liverpool operated. He described two sets of brokers, members of the LCBA, acting exclusively as intermediaries, one set solely representing the importers, the other solely representing the spinners. Ellison claimed that, until after the civil war, the model functioned as it was intended to do, admitting only that "for several years before that event [the laying of the cable in 1866] there had been, here and there, indications of a falling away from the old lines of procedure."[1] It should already be clear that there were rather more than 'indications of a falling away' and that they did not happen only 'here and there'.

The difficulty lies in proving the allegations. No business records of cotton brokers, during the period or close to it, appear to have survived. There are no primary sources that shed light on the commercial activities of Liverpool brokers at this time. There is no published work that describes in detail how the Liverpool raw cotton trade was financed, or who owned the consignments of cotton that arrived at the port, or how subsequent transactions were effected and by whom. Among secondary sources, only Nigel Hall has added to the slim body of published knowledge.[2] What exists is the theoretical model described by Ellison, together with a great deal of anecdotal evidence, much of it presented in the previous chapter, which contradicts it. There are, however, published sources, not previously evaluated, that shed substantial if indirect light on the matter. They come principally in the form of published lists of cotton brokers and, in particular, the B Lists of the Bills of Entry for the Port of Liverpool. These sources, combined with the anecdotal information, while they may not prove much definitively, enable reasonable inferences to be drawn. The concluding section of this chapter, which looks at those who were broken by the civil war, draws primarily on newspaper evidence.

However much is open to conjecture, what cannot be disputed and needs no documentary evidence is that the importing merchant, the selling broker and the buying broker had similar interests when it came to the price of cotton. The merchant naturally wanted the highest possible price. Both sets of brokers, each on a fixed commission based on the value of the consignment, wanted it just as much. The buying brokers are unlikely to have been so venal as to have deliberately paid over the odds for their cotton. No doubt they bought at the best price obtainable in the market. However, it still suited them if prices were generally high. In that critical respect, Mason was correct in saying that the brokers who bought on behalf of spinners could not have had their clients' interests entirely at heart, even when they were not selling on behalf of importers at the same time. Despite this self-evident fact, Ellison felt able to claim that the system "secured to the buyer a servant [the buying broker] whose interests were identical with the interests of the consumer [the spinner], and whose whole conduct was ... instinctively directed towards securing the welfare of the spinner".[3]

The scale of cotton imports, and variable harvests in America, meant that no one individual, or even a group of individuals, could absolutely control the price of cotton – although, after the civil war, this was notoriously attempted by Morris Ranger. An abundance of cotton in Liverpool led to a low range of prices; a scarcity led to a high range. However, within the range of prices obtaining at any moment, there were opportunities for holders of cotton to maximise the price, principally by manipulating the release of stocks on to the market. The period of credit extended by banks to the holders of raw cotton, normally 90 days, was considerably longer than the stock cover of the raw material kept by most spinners. Holders could therefore afford to hold their nerve longer than buyers. Ellison referred to "many holders having withdrawn their stocks" as if it was a regular occurrence, a statement repeated in other brokers' circulars over the period. In 1837, when Brown, Shipley & Co. were major importers of cotton, they stockpiled an entire year's worth of cotton purchases until prices rose in Liverpool.[4] The evidence that this practice was prevalent at the time of the civil war is provided in the LCBA's letter to Mason of 27 March 1867:

> It is ... the practice of most merchants to place their stocks in brokers' hands ... on arrival in the port, whether they be intended for immediate sale or to be held indefinitely for a market. But individual importers adopt a different method, and do not thus appropriate their parcels of cotton until the time arrives, which is often delayed for months, when they are to be sold.[5]

There was probably no formal cartel to keep prices high, but there did not need to be when all parties in Liverpool had the same interest. An informal cartel, or at any rate a great deal of collusion, must have been commonplace. The buying brokers must have been complicit in the practice. Besides their mutual interest in high prices, they depended on the selling brokers: the latter held the cotton they needed to buy, so complaints about their colleagues would have been inadvisable. Thus, whatever they may have said in private to their spinning clients, there is no public evidence of a direct complaint by buying brokers about the practices of the selling brokers. However, Mason's letter to the LCBA of 14 March 1867 included the words: "We are assured that an influential section of your association is as much dissatisfied as ourselves with the anomalous position you have assumed."[6] This comment referred to the dispute over the reporting of stocks and speculative sales, but it may have extended to other issues as well, and certainly suggests that some brokers privately expressed dissatisfaction with the LCBA to the spinners.

So who were the Liverpool cotton brokers, this tightly knit group who exercised exceptional influence over Britain's raw cotton trade? Anecdotal evidence suggests a dandyish group of men, eager to flaunt their wealth, self-certified members of Liverpool's elite. Mason referred, somewhat contemptuously, to "the gentlemen of Liverpool". Farnie, a Mancunian, observed that "the mere spinning and weaving of cotton was an occupation perhaps too commonplace for the attention of the gentlemen of Liverpool." Queen Victoria apparently said "she had never before seen together so large a number of well-dressed gentlemen." The anecdotes may also suggest a specialised and self-contained group, slightly aloof from the rest of the port's commercial life. When the Liverpool Chamber of Commerce was refounded in 1850, with the deliberate intent of unifying all commercial interests in the port, the LCBA did not affiliate itself to the organisation.[7]

But, while this aloofness may have existed in attitude, it did not exist in practice. The brokers were intimately connected with every aspect of the port's commerce. Liverpool Exchange, where cotton was traded, was where all other commodities were traded also. An 1846 list has survived of those entitled to vote for the committee of the Liverpool Docks. Of the 110 names appearing on the LCBA membership list of 1841, 100 were among the electors. It is clear from the exceptions that eligibility to vote in these elections was not an automatic right of LCBA membership, so many of the electors must nominally have been buying brokers, with no obvious connection to the docks. Altogether it makes more sense to regard brokers as merchants who happened to deal mostly in cotton, rather than as some rarefied species. It is, however, reasonable to regard them as an elite.[8]

Many LCBA membership lists survive. The list of founding members in 1841 is reprinted in Ellison's history, as is the final list prior to the LCBA's transformation into the Cotton Association in 1882. Annual lists exist from 1866 through to 1881, which will be discussed in the next chapter. The only

Liverpool, The Exchange, 1887: brokers on the flagstones that were the trading floor for raw cotton
(copyright: The Francis Frith Collection)

other known list is, fortuitously, for May 1864. It is pasted into the minute book of the LCBA. This, and the later LCBA lists, are especially valuable because, unlike Ellison's lists, they give the membership in the precise form in which the LCBA recorded it. The 1864 list was printed but has a number of handwritten amendments and additions that were "added since May 1864" and which, for the purpose of this analysis, have been ignored.[9]

In addition to these lists, there are the entries in *Gore's Directory for Liverpool*. These guides appeared annually, sometimes biennially, and provided lists of professions such as cotton brokers. A directory for 1864 exists, so it is possible to compare the *Gore's* list of brokers directly with the LCBA membership list. In addition to these lists, there is Ellison's account, running to 85 pages, of the origins and lineage of almost every cotton-broking firm in Liverpool, a comprehensive 'who begat who' of the fraternity. Putting this information together with the LCBA list, it is possible – with near, although not complete, accuracy – to list, for 1864, every individual who was either a sole trader who belonged to the LCBA, or a partner in a cotton brokerage that was a member of the LCBA.[10]

The first fact to emerge from Ellison's narrative is that the LCBA was the most firmly locked of all closed shops: an archetypal self-perpetuating oligarchy. Almost all brokerages had their roots in the early days of Liverpool's cotton trade in the late eighteenth and early nineteenth centuries. Few of the brokerages operating at the time of the civil war did not have links to this past. Most, sometimes in a different incarnation, had been founder members of the LCBA. Of the first 20 presidents, half had a connection with firms founded upon West Indian cotton, and thus had a connection to Britain's slave trade. Of the 110 separate surnames on the LCBA membership list of 1841, no fewer than 81 appear in the records of compensation paid to former British slave-owners. In some cases, especially with common surnames, this will be a coincidence, but the correlation is still marked.[11] There were two main routes to becoming a broker in one's own right: to have been apprenticed to an existing broker, or to have been employed, frequently as a family member, and then taken into partnership by an existing broker. All new applicants had to be vetted by the members. The LCBA was a highly exclusive club. It is striking how many new members bore middle names that were the surnames of existing or previous brokers.

The names of brokerages need to be treated with caution. They fall into two categories. Some firms carried the names of their present partners, which is why several firms changed their names as their partners changed. Others continued to trade under their founding name, despite the fact that the founding partner(s) had retired or died. Partnerships changed, or were dissolved, frequently – far more often than one would expect. Sometimes the reason was obvious, such as the death or retirement of a partner; at other times it was not, particularly when former partners formed new partnerships immediately upon the dissolution of the old one. Ellison sheds no light on the frequency of these changes. During the war, some of them may have been due to differing attitudes among the partners towards speculative risk.

Given the importance that Ellison attaches to the distinction between selling and buying brokers, it is striking that almost nowhere does he apply this distinction to the firms he is describing. On the rare occasions that he does, it relates to the origins of the firm, several decades earlier. It is possible that some of the rearrangements of partnerships were to enable firms to have a foot in both the selling and the buying camps. Perhaps Ellison found it too difficult, or too sensitive, to define a firm as either a selling or a buying broker. At any rate, it is impossible from his narrative to distinguish one from the other. Even more significantly, the LCBA's membership lists did not distinguish between the two either. Neither did the entries in *Gore's Directory*. If one is looking for confirmation that the line between selling and buying brokers was in practice blurred, this lack of evidence seems eloquent.

The brokers' role in Liverpool society is visible in Ellison's account. He records 21 brokers who were JPs, four who were MPs or the close relative of one, 5 mayors, 15 town councillors (mostly in Liverpool) and 4 deputy lieutenants. Several brokers were involved in charitable works of one kind or another. This small group exercised, over many decades, a strong influence on Liverpool's civic life. They exercised a similar influence on Liverpool's commercial life, well beyond the confines of cotton broking. Many brokers had other interests: banking, stockbroking, importing, railways. Several brokerages were merely departments of large merchant houses. Liverpool businessmen had fingers in all sorts of pies, most of them involving little capital. In this way, raw cotton differed from manufactured cotton. The trade required little or no capital, no factories and no machinery. What it needed was credit. Enough to pay for a few bales of cotton and its warehousing. Enough to start spinning a whirligig of a business.[12]

Two questions about LCBA membership must be answered. Was it possible for someone to act as a cotton broker without being a member? Was membership individual or corporate? Two resolutions of the LCBA on 18 February 1842 shed light on both issues. Hall has written that "all cotton brokers were, and indeed had to be, members of the Association in order to operate as a Liverpool cotton broker", but this was not true until very late in the LCBA's existence. One of the resolutions states that "no individual shall be admitted a member of the Association unless he shall have ... been in business at this port for three years at the least as a cotton broker." Ellison wrote, anonymously, that "a number of brokers carried on business for many years without joining the association; and it was not until within very recent times that ... [it] became necessary for every broker to become a member." This confirms, as do multiple press references, that there were brokers who were not members of the LCBA. Some may still have been employed by member firms; others may have constituted a second tier in the market which did not sell cotton upon its first arrival in the port, but which traded it thereafter.[13]

The wording of the resolutions also seems to suggest unambiguously that membership was vested in the individual, not in the firm. Yet the LCBA's 1864 membership list appears to contradict this. It is not a list of individuals. Membership falls into three categories: firms and partnerships (56 members of the total of 152); individuals who were sole traders (32 members, as far as one can tell); individuals who were members of firms or partnerships, with the corporate name listed in brackets afterwards (64 members). The most likely explanation is that membership was indeed individual but that, where all partners in a firm were members, it was felt sufficient to list the firm as an entity rather than give the names of the individual partners. In which case, those names listed as individuals with their firms in brackets afterwards were presumably partners in a firm where not all the partners were individual members, which would have included the heads of cotton departments in firms with wider merchant interests, as provided for in the resolutions.

Of the 152 brokers or 151 broking firms (one firm had two named members) who were members of the LCBA in 1864, 128 are noted in Ellison's genealogy.

Figure 10 Recorded Liverpool cotton broking firms, 1864

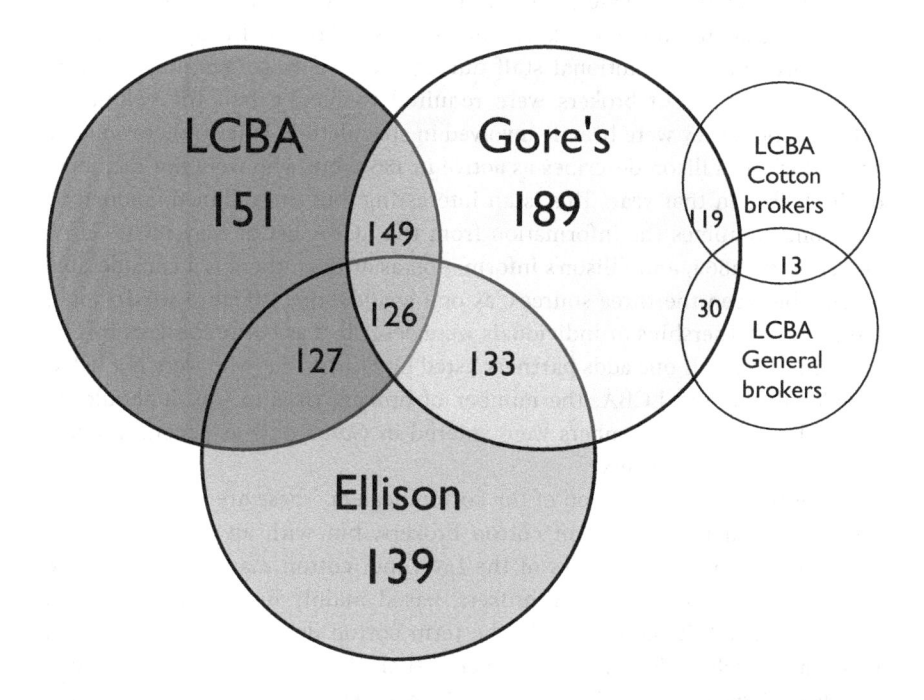

[Venn diagram showing: LCBA 151; Gore's 189; Ellison 139; LCBA Cotton brokers; LCBA General brokers. Overlap values: 149, 126, 127, 133, 19, 13, 30.]

Sources: Constitution, Laws and Usages of the Liverpool Cotton Brokers Association, 1871 (Liverpool: Joseph A. D. Watts & Sons, 1871) (Liverpool Record Office, 380/COT/1/1/1); *Gore's Directories*; Thomas Ellison, *The Cotton Trade of Great Britain* (London: Effingham Wilson, 1886).

The lack of a complete correlation is not surprising, since Ellison's object was to describe the lineages of the 90 founding members from 1841. However, Ellison claims that only "about a dozen other firms were added in later years" which, even with name changes and begettings, seems to be a considerable understatement. It may be significant that those individuals on the LCBA list with their firm's name in brackets afterwards, while accounting for only 42 per cent of the membership, include most of the names that fail to appear in Ellison's genealogy. This may suggest that, during the civil war, firms that were either new, or new to cotton broking, took on a partner with LCBA membership as a short cut to becoming member firms. Ellison reported that, at this time, "many general brokers added cotton to the other branches of their business." According to *Gore's*, the number of cotton brokers increased by 20 per cent between 1860 and 1864. Ellison said there were "nearly double the number of brokers" during the war. The reason for the discrepancy is that *Gore's* listed businesses, while Ellison was referring to individuals. This would suggest that many brokerage firms, most of them already members of the LCBA, took on additional staff during the civil war. One may ask why twice the number of brokers were required to handle half the volume of cotton, unless they were heavily involved in speculation. Finally, there were 12 brokers whom Ellison describes as active in 1864, but who were not members of the LCBA in that year. This is an interesting, but unexplained, anomaly.[14]

If one combines the information from the LCBA list of May 1864, *Gore's Directory* for 1864, and Ellison's information as at 1864, there is a considerable overlap between the three sources, as one would expect (Figure 10). In total, 196 firms, partnerships or individuals were described as cotton brokers by one or more sources. If one adds partners listed by Ellison, but who were not listed individually by the LCBA, the number of brokers rises to 339. It should be noted that 17 LCBA members were entered in *Gore's* only as general brokers and not as cotton brokers.

Then there is the question of the cotton dealers. These are listed by *Gore's* under the general heading of cotton brokers, but with an asterisk against their names. In the early days of the Liverpool cotton market, dealers were the forerunners of the buying brokers, based mainly in Manchester. Later, as Ellison haughtily commented, "the term cotton dealer became associated with an entirely different class of men." There is no overlap at all between the lists of dealers and the 1864 LCBA membership list. The dealers were effectively unofficial brokers, as indeed were some of the brokers themselves. Some of the dealers later chose to list themselves in *Gore's* as brokers, but none of these has yet been found on an LCBA membership list either. They seem simply to have decided to call themselves brokers. There was a huge increase in the number of dealers during the civil war, especially in the latter stages and during the speculative fever after the war. Of the 53 dealers listed in the 1864 directory, 22 had names of Irish origin. A cursory reading of the names of LCBA members suggests that few, if any, of the brokers were Irish. While this may reflect economic status, it may also reflect an anti-Irish or anti-Catholic prejudice within the LCBA. Evidence from a variety of sources suggests that most brokers were Liberal in their politics and non-conformist or Anglican in their religion. In these respects, they mirrored the mill-owners.[15]

Many dealers were bankrupted after the war. A lot of them seem to have been small-time traders, who saw the mouth-watering profits from cotton in the early years of the war, decided to join the stampede and chose the wrong moment to do it. However, for these people to deal, someone had to have sold them the cotton in the first place. The inference must be that the dealers, and perhaps many other unrecorded people and businesses, were speculative traders, with little or no capital behind them, buying either from

LCBA members or from other speculators and forming a second tier in the market, even less well regulated than the first.

Taking the information from the lists as a whole, a picture emerges that is much less clearly segregated than the one Ellison presents. In a satirical piece from 1870 that reflected changing times in Liverpool, the *Porcupine* wrote that "Mr Barnacle is a specimen of the old-fashioned buying brokers, who buy for spinners and do nothing else. There are not, however, many of them left. ... The majority ... have become general brokers."[16] The lack of any published indication as to which were selling brokers and which buying brokers surely suggests that the dividing line between the two was thin and at times non-existent. Not all the cotton brokers in Liverpool belonged to the LCBA. The dividing line between the cotton dealers and the non-LCBA brokers must also have been thin or non-existent. It is difficult to avoid the feeling that LCBA members, other brokers, cotton dealers and general traders were all part of the amorphous and shifting scenery that constituted Liverpool's cotton community. The list of bankruptcies after the war confirms this impression.

Neither is there any evidence that this situation was created by the circumstances of the civil war. As Liverpool's cotton trade expanded through the century, it must have become harder for its founding fathers to retain control of what they had started. It may have been an attempt to assert control that led to the establishment of the LCBA in the first place. Any club is, by definition, an organisation that excludes people. By 1841, the list of those that the established brokers wished to exclude had lengthened. In particular, they wanted to exclude the general brokers. According to Ellison, "down to 1841 the cotton and general brokers were included in one association, but in that year the cotton brokers had become a sufficiently important body to form a separate association."[17] During the war, many general brokers seem to have found the means, within the LCBA's regulations, to inveigle themselves back into membership.

The final aspect of the role of cotton brokers to be examined concerns the part they played in shipping consignments that arrived in Liverpool. The Port of Liverpool Bills of Entry provide the source material for this study.[18] The Bills were published daily in two parts, the A List and the B List. The A List dealt primarily with the ships and the B List with the incoming cargoes. Negligible study has been made by historians of the A Lists and, so far as is known, none at all of the B Lists. Each list features names entered against consignments. The two lists of names vary considerably for consignments of cotton, and there is no key or heading to explain what they were. It has been assumed that the names on the A Lists were the consignees, and this seems to be correct, although one should add 'and/or proprietors'. No one has explained the divergent list of names on the B Lists because no one has examined them.

A contemporary source provides the explanation.[19] The original Bill of Entry was a document completed by the person taking responsibility for a consignment, or part of a consignment, when it arrived in Liverpool. Hundreds of such documents would have been submitted to the port authorities every day. From the information contained in them, the authorities then produced a composite Bill of Entry for the day, split into the A List and the B List, each containing different information. The person submitting the Bill of Entry was not the same, or not necessarily the same, as the proprietor or consignee of the goods, which would explain the discrepancy between the two lists of names. As historians are aware, the list of names on the A Lists is incomplete, with many cotton consignments – up to 70 per cent in some years – being shown enigmatically as 'consigned to order'.[20] However, the list of names on the B Lists *is* complete: of more than 21,000 cotton consignments examined, only three did not have a name against them. If there was one list of names that the port authorities needed to be complete, it was surely the list of those who would take charge of the goods and – where relevant, which it was not for cotton – pay the duty on them. It must therefore be concluded that the names on the A Lists were the proprietors and/or consignees, where they were given, and the names on the B Lists were the authorised agents of the proprietors and/or consignees, with responsibility for taking charge of the cotton in Liverpool.

Studying the names on the B Lists is perhaps more rewarding than studying those on the A Lists. Not only is the A List of names incomplete, but it is impossible to know their precise status, whereas the B List of names is complete and one knows precisely their status: they had immediate responsibility for the cotton that arrived. Had a list of the owners of the consignments been compiled, that would have been more interesting still, but it was not. Ownership was seldom known, even at the time. When the Liverpool branch of Barings Bros was asked by its head office in London to produce a list of the port's main cotton traders, it replied that it could not produce an accurate list because "so much comes to parties whose names do not appear, for which the broker makes the customs house entry."[21] If the information did not exist at the time, historians will never know who owned what, or who paid for what.

A full study has been made of the B Lists of cotton consignments in 1864 and – for pre-war comparison – in 1860. Before looking at the names on those lists, hereafter called 'the recipients', it is worth noting how the overall shape of the trade was affected by the war. Although the volume of cotton imported into Liverpool was 38 per cent lower in 1864 than in 1860, the number of individual consignments was actually higher (by 12 per cent) and the number of individual recipients was also higher (by 28 per cent). The volume per consignment and the volume per recipient were thus roughly halved. The numbers receiving small amounts of cotton increased dramatically. In 1860,

52 recipients had received less than 20,000 lb of cotton each in the full year; in 1864, the number was 203. In 1860, there had been 230 consignments of fewer than 10 bales; in 1864, there were 837. This information provides dramatic evidence of two points, neither of which is surprising in the light of what has already been described. The first is that the civil war brought into the cotton market a great many people who were not in it previously, many of them operating on a small scale, and many of whom must have been speculators. The second is that the war period saw a scramble by all operators to lay their hands on whatever cotton they could locate, in whatever quantity they could get it, wherever they could find it.

A vast amount of information has been derived from this analysis of almost 10,000 raw cotton consignments in 1860 and more than 11,000 in 1864. Most of it is too detailed to be reproduced or is beyond the scope of this study.[22] Two further issues are relevant here: the most significant non-broker recipients of raw cotton in 1860 and 1864, and the role of the cotton brokers as recipients.

Table 9 Non-broker recipients of cotton consignments, 1860 and 1864 (000 lb)

Recipient	1860	1864	Recipient	1860	1864
Finlay, Campbell & Co.	6,562	22,891	Asia Minor Cotton Co.	0	2,762
Cama, B. & Son	0	19,186	Hodgson, Mather & Co.	0	2,637
Forbes, Forbes & Co.	6,521	18,491	Harrison, J.	0	2,623
Fraser, Trenholm & Co.	38,769	13,707	Schuster, Leo, Bros & Co.	164	2,607
Clover, J. & W. W.	0	13,374	de Jersey & Co.	677	2,561
Thomson, Finlay & Co.	7,189	13,084	Leech, Harrison & Co.	12,734	2,264
Rennie, Clowes & Co.	12	10,462	Schroder, J. H. & Co.	20,855	2,087
Hanlon, T.	0	9,849	Cropper, Ferguson & Co.	5,248	2,043
Cowan, R.	23,376	8,680	Melly, Forget & Co.	15,004	1,999
Poonjabhoy, D.	0	7,716	Baring Bros & Co.	8,505	1,637
Comber, E. & Co.	0	7,514	Maxwell, W. A. & G. & Co.	6,121	1,197
Turner, W. D.	11,079	7,305	Zizinia & Co.	7,816	1,088
Ralli & Psicha	2,343	7,076	Hennings, Gosling & Co.	6,905	1,062
Cowie, C. G. & Co.	731	6,999	Mason, W.	4,419	842
Cardwell, T. & Co.	3,177	6,906	The Merchants' Co.	5,921	836
Gibbs, Bright & Co.	712	6,858	Guion & Co.	5,622	835
Menasce Bros & Co.	94	6,390	Fachiri, A. & Son	6,281	508
Nicol, Duckworth & Co.	54	6,387	Stolterfoht, Sons & Co.	6,743	404
Peel, J. & Co.	0	6,279	Hill, C. & Sons	4,174	396
Mody & Co.	0	5,918	Malcolmson, J. & D. & Co.	21,743	226
Hankey Bros & Co.	0	5,774	Cater, J. W. & Co.	4,137	192
Huth, F. & Co.	18,917	5,188	Fielden Bros & Co.	16,916	156
Drake, Kleinwort & Co.	15,601	5,161	Jackson, W. & Sons	8,289	138
Daniell & Co.	3,790	5,149	Melhuish & Dela Rue	5,333	101
Cama, B. F. & Co.	8,839	4,849	Rathbone Bros & Co.	15,235	73

Recipient	1860	1864	Recipient	1860	1864
Lyon, F. & Bros	2,915	4,792	Blessig, Braun & Co.	15,861	51
Robinson Bros	0	4,272	Green, G., Son & Co.	5,150	42
Bell, Miller & Co.	0	4,190	Thomson, H. M.	9,482	19
Saunders, C. & Co.	3,807	4,128	Moore, C.	4,898	8
Gunston, Wilson & Co.	73	4,070	Heath, E. & Co.	4,623	1
Gilliat, J. K. & Co.	4,050	3,920	Babcock, B. F. & Co.	6,643	0
Nathabhoy, C., Sons & Co.	0	3,903	Benn, R. & G.	4,955	0
Ayre, J.	0	3,901	Boyd, Edwards & Co.	6,968	0
Dickinson, W. & Co.	1,015	3,878	Buchanan, Browne & Co.	3,950	0
Lunds & Vernon	0	3,862	Franghiadi & Co.	7,270	0
Duranty, A. & Co.	269	3,810	Higgin, R. & Co.	5,398	0
Duff, Cadell & Co.	320	3,669	Isaac, Low & Co.	23,773	0
Burstall, J. W. & Co.	0	3,528	Jackson, J. A. & Co.	10,657	0
Eccles, Cartwright & Co.	297	3,387	Meadows, Frost & Co.	7,244	0
Crawford, Colvin & Co.	0	3,351	Moon, E. & Co.	6,314	0
Prange & Son	0	3,113	Oxley, W., Son & Co.	6,104	0
Mellor & Southall	1,468	2,940	Richardson, Spence & Co.	5,204	0
Oxley, J. S. & Co.	0	2,874	Swire, J. & Sons	4,801	0
Hewitt, J. & Co.	11,834	2,833	Zwilchenbart, E. & Co.	6,305	0
Dixon, C. E.	2,174	2,767			

Source: Custom Bills of Entry, Liverpool B Bills, Merseyside Maritime Museum, C/BE/Liverpool.

The 50 largest non-broker recipients in 1860 and the 50 largest in 1864, ordered in rank according to 1864 volumes, are listed in Table 9. These firms received 71 per cent of the cotton in 1860 that was not received by brokers, and 75 per cent in 1864. The salient point that emerges is the enormous turnover between the two years. The nature of the data means that one cannot draw absolute conclusions. It is possible, for example, that the absentees from either the 1860 or 1864 lists were still active in cotton merchanting in the other year, but had their cotton received in Liverpool by other firms. But even allowing for this, and for changes in partnerships, which make direct comparisons difficult in some cases, the vast turnover shows that the civil war led to a huge change in the personnel involved in the raw cotton trade in Liverpool and to the scale of their operations.

Only 11 of the 50 largest recipients in 1860 were among the 50 largest in 1864. The big losers, unsurprisingly, were those who had been recipients of American cotton. Fourteen of the top 50 firms from 1860 received no cotton at all in 1864. All of these had received their 1860 cotton exclusively, or almost exclusively, from America. The big winners were those who dominated the Asian trade in 1864. Twenty of the top 50 firms in 1864 had received no cotton at all in 1860. Of these, 18 were large recipients of Indian cotton. The names on the list seem to be mainly traders and merchants, mostly British, some based overseas. There are several banks amongst them (Barings; Drake, Kleinwort; Gilliat; Huth; Schroder). A few may have been firms related to cotton brokerages. The one thing they would have had in common is a head office, a branch office or an employee in Liverpool: someone, in other words, to receive the cotton on the firm's behalf.

Of the cotton that arrived in Liverpool in 1864, 44 per cent was received directly by known cotton brokers, and 43 per cent by brokers who were members of the LCBA. This is not surprising: one would expect the selling brokers to act as agents for their principals in the port. What is surprising is that as many as 129 of the 152 brokers on the membership list received cotton in 1864, some of them in relatively small quantities, as well as 39 brokers who were not on the LCBA list. Most of the latter were identified by Ellison as partners in a brokerage, but they still received cotton consignments in their own name. In every case, their firms had also received consignments under the corporate name. It is difficult to conceive of any reason for this unless the individual partners were trading and speculating on their own account.[23] A great many who received cotton must theoretically have been buying brokers. Under Ellison's model, buying brokers would not normally have received a cotton consignment directly from an incoming vessel and taken responsibility for it. In that case, either most buying brokers were also selling brokers, or they were trading on their own account, or they had clients who were buying directly, bypassing the selling brokers, or who were also trading on their own account. In practice, it seems likely that all four alternatives were to some extent true.

This situation was not created by the war. The same analysis is difficult to make for 1860 because no LCBA membership list exists for that year. However, by taking the 1864 list and adjusting it for known partnership changes described by Ellison, it is possible to come close. On that basis, 112 LCBA members received consignments of cotton in 1860, accounting for 42 per cent of all cotton imports. In practice, both figures would have been slightly higher had full data been available. Again, many of the recipients must have been buying brokers. A few brokers who were recipients in 1860 did not receive cotton in 1864.

Overall, 138 members of the LCBA, 91 per cent of the 1864 membership, took delivery of raw cotton from Liverpool docks in either 1860 or 1864 or both.

Table 10 Cotton received by members of the Liverpool Cotton Brokers' Association, 1860 and 1864 (000 lb – average of both years)

Joynson, T. & Co.	21,927	Armour & Co.	1,856	Bateson & Hilton	392
Joynson, P. jun	18,064	Bulley, Samuel (& W. Raffles)	1,814	Mayall & Andersson	391
Holt, G. & Co.	17,909	Webster, H. J.	1,797	Broom, W. T. & Co.	372
Swainson, A. & Sons	17,601	Wolstenholme, C.	1,693	Curry, P. W. & Co.	338
Haigh, T. & Co.	17,038	Houghton, Vance & Co.	1,613	Hall & Jones	298
Hollinshead, Tetley & Co.	16,489	Bright, W. & Sons	1,542	Lloyd, L	216
Littledale, T. & H. & Co.	16,293	Cruttenden & Oulton	1,509	Gaskell, J. & Son	209
Duckworth & Rathbone	15,799	**Waterhouse, N. & Sons**	1,457	Harpin & Bower	206
Titherington, Gill & Co.	14,674	Mussabini, P.	1,434	Raffles, W. W.	205
Marriott & Co.	13,937	Bulley, S. M.	1,334	Hornby & Robinson	175
Browne, Hunter & Co.	12,909	Haywood & McViccar	1,316	Thompson & Bradbury	174
Molyneux, Taylor & Co.	12,770	Reede, J. S. M. & Co.	1,312	Agelasto, A. S.	174
Bateson, J., Sons & Co.	11,050	Shakespeare, I. & Co.	1,273	Strafford Brothers & Co.	161
Rogers & Calder	10,830	Gaskell, T. & R.	1,256	Williams, O. H. & Co.	152
Bushby & Co.	9,309	Trepplin & Rome	1,249	Meugens & Forwood	127
Cunningham & Hinshaw	9,116	Joynson, J. & M.	1,237	Parkinson, Hamilton & Ingleby	112
Thomson, J. B. & Co.	8,778	Corrie & Co.	1,222	Farrer, W.	97
Whitaker, Whitehead & Co.	8,223	Morgan, J. B.	1,103	Willis, J.	92
Belcher, M. & Co.	7,977	Hollins, F. & Co.	1,092	Seville, W. & Co.	86
Cowie, Smith & Co.	7,935	Logan & Shaw	1,061	Given & Braddyll	80
Eccles, A. & Co.	7,167	Clark, H.	1,055	Lees, W. P. & Co.	75
Newall & Clayton	6,195	Armstrong & Berey	1,024	Bayley & Norbury	69
Musgrove, E. & Co.	5,899	**Wrigley, J. & Sons**	948	Cookson & Co.	57
Livesey & Thorpe	5,667	**Stock, J. & Son**	929	Meeson, W. & Co	53
Clare, W. & Sons	5,617	Percival Bros & Co.	909	Peers, J.	50
Campbell, C. & Son	4,563	Tipton, R. S.	894	Pearce, H.	48
Shand, Higson & Co.	4,272	**Gath, S. & Son**	846	Howell, J. & Sons	43
Chambres, Holder & Co.	4,082	Melladew, R.	803	Holland, J.	39
Postlethwaite, T. & Co.	3,913	Davies, J. H.	726	Brown, W. J.	29
Mason & Lister	3,781	Dean, C. & Co.	724	Griffith, Sons & Palethorpe	21
Salisbury, Turner & Grey	3,426	Schofield & Blackburn	711	Hall, R. C.	19
Buchanan, D. C. & Co.	3,373	Paton, D.	702	Blundell, J. & Co.	18
Stead Bros	3,275	Williams, M.	691	Comer & Harrison	14
Finlay & Lance	3,138	Fox, W.	671	Robson & Eskrigge	12
Reynolds & Gibson	3,068	Kearsley & Cunningham	656	Lea & Walthew	1
Campbell, J. P.	3,048	Good, J. W.	651	Bousfield & Johnson	<1
Smith, Edwards & Co.	2,940	Sheppard & Hyslop	643	Hutchinson, J. H.	<1
Eason, Barry & Co.	2,857	Jardine, E. & Co.	636	Chinn, F. F.	0
Cox, E. & Sons	2,838	Joseph Brothers	628	Cox & Radcliffe	0
Mellor & Co.	2,750	Jowett, S.	596	Cox & Young	0
Bell, Nott & Co.	2,732	Rushton, Johnson & Co.	582	Danson & Wild	0
Gladstone & Serjeantson	2,728	**Barton, M. & Son**	578	Ellison & Haywood	0
Withers & Co.	2,667	**Nicholson & Wrigley**	520	Hooton & Wilkinson	0
Buchanan, Wignall & Co.	2,373	Coupland & Thorburn	516	**Jee, M. & Son**	0
Bower, W. & Son	2,338	Blythe & Harvey	509	Martin, Studley	0
Cooke, I. & Sons	1,999	Thornely & Pownall	496	Rew, John	0
Jefferson & Taylor	1,964	Shaw, R. & Co.	489	Rickman & Tobias	0
Hodgson & Ryley	1,952	Tomlinson, W. D. & Co.	484	Rowlinson, R. B.	0
Coddington Bros	1,915	Peers, W. & Son	479	Rylands Brothers & Boult	0
Mellor, Cunningham & Powell	1,907	Whitehead & Hetherington	405	Sleigh, A. & Co.	0
				Tarleton & Cherry	0

The names in bold indicate those firms that supplied the Presidents of the LCBA from 1850 to 1869
Source: Custom Bills of Entry, Liverpool B Bills, Merseyside Maritime Museum, C/BE/Liverpool.

It can only be a provisional exercise, but it is worth attempting to categorise the Liverpool brokers according to whether they are likely to have been predominantly selling or predominantly buying brokers. The 1864 list of LCBA members has been divided into three columns according to the volume of cotton they received (Table 10). The third column includes those brokers who received no cotton in either year. To take account of the fact that many brokers will have suffered disproportionately from the collapse of the American trade, an average of 1860 and 1864 volumes has been used in compiling the rankings. When a firm changed its name between the two years, the name shown on the printed LCBA list of 1864 has been used.

The nature of the data means that caution must again be used in interpreting them. An extreme possibility would be that one of the firms shown as receiving no cotton might still have been a large selling brokerage, but one whose importing clients chose to receive cotton in their own name. For the same types of reason, the list will not accurately reflect the relative sizes of brokerage firms that did receive cotton. However, it remains probable that most, if not all, of the names in the first column were nominally selling brokers and most, if not all, of the names in the third column were nominally buying brokers. With the second column, it is impossible to say. Many firms in the third column still received a great deal of cotton. Hornby & Robinson, for example, received cotton to a value of almost £40,000 (£4 million today) in 1864. The names in bold in Table 10 indicate those firms that supplied the Presidents of the LCBA in the years 1850–69.[24] The great majority are to be found in the first column; all but one of the remainder in the second column. It is possible that the only genuine buying broker to become LCBA President in those 20 years was Matthew Jee. He was also one of the few not to be among the Dock committee electors.

As with almost everything that concerns the cotton brokers of Liverpool, the evidence is either anecdotal or needs to be inferred from data such as these. Cumulatively, the information suggests a reality different from and more diffuse than Ellison's model. The cotton brokers were not a breed apart. They were members of the wider merchant community, with blurred lines between several different functions. Many brokerages were departments of large trading houses. Several of the individual surnames on the list of non-broker recipients are the same as surnames on the lists of brokers. In some cases this may have been coincidental. In others, it seems likely that brokers either ran merchant firms in parallel with their broking business or had relatives engaged in merchanting.[25] It was a world of incestuous trading relationships.

The war years offered an unprecedented temptation to all brokers to cash in, and many seem to have been unable to resist it. But the opportunity was far from risk-free. As the price of raw cotton doubled, tripled, quadrupled during the war, many of those engaged in Liverpool's cotton trade – brokers, merchants and speculators – were sucked into a vortex of ever-increasing danger. Many would be ruined by it. It may reasonably be asked why the selling brokers, in particular, should have allowed themselves to be placed in this position. They were not unaware of the speculative fever in which they were operating, nor of the questionable substance of many of those with whom they were dealing. Nor should they have been unaware of where speculative fevers invariably lead. It is hard to avoid the conclusion that, in the pursuit of still greater profits, they became careless of the ever-increasing risks they were running.

The role in the cotton market that the selling brokers had progressively carved out for themselves was not far short of a licence to print money. However, the means through which they had acquired their dominance left them vulnerable to the types of risk that bankers carry, but without the bankers' capital to cushion them. It can be seen from the method of financing the trade, described in Chapter 6, that the failure of his own speculations was not the only way for a Liverpool broker to be ruined. Over the years, going back to the start of the century, the selling brokers had become the de facto bankers to their clients, the importing merchants. Backed by their own banks, the brokers advanced up to 80 per cent of the shipment value to the importers. In unexceptional times this represented little or no risk: the broker earned interest on the advance, and if there was a slippage in price, there was a 20 per cent protection for the broker, which was normally more than enough. In Ellison's words, "where ordinary care was exercised the losses … were not serious." Technically, the planter or the importer still owned the cotton until it was sold to a spinner. However, the broker was the account holder at the bank and the cotton was the collateral on which the advance had been made. In the event of default, the bank would have had recourse to the broker, not to the merchant, and it would then become a question of whether the broker could obtain payment from his client.[26]

In calm times, these remained largely hypothetical issues. They ceased to be hypothetical during the civil war. The LCBA imposed no requirement on a purchaser to prove creditworthiness. In the long chain of contracts for the same consignment of cotton, usually sold on at ever increasing prices, the person left with the last contract was the one who had to pay for the cotton when it arrived. If that person could not pay, the cotton passed back up the chain until it found a buyer who could pay. When the market collapsed in September 1864 – and at several points thereafter – this frequently turned out to be the importer, usually funded by his broker and the broker's bank. Milne has commented that "bills of exchange, when discounted and signed on frequently in times of extreme financial speculation, could be used to construct houses of cards, liable to collapse should any of a number of parties involved in complicated transactions suffer a commercial setback."[27] The brokers T. & H. Littledale explained what happened:

> Cotton had been sold "to arrive" at the very highest point of the market, and in many instances to men of straw – the first struggle of course was to re-sell at almost *any* price, to enable them to meet the prompts, but the differences were soon found to be too heavy for such weak hands, and the Cotton fell back to the Importers, causing a state of confusion and ruin that baffles description. ... Had this Cotton not been sold to these gamblers ... probably not an Importer or Broker would have been placed in difficulties.[28]

Importers were obliged to pay a higher price to buy back their own cotton than it was now worth. This ruined some of them, and their brokers in turn. As Williams sourly remarked in 1867, "it will ... be seen if our Bankers have exercised a wise discretion in withdrawing their confidence ... from Cotton, and which has resulted in the utter ruin of so many of their customers."[29]

According to Crick and Wadsworth's study, from the late eighteenth century, "the textile trades had evolved a system of credit and currency ... and they continued to employ methods which to some extent acted as a substitute for the more usual development of banking." Credit was already integral to the system well before the civil war. The financial downfall of some brokers towards the end of the war and after it needs to be considered in the context of the finance that would have been available to them with which to speculate. Again, detailed information is scant, but not altogether lacking. Although it is commonly agreed that the banks of the mid-nineteenth century were not the major source of long-term capital for business that they subsequently became, they were often the source of substantial short-term credit. Provincial banks at the time were overwhelmingly local. In 1831, nearly 60 per cent of the Bank of Liverpool's shareholders lived in the Liverpool area, and only 10 per cent outside Lancashire. The banks were inextricably linked to the trade of their region. Thus, merchants and brokers were active in establishing and maintaining the banks in Liverpool and formed the majority of directors in all but one of its banks. Three cotton brokers were among those who established the Bank of Liverpool. It is reasonable to conclude that the relationship between the Liverpool banks and the traders of raw cotton was extremely close.[30]

To preserve their liquidity, the banks preferred to make short-term advances. One form was through discounted bills of exchange, which is how the brokers made their advances to importers, and how they financed their regular business. However, there were two other methods of bank borrowing, either of which could have been available to a Liverpool broker. Banks were prepared to offer unsecured loans to customers who were considered reliable. The Bank of Liverpool lent up to £50,000 unsecured (£5 million today) and the Liverpool Union Bank up to £10,000. The second method was through a bank overdraft. It was normal for Lancashire banks to allow current accounts to be overdrawn for an undefined period of time up to a limit of 10 per cent of the account's annual turnover, and many account-holders used this facility as a permanent credit reserve, drawing on it whenever they needed the money.[31]

A rough calculation will show how valuable this facility could have been to a cotton broker. In 1863, before the height of the speculative boom, British annual raw cotton imports were worth nearly £60 million. A medium-sized brokers' firm could expect to handle 2 per cent of this total. This would yield the broker a minimum income of 0.5 per cent, or £6,000. However, because of the way that the trade was financed, the entire value of the transactions, not just the broker's commission on them, would form the turnover of a selling broker's account. In which case, the 10 per cent overdraft limit would theoretically enable such a broker to have a permanent overdraft facility of £120,000 (£12 million today). In total, brokers could have had access to many millions of pounds of unsecured credit at today's values.

The figures above are merely extrapolations from the lending policies of Liverpool banks at the time. The information does not exist to show to what extent cotton brokers chose, or were allowed, to take full advantage of them, but Hemelryk said that the credit obtained was considerable:

> Banks in Liverpool ... gave credit with very great readiness to respectable people. ... The banks at that time had no tangible security; they simply had the cotton morally hypothecated to them. ... As business was so profitable on all sides, large credit was given to those engaged in the cotton trade. ... A great many [banks] offered open credits for ten, twenty, and thirty thousand pounds, and one went so far as to offer to accept up to £100,000 without security.[32]

It would seem, therefore, that brokers would not have struggled to raise significant finance for speculation, as long as their bankers considered them a good risk. Most members of the LCBA had a long and successful pedigree in the cotton trade. That trade was huge, established and profitable. The rise in prices after 1861 made cotton an appealing investment. Brokers would surely have had little problem in borrowing money in the early years of the war. Only in September 1864, and at various points thereafter when prices collapsed, was confidence likely to evaporate. As indeed it did, as exemplified by Williams's quote above.

The only sure way for a broker to make money in the civil war years was to have a brokerage business that represented only spinners and to eschew all speculation. Perhaps a few brokers did satisfy both criteria. Others, such as Smith, navigated the minefield and made great fortunes. He was not the only one. A study of the probate records for 52 Liverpool cotton brokers active at the time of the civil war shows that the average size of each of their estates was more than £6 million at today's values. Twenty-four of these brokers left more than £5 million and 10 more than £10 million, one of whom was Samuel Smith. James Macrae was said to have left each of his three daughters £100,000 (a total of £30 million today) upon his death.[33]

But many were less skilled or less lucky. Ellison wrote that "palatial mansions were given up. Carriages and horses were sold. ... Many familiar faces disappeared from the Flags."[34] Smith recalled that:

> Most ... speculators lost all they had when the tide ebbed away, and the recoil came after the war. They had lost their legitimate business and their habit of patient industry, and many of them sank into chronic poverty. It was pitiable to see men who had bought fine mansions and costly picture galleries, hanging about "the flags", watching the chance of borrowing a guinea from an old friend.[35]

It can be assumed that William Forwood agreed with Smith's description, since he cribbed it word for word in his own autobiography.[36]

Reckless speculation, which had mushroomed during the war, had become a habit for Liverpool's cotton traders, and it proved a hard habit to break. There were now many more brokers, accustomed to inflated incomes and extravagant lifestyles. As prices fell after the war, commissions reduced too. Speculation must have seemed the easiest way to make up the shortfall. But, although prices fell, they did not fall evenly. For many years, as American cotton gradually came back on to the market and as Indian imports ebbed and flowed, both volume and price continued to fluctuate substantially, from year to year, from month to month. These were not the easiest of times in which to speculate. Crick and Wadsworth wrote that "the immediate revival in the cotton industry following the restoration of peace ... was accompanied by a burst of speculation in the raw material, which brought disaster to some Liverpool banks." They went on to say that the bank directors' reports for 1867 and 1868 had referred to "the fall in the level of ... common morality" and that 1871 saw the end of a period in which five Liverpool banks had failed.[37]

The Royal Bank of Liverpool suspended payments in October 1867. Amongst its shareholders in 1862 were the merchant families of Bibby, Brancker, Hutchison, Tomlinson and Zwilchenbart, and the broker families of Duckworth, Gill, Littledale, Shand, Molyneux and Taylor. The cotton merchant Robert Hutchison, a former Mayor of Liverpool, was a director of the bank. In 1868, he became bankrupt. He owed £33,705 to the bank (£3.4 million today),

£43,500 to his brokers and nearly £55,000 to the Molyneux family, connected with the brokers Molyneux, Taylor & Co., from whom he had borrowed. His losses on cotton were stated to be £51,183 in 1866 and 1867. At the bankruptcy hearing, Hutchison said that "all the directors were aware that he owed that sum to the bank, for the accounts were laid before them every Friday. Never heard any remark about his balance while he sat at the Board."[38]

As far as is known, Hutchison's failure did not lead to the failure of his brokers, Parkinson, Hamilton & Ingleby, nor to any member of the Molyneux family, which gives a good idea of the resources of both. However, there were plenty of other failures. An online search of the Liverpool press for the bankruptcies of cotton brokers and dealers between January 1864 and December 1872 revealed 113 separate instances. None occurred after March 1871. None can be blamed directly on the civil war. However, without the civil war and the price volatility and speculation it induced, perhaps few, if any, of them would have happened. The situation was not helped by severe problems in financial markets, including the collapse of the bank Overend, Gurney & Co. in June 1866. But this banking crisis was itself related to cotton. John Mills believed that the problems caused by the fall in cotton's value had been greater than those caused by its rise: "The price has settled down through a series of embarrassing fluctuations or jerks, caused by speculation, false reports ... and the difficulties of a new labor-system."[39]

The bankruptcies shed considerable vicarious light on dealings in the raw cotton market. Of the 113 bankrupts, 60 were cotton dealers, of whom only 12 were listed in *Gore's Directory*. One reason is that most of them were based outside Liverpool. The old-fashioned cotton dealer, who lived in Manchester or the spinning towns and sold small quantities of cotton to local spinners, was far from an extinct species in the 1860s. It is also clear that the term 'dealer' could conceal huge variations in the scale of operations. At one end were T. Wood, a "coal and cotton dealer of Saddleworth" and Charles Thompson, "provision and cotton dealer and butcher, Blackburn". At the other were James McMonnies, who numbered the large merchant house of T. & H. Littledale among his clients, and Louis Speltz, who failed with debts of £320,000. Cotton dealers were not necessarily small-time operators.[40]

Of the 53 broker bankruptcies, 35 were known members of the LCBA – nearly 20 per cent of the membership. This figure includes both entire firms and partnerships where only one partner failed. A further nine were listed in *Gore's* as cotton brokers, while the remaining nine were not listed anywhere. This strengthens the view that there were many non-LCBA brokers in Liverpool, their names still unknown. It is probable that the search did not reveal every failure, and certain that there must have been many people who faced financial difficulties or even ruin without formally becoming bankrupt. Several other long-standing members of the LCBA disappeared from the membership lists in these years yet are not to be found in the press reports of bankruptcies. Equally, several of the firms or individuals who were reported as bankrupt found ways of continuing in business and remained members of the LCBA. Altogether, the bald statistics reported here probably understate the level of carnage, particularly in the period 1869–71.[41]

Amongst the casualties were five firms, or partners in them, that had supplied past Presidents of the LCBA: William Clare & Sons, Isaac Cooke, Samuel Gath junior, Anthony Swainson & Sons and Titherington & Gill. In addition, the scion of a sixth firm, Charles Campbell of Colin Campbell & Sons, was "charged ... with having obtained from the National Bank of Liverpool an advance of £10,500 by fraudulent pretences". The National also offered him a facility of £30,000 on the verbal and untruthful assurance that there would be cotton to cover it. To these failures of LCBA luminaries may be added two others. One was Maurice Williams. According to Ellison, "after prices had fallen to what he considered to be a safe level, he recommenced operations on a large scale. ... Eventually there came a collapse, and, as he held a large stock ... the whole of his fortune disappeared before he got rid of his cotton." The other was Peter Joynson Jr, the second largest recipient of all cotton consignments in 1860. Ellison related that he was "one of the most genial 'characters'. ... His invariable ... salutation ... was 'Good morning. It's very fine to-day'." This description can be considered alongside Hemelryk's remembrance of "an old broker, who ... used to say to everybody: 'It is very fine to-day.' He had a bad end, that courteous man; he left suddenly for Spain, and his banker could have told you the reason why." The bank in question was the Liverpool Commercial Banking Co., which repossessed Joynson's property in Wallasey in 1874.[42]

When William Titherington, cotton broker, former partner of Titherington, Gill & Co., one of the largest recipients of cotton in both 1860 and 1864, looked out from his cell window at Lancaster Castle on 14 May 1868, wondering if he would be released the following day, he may have reflected on how the mighty had fallen. His case is a vivid example of how the tentacles of greed and corruption extended throughout Liverpool's elite. Titherington had been jailed following a petition from his own former company for the return of corporate funds that he had used for private speculation. "The debt was ... in respect of the joint speculations of Mr Titherington, Messrs. Mozley, Mr Price Edwards, and Mr Atwool." 'Messrs Mozley' were Charles Mozley, Mayor of Liverpool in 1863–64 and former chairman of Barned's Bank, Liverpool, which had failed in 1866, and his son Albert Charles Mozley, briefly a member of the LCBA and bankrupted in 1867. Samuel Price Edwards had been the Collector of Customs at Liverpool Docks until 1865 and was believed to have colluded in the escape of the *Alabama*. Upon retirement, he became a director of Barned's Bank. In 1867, Titherington, Gill & Co.

MEMBERS OF THE
LIVERPOOL COTTON BROKERS' ASSOCIATION.

MARCH, 1866.

COMMITTEE.

DANIEL CRANMER BUCHANAN, President.
FLETCHER ROGERS, Vice-President.

MICHAEL BELCHER.	THOMAS HOLDER.
PETER S. BOULT.	JAMES HARDY MACRAE.
SAMUEL MARSHALL BULLEY.	EDGAR MUSGROVE.
ALFRED H. COWIE.	HUGH H. NICHOLSON.
ROBERT HINSHAW.	SAMUEL WITHERS.

*N.B.—Those Gentlemen before whose names an asterisk * is prefixed have served the office of President.*

Titherington, Gill and Co.   * Wm. Titherington

Liverpool Cotton Brokers' Association Membership List, 1866, with William Titherington shown as a past President
(LRO 380 COT/1/7/1, reproduced by permission of the International Cotton Association)

had sued Price Edwards for reneging on a purchase order. During the trial, he said: "I should think Titherington has been speculating in cotton from the earliest period of his existence as a cotton broker." David Atwool had been the tenant of a warehouse at Liverpool Docks and was a friend of Price Edwards. The investment was under his name because "Messrs. Mozley as bankers ... and Mr Titherington as a broker ... did not wish it divulged ... that they were engaged on their private account in extraordinary cotton speculations." Titherington "could not give any idea of the amount of his liabilities ... but he thought they were not more than £100,000" (£10 million today). The largest creditor was the North-Western Bank; the next largest was the merchant house of Thomson, Finlay & Co., the twelfth largest recipient of cotton in 1864 and now in liquidation itself.[43]

William Titherington was not released from jail the following day, or for some time to come. It is superfluous to add that, apart from the downfall of Williams, no information in the preceding paragraphs was mentioned by Thomas Ellison.

There is an intriguing codicil to Titherington's story. The LCBA membership lists from 1866 onwards denote the names of past Presidents who were still active cotton brokers. The 1866 list clearly shows William Titherington as a past President. On the 1867 and subsequent lists (by which time his legal travails had begun), he is not so shown, although he remained a named LCBA member for many years to come. Neither does Titherington's name appear on the complete list of LCBA Presidents in Ellison's *Cotton Trade*. It is possible that the LCBA made an error on the 1866 list. However, it seems unlikely that it would mistake the name of a past President, especially as the list must surely have been checked, if not created, by Studley Martin, its long-serving Secretary and a broker himself. If it was not a mistake, then – following Titherington's disgrace – the LCBA must have decided to rewrite its own history and expunge his name from the roll of honour. In that case, Ellison was complicit in falsifying the historical record.[44]

If this is what happened, then another name, probably that of the Vice-President, must have been substituted on Ellison's list. Most candidates can be ruled out because they are either denoted as past Presidents on the 1866 LCBA list or were specifically mentioned by Ellison in his narrative as having been elected President. There is a single exception within the probable time-frame: Thomas B. Blackburn of Blackburn, Schofield & Co., whom Ellison listed as the President in 1856. Blackburn was still an active broker in 1866, present on the LCBA list, but not denoted as a past President in that or any subsequent year. Nor does Ellison mention him as a President in his narrative, which he does for most, although not all, of the others. The strong suspicion is that William Titherington, not Thomas Blackburn, was President of the LCBA in 1856.

This may seem a trivial issue, but it is revealing. It does nothing to inspire confidence in the truthfulness of either the LCBA or Thomas Ellison about any matter which caused them shame and embarrassment. It is significant that the articles that Ellison wrote anonymously for the *Liverpool Post* in 1881–82 and which formed the draft of his chapters on brokerages in *Cotton Trade* included no mention of William Titherington or Thomas Blackburn, and made only cursory references to their firms, both of which had been founder members of the LCBA.[45] This must make one wonder what other information has been falsified or omitted.

CHAPTER VIII

When Johnny Went Marching Home
Aftermath and conclusions

The years of the American Civil War produced utter turmoil throughout the British cotton trade and the Liverpool raw cotton market. But, as the bankruptcies and financial collapses described in the previous chapter show, the turmoil did not stop with the end of the war. The statesman and businessman George Goschen later wrote that "whoever held [cotton] stocks felt the ground giving way beneath his feet. No branch of trade connected with the article has been exempt, and we have heard the saying in Liverpool that 1865 ruined the speculators, 1866 the merchants, 1867 the producers."[1] Manchester might justifiably claim that it had been damaged constantly during the war and after it, but would not have been surprised at Liverpool's forgetfulness of its misfortunes.

The minute book of the LCBA gives vicarious evidence of the pressures its members were under once the war had ended. From early 1865, there was an escalating incidence of expulsions, disputes and threats of legal action between brokers. In April 1865, the behaviour of Messrs Topp and Coupland was described as 'disgraceful'. In April 1866, the resignation of Mr Norbury was refused, and he was instead expelled. Later that month, the actions of Mr Giannacopulo were described as 'reprehensible'. In June, the firm of Lea & Walthew was reprimanded for its behaviour towards the firm of Newall & Clayton. In July, upon the motions of members, the names of Samuel Gath Jr and Godfrey Barnsley were erased from the list of members. In June 1867, Mellor & Co. warned of their intention to make a complaint against Mayall & Andersson.[2]

The LCBA had somehow managed to exist without written rules until 1863, when the civil war forced an attempt to tame the jungle. In that year, wrote Ellison, "it became necessary to do something ... in consequence of the numerous disputes arising out of the gigantic speculative transactions developed by the occurrences incidental to the American war." But the end of the war did not halt the unravelling of Ellison's pristine system. The laws of the LCBA, non-existent until 1863, then consisting of a single sheet of paper, had expanded to 16 pages by 1871 and to 31 pages by 1879. This simple fact is evidence of the pressure the LCBA was under to improve its self-regulation. By 1879, it was felt necessary to require each broker to append his signature to the laws, presumably to prevent subsequent pleas of ignorance. In retrospect, the preceding hundred years or so can be seen as one continuous process. The civil war period may have been uniquely dramatic, but the system was constantly evolving and losing its cohesion over many years, despite the best efforts of the LCBA to control it.[3]

Ultimately, the convulsions in the Liverpool raw cotton market destroyed the LCBA as it had existed since 1841. Yet the immediate aftermath of the war had seemed full of promise for those brokers who had managed to avoid ruin. The first major event was the successful completion of the transatlantic cable in 1866, which enabled almost instant communication of market information, and especially prices, between America and Liverpool. In Ellison's passive words:

> The change suggested to some members of the CBA the feasibility of doing business direct with America, without the intervention of a merchant; of being themselves importers, instead of selling for importers. In time an extensive business sprang up in this way, and, of course, whatever consignments went to brokers direct were lost to the merchants who had previously received them. The broker, instead of being the servant of the merchant, became his competitor.[4]

Ten years later, a clearing house was established in Liverpool through which all futures trading had to be conducted and to which access was a monopoly privilege of LCBA members. This change, enforced by the LCBA, had the effect of handicapping the importing merchant by 1 per cent vis-à-vis the selling broker, with the result that direct trade between America and the selling brokers increased still further. Importers then applied to join the LCBA, but were rebuffed, as were their attempts to have the cost penalty removed. Meanwhile, some buying brokers had already approached the importers to buy directly from them, which the latter agreed to do with apparent reluctance. The upshot was that, in 1881, the importers set up a rival organisation, the Cotton Exchange, through which cotton could be sold and bought only by brokers who were not members of the LCBA. Eventually, the two organisations buried the hatchet and, in 1882, merged into a single Cotton Association, ending the brokers' monopoly.[5]

This, at least, was the theory. Tangential evidence from the LCBA's membership lists in the 1860s suggests that the situation was more complicated in practice. These lists confirm the convulsions that took place in the raw cotton market during the financial crises after the war and demonstrate substantial changes both to the LCBA membership list and to the way in which the membership was recorded. The greatest convulsions are evident in 1870 and 1871. In other years, an average of three or four brokers disappeared from the list each year. In 1870, 15 firms or individuals disappeared and, in 1871, 17. Mention of many of these can be found among the press reports of bankruptcies.[6]

As described in the previous chapter, in 1864 (and through to 1867) the membership was reported in three categories: entire firms or partnerships; sole traders; and individuals who were members of firms or partnerships, with the corporate name listed in brackets afterwards. The last category had consisted of more than 40 per cent of the membership. In 1868, that reduced to 3 per cent: only five members were reported in that way, which begs the question as to why *any* were. The others were all transferred to the first category: entire firms or partnerships. The reporting of sole traders was unaltered. This was a substantial change and must surely have been implemented for a substantial reason. It is impossible to know what that reason was, or why, a year later, the decision was reversed. In 1869, and in subsequent years through to at least 1872 (the limit of this study), there are only two categories of member: sole traders and companies or partnerships with named individuals against every one of them.

Any comment on these changes can only be speculative. But, with the already complicated membership structure of the LCBA and with a doubling of the number of brokers during the civil war, it would not be surprising if, by the mid-1860s, there was considerable confusion as to who exactly was a member of the LCBA. It may be that, in 1868, the LCBA simply gave up trying to distinguish between firms where all partners were members and firms where only some were members, so it listed only the firms (except in five cases). It may then be that this caused even greater confusion, so that, in 1869, the membership list became what, by the LCBA's own rules, it always should have been: a list of individuals.

These post-war membership lists highlight another important issue. It has already been shown that the demarcation line between selling and buying brokers was blurred. It begins to become apparent that the demarcation line between selling brokers and importers could also be blurred. Between 1866 and 1872, seven individuals who had been substantial recipients of raw cotton in 1864 but who were not cotton brokers in that year, were admitted to LCBA membership. The names were Stitt (1866), R. Christie Jr (1867), Giannacopulo (1868), Ralli (1868), James Spence (1869), Hime (1871) and J. P. Schilizzi (1872). Together, these seven received more than 12 million lb of cotton at Liverpool docks in 1864. For the reasons described earlier, it is possible that, where first names or initials are not given, the LCBA member was a relative of the importer rather than the importer himself, but it still seems improbable that any of them would have become brokers other than in connection with their, or their family's, importing business.

Because there are no surviving LCBA membership lists between 1841 and 1864, it is impossible to know how many other members may have started as importers and then become brokers as well, or vice versa. But the available evidence, including the duplication of surnames between importers and brokers, suggests that importers may always have formed a significant part of the LCBA's membership. In which case, Ellison's description of the post-war developments, in which he refers to importers and selling brokers as two discrete groups, needs to be treated with caution. When he writes that importers "suggested that ... merchants should be admitted to the privileges of the Association", he does not mention that many importers, or their relatives, were already members, with a clear interest in keeping out the competition.[7] The picture that begins to take shape is not so much a struggle between distinct interest groups as a melee in which a large number of businesses and individuals, with interests that were varied and overlapping, were competing for a share of the new opportunities that the momentous post-war changes were rapidly enabling.

These conclusions would remain largely conjecture were it not for Ellison's anonymous articles for the *Liverpool Post*, which confirm not only that the status of brokers was confused, and always had been, but that Ellison was either confused himself or was unwilling to clarify the confusion.

Writing of the early nineteenth century, prior to the LCBA's existence, Ellison states that "some of the dealers [the forerunners of the buying brokers] were in a very large way of business, and many of them imported extensively on their own account. They were, in point of fact, merchants." By the time of the LCBA's formation, "if any of [the brokers] had been merchants as well as brokers [this] ... would not have given them any advantage over merchants who were not members." This might suggest that some brokers were indeed merchants, but that Ellison did not want to say so explicitly. However, he then reports that "[the LCBA] was not, nor was it intended to be, an association of all sections of the trade ... importers [not] ... being eligible for membership." Finally, in 1882, he acknowledges that "by almost imperceptible degrees the [LCBA] has become something very different from what was intended or anticipated at its original formation."[8]

In the closed world of Liverpool's cotton brokers, it beggars belief that the LCBA would not have known if any of its members were also importers. Why was a single one admitted if importers were ineligible? How could the process have been "almost imperceptible"? Even in anonymous mode, Ellison does not answer these questions directly. However, one comment offers an insight into what probably happened: "If one man applies for admission as a broker, and after his election turns merchant, all is right; but if another who intends to do the same kind of business applies for admission as a merchant, all is wrong, and he is rejected."[9]

If one assembles the available information, some of it conflicting, a probable truth begins to emerge. Some founding members of the LCBA were already importers as well as brokers, with sufficient clout to insist on being admitted to membership. As time went by, other brokers became importers too, and the initial precedent made it impossible to debar them. This process was accelerated by the American Civil War when many more brokers began to import, to a greater or lesser extent. It then accelerated further with the establishment of the clearing house, which for the first time gave importers a direct financial advantage in being members of the LCBA. The culmination of all this, in Ellison's bleak, anonymous words, was that "the [LCBA] has ceased to be what it is called, and has developed into an association of brokers, importers [and] exporters."[10]

Although the cable and the clearing house gave the impetus to these changes, the relative underlying strengths of the factions, and the tensions between them, did not develop from nothing in little more than a decade from the end of the civil war. Two things are evident from the subsequent chain of events. First, until they over-reached themselves, the selling brokers were the real power in the market: more powerful than the importers, able to bully them at will, and also able to dominate the buying brokers. Second, although the line between selling and buying brokers might have been blurred, there *was* a line, and ultimately the LCBA split partially along it. The available information suggests that there was a continuum of change from the late eighteenth century until 1882. Over time, the selling brokers progressively came to dominate the importers, until they metamorphosed into importers themselves, while bending the buying brokers into serving them rather than their spinner clients. The four key events in this process were the formation of the LCBA, the American Civil War, the laying of the transatlantic cable and the formal establishment of futures trading and the clearing house. In the end, the system fell apart because the selling brokers became too greedy, and because the size and complexity of the trade made it increasingly impossible for a small group of middlemen to retain absolute control.

It is not hyperbolic to compare changes in the Liverpool cotton market in the late 1870s to changes in the City of London in the late 1980s after Big Bang, even if the scale was very different. In both cases, a hugely successful commercial powerhouse had grown up over many decades, with its own idiosyncrasies and methods of business, presided over by a small group of people from similar backgrounds, who trusted each other and controlled everything. Then, and in both cases as the partial result of technological innovation, these traditional, self-contained worlds were blown apart by a whirlwind of change. New ways of doing business needed urgently to be devised. New institutions were required to police them. And new people came to prominence in the market, with different ethics and different ways of viewing and conducting business, to the acute discomfort of the old guard.

However, these upheavals in Liverpool paled into insignificance compared with the upheavals in America, as the South attempted to resuscitate its cultivation of cotton and to retrieve its domination of the world market.

After the civil war, the South was broke. Most of its capital had been wiped out, since it had consisted mainly of slaves. The value of land plummeted. Most planters had always been improvident and permanently in debt. Hardly anyone, however rich at least on paper before the war, now had either ready cash or substantial assets. It has been estimated that, even when the value of slaves is excluded, Southern wealth fell by 43 per cent between 1860 and 1865. Before the war, Mississippi had been America's fifth richest state; after the war, it became the poorest. For most in the countryside (and most of the South *was* countryside), the only remedy appeared to lie in growing and selling cotton. There was no industry to speak of and, although immediate attempts were made to create more, most of them failed. The African American population in the South had always been slaves to cotton; now much of the white rural population became slaves to it as well. Meanwhile, the extreme racial prejudice of white Southerners that had underpinned slavery was unaltered. During 1865 and 1866, around 500 white men were indicted in Texas alone for the murder of African Americans. Not a single one was convicted by a jury.[11]

From a cotton perspective, the civil war did not end in April 1865. On the islands off South Carolina, home to the premium Sea Island cotton, it ended in November 1861. In New Orleans it ended in April 1862. In the Mississippi valley it ended in July 1863. In these and other parts of the South, the war ended when Union occupation began. And slavery did not end abruptly in 1865 either. Instead, it withered and crumbled throughout the whole period of the war, and not only in the areas of Union occupation. With these various endings came the urgent need for economic activity to resume, with implications for both the planters and their former slaves. Many plantations had been abandoned; the owners of most were destitute, or close to it, and needed to sell or lease out their land. One consequence was an immediate influx of Northern entrepreneurs to exploit the apparent opportunities. Much cotton land was nearly worthless and the owners so impoverished that almost any offer was a good offer. The price of cotton still reflected its wartime scarcity. Thus began vast speculative ventures that rivalled anything that Liverpool could offer. Even more frequently than in Liverpool, however, they ended in ruin.[12]

The planters hoped to use the Northerners' cash to rebuild their cotton businesses and their own wealth. The Northerners hoped to exploit a shortage of cotton, an inflated price and the cheap and ready availability of plantation land to make quick money. Like speculators in Liverpool, the incomers made big eyes at the price of cotton without appearing to understand the treacherous volatility of the cotton market. But they were unlucky too. Because of the dereliction of cotton cultivation during the war, the quality of the seed was poor. There was atrocious weather in 1865 and 1866, with widespread flooding in the Mississippi valley. By the end of the 1866 season, many incomers were in difficulty, and a fall in prices in 1867 finished them off. Most of them returned North. This brief experience did, however, have some enduring consequences. It enabled the quick resurrection of Southern cotton. It enabled more of the old planters to retain their estates. It demonstrated, as every other section of this book has done, the paramount importance of price in anything to do with cotton. And it proved how difficult it would be to persuade the freedmen to return voluntarily to the plantations on any basis, but especially as wage-hands.[13]

In the immediate aftermath of the Union victory, many freedmen simply stopped working. William and Henry Neill travelled extensively through the South in late 1865 to assess the state of cotton cultivation. William Neill wrote home that "the negroes seem to be nearly all leaving the plantations & wandering about." Many migrated to the towns. One way of looking at the post-war situation is to envisage a vast commercial enterprise, on which the entire Southern economy depended, and from which the whole workforce had conceptually vanished. There was an imperative for the freedmen remaining in the countryside to work and to acquire the means of subsistence. This inevitably raised the question of land tenure and ownership. Many freedmen hoped and expected that the Federal government would give them land after emancipation. But widespread amnesties for former Confederates, and the consequent restoration of their estates, put paid to these notions. Without redistribution, few freedmen could afford to buy land, few white land-owners would sell to them, and those who did were often subjected to physical violence. So land remained almost entirely a white preserve.[14]

Without land, it was impossible for the freedmen to achieve full independence. However, they did retain one weapon in their fight to escape a resurrection of the former plantation system: their labour. As long as the freedmen were prepared to hold out against the progression from slavery to wage slavery, the planters needed to make concessions if any cotton was to be grown. Increasingly, the freedmen refused paid employment. They were disillusioned by already low wages, further reduced by 25 per cent to 40 per cent in 1868. They were affronted by arbitrary deductions for infringements real or imagined (as high as 25 per cent or 30 per cent, according to one study) and by the widespread obligation to buy provisions from the planter's own store at inflated prices. Different forms of land tenure on the plantations developed as a consequence of this stand-off and, in particular, sharecropping – a distant cousin of tenancy, whereby the cropper was paid for his labour via a share of the proceeds of his own crop at the end of the harvest year. From the early 1870s, there was a move away from the rigid wage contracts that had been imposed during and immediately after the war towards more diverse forms of land tenure. "On twenty plantations around me," said an Arkansas planter, "there are ten different styles of contracts." But sharecropping increasingly predominated. By the late 1870s, insofar as it can be established, about 5 per cent of the freedmen owned their own land, 20 per cent rented, 20 per cent worked as employed labour and 55 per cent were sharecroppers. By the end of the century, it was estimated that, in six key cotton-growing states, more than 75 per cent of African American farmers were sharecroppers.[15]

To regenerate their plantations, the planters needed more than labour: they needed credit. Although, as a generality, Southerners were impoverished by the war, there were exceptions. As in any war, some people found the means to make a fortune, and in this case they were the ones who had understood the significance of cotton as a currency and had managed to acquire it in bulk. Those who had hoarded it, those who had stolen it, those who had failed to burn it but had instead sold it surreptitiously to the Union for hard currency, those who had continued to grow it when they were instructed not to by the Confederacy – these were the people who were rich at the end of the war, who formed the bedrock of what little prosperity there was in the South in 1865, and who were in a position to expand their fortunes in the years afterwards. Some were planters, but most were entrepreneurs, from both South and North, who collectively formed a new merchant class after the war that had not existed before it. They were the ones who oiled the wheels of renewed cotton cultivation. In time, the lien laws – introduced after the civil war to help the planters get credit – led to the merchant selling directly to tenants and sharecroppers without reference to the planters.[16]

Cotton prices tumbled throughout the 1870s and continued to fall for most of the rest of the century. This necessitated further recourse to the credit merchants, further liens on the crop and further debt. Increasingly, the same crop had liens upon it for rent or labour and for supplies advanced, sometimes by more than one provider. When the crop was good and prices high, all claims could be satisfied. When they were not, which was progressively the case from the 1870s onwards, they could not. The freedmen were forced back into dependence, at least until the next crop was harvested. Servitude for life was commuted to servitude for a year. Unless a better alternative could be found at the end of that year, it would become servitude for another year. In many instances, slavery became peonage – debt servitude. This was the reality of post-emancipation life for most freedmen.[17]

But cotton's revival after the war did not depend on the planters and the freedmen alone. The five traditional cotton states (Alabama, Georgia,

Louisiana, Mississippi and South Carolina) had produced 74 per cent of the nation's cotton in 1859. In 1899, it was 55 per cent. They did not collectively exceed their pre-war volume until the late 1880s. Instead, the growth came from new areas, and especially from Texas, which had grown 8 per cent of the nation's cotton before the war and was growing 27 per cent at the end of the century. And the growth came, not from large plantations with freedmen supplying the labour force, but from the small farms of white farmers. Before the war, these farmers had produced 17 per cent of America's cotton at most; by 1880, that share had increased to 44 per cent. These white farmers also lacked the capital to invest in cotton production, so they too borrowed from merchants, on the merchants' terms. The accumulation of debt caused many of them to lose their lands and turned them into tenant farmers or sharecroppers. By 1880, 40 per cent of all one-family cotton farmers were white, and 81 per cent of those were sharecroppers. For everyone involved in growing cotton, the dependence on the credit merchant was principally responsible for the desperate plight of the cotton South in the decades after the civil war.[18]

Almost everyone needed credit. The Georgia State Department of Agriculture reported that, in 1875 and 1876, only a quarter of farmers had no recourse to it during the year. The need was supplied by thousands of local merchants, scattered throughout the South. They also provided food, clothing and implements to the farmers through the year and sold cotton on their behalf at harvest time. They charged high interest rates – from 30 per cent to 70 per cent p.a. For anyone already operating on the breadline, the debt frequently became unpayable. The logical solution would have been for the farmers, both African American and white, to have planted less cotton and produced more food, but the merchants would not allow it because it would have undermined most of their sources of income. The terms of their loans imposed increased cotton production on the farmers, despite the tumbling prices and despite the fact that it was a barely profitable activity. This situation, with small farmers in thrall to money-lenders, was similar to the position of the *ryots* in India. And, in a different way, it was similar to what had happened in Egypt during the American Civil War: a region that had once been self-sufficient could no longer feed itself.[19]

The simplest way of viewing the Southern cotton economy in the decades after the civil war is as a vast system of payday loans, with the difference that the payday came only once a year and was often insufficient to pay the loan.

An oblique testimony to the desperation of cotton-growers can be seen in the newspaper treatment of Henry Neill. After the civil war, Neill returned to New Orleans, where he became a cotton merchant. He also produced a newsletter for the British cotton trade, advising them on the size of the current crop and the likely movement of prices. By the 1890s, Neill's influence was enormous. According to the *Atlanta Constitution*:

One blast from his horn has been known to knock the price of cotton down 50 points, which meant an apparent reduction of nearly $20,000,000 in the value of the crop. The spinners had the most absolute faith in his predictions, and his influence so dominated the market that, regardless of what conditions might seem to indicate, the price of the south's great staple was practically dominated by this one man's opinion.[20]

The problem for the growers was that Neill's predictions were usually accurate, which did not stop their newspapers turning on him with a vengeance. "Henry Neill has damaged the cotton farmers more than all the boll worms, rust, floods and drouths [sic]." "[His] outrageous and inexcusable prophecies." "Fabric of guess work." "[A] commercial Judas, who undertook to deliver the hard-working producers into the hands of sharp men." "An enemy of the public welfare." "[A] prophet [who] is an agent of evil." "A demon of destruction." "He knows as much about the output of the coming crop as a chimpanzee."[21]

The perennial question for British cotton manufacturers before and during the civil war had been whether cotton grown by free labour could be produced as efficiently as cotton grown by slaves. It had been supposed, not unreasonably, that the answer to this question would determine the price of raw cotton after the war. It did not. This issue was made a theoretical abstraction by the excessive volume of cotton grown, which had a far greater impact on its price than the cost of production. The peak period of growth for cotton manufactures was now over, yet America was increasing its supply of raw cotton faster than the worldwide market was consuming it. The cotton could still be sold, but only at prices that were so low that they barely covered the costs of production, if that.[22]

Statistics for the acreage of cotton cultivation do not appear to exist prior to 1867, so a comparison of the productivity of the land, pre- and post-war, is impossible. However, Samuel Smith, a usually reliable source, stated that the pre-war American yield ranged from 200 lb to 400 lb per acre. In the years 1867–69, the yield averaged 193 lb. In the 1870s, it averaged 175.5 lb; in the 1880s, 171.2 lb; and in the 1890s, 178.1 lb. Figure 11 shows the combined effect of the fall in price and the fall in yields. The dollar return of each acre under cotton cultivation reduced by 75 per cent between 1869 and 1896. Even if one strips out the artificially high prices after the war, the return still reduced by 61 per cent between 1875 and 1896.[23]

There seems no reason, if the price of cotton had remained stable at a farm-gate level of about 12 cents per lb, its value in 1870, that it could not have been a profitable activity for all the different forms of labour by then involved in it. The reason the price did not stabilise at that level, and had in fact more than halved by 1898, was that too much cotton was being grown. When the

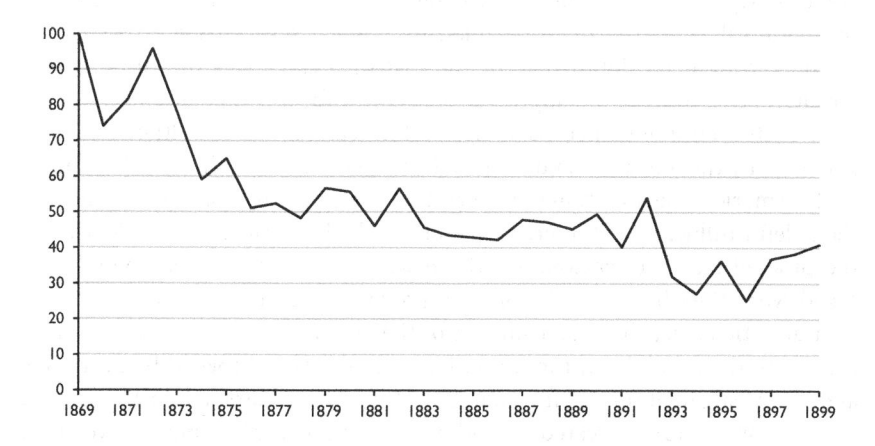

Figure 11 American cotton earnings per acre, 1869–1899 (Indexed on 1869)

Source: US Department of Agriculture, 'Cotton Crop of the United States, 1790–1911' (Washington, DC: US Government Printing Office, 1912), Circular 32.

crop became unprofitable, its operatives could not switch their labour into other, more profitable alternatives, because there were no alternatives. The option of becoming subsistence farmers was closed to most by the dictates of the credit merchants. Collectively, the South had a near monopoly of the supply of raw cotton to the world market. But, collectively, the South had no meaning. It existed only as an assortment of desperately poor individuals, with no means of using their combined power to raise prices. On a macro level, a decision to grow less cotton was imperative; on an individual level, it was impossible. This was not so much a failure of free labour as a catastrophic failure of the free market.[24]

None of this seems to have concerned the British cotton trade unduly. There were frequent and lengthy press commentaries on American cotton cultivation immediately after the war, while the future remained uncertain. But once cotton started to flow again from America, cheaply and in quantity, the comments became fewer. All the British cotton trade had ever cared about was obtaining a large volume of raw cotton at a low price. How this was achieved had been a matter of indifference under slavery, and it remained a matter of indifference after slavery.

In this way King Cotton resumed his throne after the interregnum – not as the constitutional monarch that many had hoped for, but as the autocrat of a new form of tyranny. The rural population of the American South remained his vassals, while the British cotton trade remained the principal beneficiaries of his largesse. The imports of American cotton crept slowly up and its price crept slowly down. The volume regained its pre-war level in 1871, but not reliably until 1878. The price regained its pre-war level in 1876.[25] American cotton retrieved its dominance of the British market and the futile search for alternative sources of supply was suspended for a while, although not for ever. Cotton famine turned back into cotton feast in Britain, although not in America. By the mid-1870s, nothing had changed. Yet everything had changed.

In America, the abolition of slavery, the development of sharecropping and the baleful influence of the credit merchants had transformed the South and the production of its cotton. Yet those who grew it might reasonably have asked what they had gained from the process. In Britain, the laying of the transatlantic cable, the establishment of the clearing house, the regulation of futures trading and, later, the formation of the Cotton Brokers' Bank in 1878 and the amalgamation of all elements of the cotton market into the Cotton Association in 1882, created a trading environment that must have been unrecognisable to its pre-war participants. If cotton speculation could not be prevented, at least it could be controlled. The changes were not universally welcomed. But, as Ellison commented, passively as ever, "eventually the old method (or want of method) of conducting the arrival business became so thoroughly unbearable, that it was decided to give the new plan a trial."[26]

The changes in Liverpool would have happened, and would have needed to happen, in any event. The American Civil War did not cause any of them. But the extreme circumstances of the war hastened the process: they magnified the excesses and irregularities of the Liverpool raw cotton market and made them unsustainable. In retrospect, the civil war marked a watershed in the British raw cotton trade between buccaneer capitalism and self-regulated capitalism.

* * *

In conclusion, it was the scarcity of raw cotton during the war, as well as its engorged price, that was the catalyst of this process. As has been definitively shown, Britain's production of yarn in the years 1862–64 was at 46 per cent of the level of the preceding three years and, if one makes a reasonable allowance for lost market growth, at 36 per cent of the consumption demand. Compared with the average price in 1860, the average price in 1862–64 was three and a half times higher and, at its peak on 21 July 1864, nearly five times higher. Much of that increase in price was the result of speculation, but most was due to the demonstrable absence of by far the world's largest cotton crop from the world market, which in turn fuelled the speculation. Throughout the civil war, a cotton scarcity co-existed with a cotton famine. Yet, according to Farnie, the notion that the two might be related is a "a stupefying misconception. ... There was no real shortage of cotton in Lancashire even during 1862."

Instead, the blame has been placed on the mill-owners for over-producing before the war – a judgment that Ellison and Arnold originated, to which Brady contributed a spurious and ill-informed statistical justification and Farnie a few selective and misleading facts, and which has been repeated without research or justification by almost every historian since. Under no scenario can over-production be blamed for the cotton famine. But for the war, there would have been a limited recourse to short-time working as a result of the short American crop of 1860–61. That is all. So one is left with Wright's conclusion that there was a sudden and inexplicable plunge in the worldwide demand for cotton goods, which just happened to coincide with the war. To which the riposte is: what do you expect to happen when the price doubles or quadruples, and the supply halves? It is true, of course, that demand did fall. As one would expect, it adjusted itself to the supply through the mechanism of price. In that sense, and in that sense alone, there was no scarcity. But this line of argument, which would have appealed to Liverpool's cotton brokers, is pure sophistry.

Sometimes the obvious explanation is the correct one. The outbreak of the civil war caused an immediate fall in the worldwide demand for fresh supplies of cotton goods, which led to short-time working in late 1861. The absence of American cotton as a result of the war caused the cotton scarcity, which in turn led to the famine. The global cotton trade operated, and needed to operate, with a substantial pipeline of stocks at every stage. The pipeline was well stocked when the civil war started. Because of the uncertainty over its duration, and because of shipping times of up to six months, the worldwide trade began to sell from stock in the summer of 1861. The pipeline drained through 1862. Until the supply and the price became dependable again, the trade bought only for immediate requirements. There was no refilling of the pipeline. Instead, there was a temporary, provisional market throughout the war, created by the related symptoms of a scarce supply and an inflated price. This is where any analysis of the cotton trade during the war needs to be centred. Once this market had emerged in late 1861, any retrospective comment on pre-war levels of production became meaningless.

There are two original findings about Liverpool in this book. The first is that it was not a solidly pro-Confederate town and that, whatever the emotional sympathies of its merchants, as a body they were strongly in favour of neutrality and non-intervention. The second is the vicious dispute between the LCBA and the spinners. This antagonism later softened for a while. In May 1868, the brokers even said they were "greatly indebted" to Hugh Mason; in January 1869, a meeting between them and the spinners "had passed off in a very friendly spirit". But it was too good to last. A few days later, Mason was back on the warpath.[27]

Otherwise, the detailed material in Chapters 6 and 7 does not advance a new hypothesis; it puts layer upon layer of information upon a previously hazy framework. It has always been known that some brokers were simultaneously buyers and sellers of cotton. It has always been known that some traded cotton on their own account. It has always been known that speculation was rife in the market during the war. It has always been known that there were many business failures after the war. But these things have been known in a sketchy way, with a lack of hard data, and especially with a lack of data for the years of the civil war. With the help of some unexamined primary sources and a great deal of anecdotal evidence, it has been possible to build a more complete, more vivid picture. The difficulty is in knowing what conclusions to draw when so little of the information is quantified, and when that which is quantified – principally the Bills of Entry – is to some extent open to interpretation.

The conclusions therefore need to be more circumspect than some of the evidence. There was an orgy of speculation in Liverpool during the war, much of it reckless gambling. Members of the LCBA were directly implicated in it, but how many, and to what extent, cannot be answered definitively. Without doubt, the Liverpool brokers traded extensively on their own account. Whether most of them represented both sellers and buyers of cotton is a harder question to answer. In other findings, the gothic gravitas of Victorian statistics has provided the evidence. Here, it is proposed to rely on two words written by one somewhat intemperate man. The man was Hugh Mason, and his words were contained in the allegation that "very many" of the brokers acted for both importers and spinners. Given Mason's nature and the context of the remark, it seems significant that he did not use the word 'all' or even 'most'. The probability must be that 'very many' brokers did perform both functions, but not all of them.

However, and in a final act of disaggregation, Liverpool cotton brokers, while ostensibly performing the simple role of middlemen, had three separate business activities. It would be hard to say which of the three was the most lucrative, and it probably varied over time. One part involved selling for importers and/or buying for spinners. Another part involved all manner of trading and speculative ventures of their own, sometimes in conjunction with third parties. The third part involved acting as brokers for the speculative transactions of others. In this part of their business, brokers both sold to speculators and bought from them as a matter of course. During the war, every broker would have dealt with speculators. It was thus possible for them to act for both buyers and sellers simultaneously, without necessarily acting for both importers and spinners.

Confirmation that this is what happened is provided, anonymously, by Ellison himself:

> The widespread and demoralising spirit of speculation to which [the American war] gave rise almost completely swept away the old landmarks of the market, and introduced a style of business altogether antagonistic to the interests of the consumers of cotton. ... On the outbreak of the war the speculative department of the market assumed such vast dimensions that nearly the whole of the brokers became, either directly or indirectly, connected with its operations.[28]

This was the final wrench of the bolts that opened the floodgates and washed away the demarcations that Ellison proclaimed in public.

Chapter 7 substantiates the fact that there was a vast confection of raw cotton trading in Liverpool, and that the LCBA was merely the icing on the cake. It certainly contained all the most important brokers, and it controlled the raw cotton market to an overwhelming extent. There was a lot more icing than there was cake. But the cake was not negligible. There was a large swathe of non-LCBA brokers, dealers and other traders: a nebulous secondary market that bought and sold cotton, sometimes in large quantities. If the cotton industry dominated the British economy, the trade in raw cotton dominated Liverpool's economy. The town's brokers were an integral part of Liverpool's trading community, more so as time went by, as more importers became brokers, and as more general brokers added cotton to their interests. Ellison's description may yet serve as a template for how the system was intended to work, but it can no longer be regarded as an accurate description of how it did work by the time of the civil war.

A major theme of this book has been the disaggregation of interests. The British cotton trade was not a harmonious single entity. The interests of Liverpool and Manchester were fundamentally opposed. Within Liverpool, the interests of selling and buying brokers, and of importers, were not identical. Many brokers and importers had varied and conflicting interests. Attitudes to the civil war were similarly diverse. Further afield, the interests of Manchester were in conflict with the attitudes of government, both in Westminster and in India. And, of course, the interests of those who grew cotton were in conflict with the interests of those who processed it. In every case, it is necessary to ask what the self-interest was of each of the groups. They seldom coincided.

The best means of judging how much the escalation in the price of raw cotton was due to its scarce supply, and how much to speculation within the Liverpool market, is to look at the respective price movements of raw and manufactured cotton. From the onset of war in April 1861 to the peak in July 1864, the price of cotton goods rose by a multiplier of 2.52. This suggests where the true equilibrium lay between supply and demand. Yet, over the same period, the price of raw cotton rose by a multiplier of 4.20.[29] As a rule of thumb, therefore, distortions in the Liverpool market raised the price of raw cotton by a further two-thirds above its natural level. The war would have created a windfall for Liverpool in any event. The brokers not only received their due share of it but helped reduce the manufacturers to penury into the bargain. As Ellison anonymously admitted, "while Lancashire millowners were reduced to the verge of bankruptcy, Liverpool brokers were rapidly accumulating wealth."[30]

Severe criticism needs to be made of Liverpool's cotton brokers, unless one believes that the pursuit of unbridled self-interest should be the only principle of commerce. Even if it was the case that many members of the LCBA abided by its (unwritten) ethical standards – and this may have been true, especially of the more established brokerages – they have a heavy collective charge to answer. By selling freely to speculators, even when they were not speculators themselves, the brokers enabled a massive distortion of the raw cotton market, leading to a rise in price way above the natural consequence of a short supply. They profited indirectly from this speculation, through their commissions, even when they did not profit directly. They did all this when the county of which they were nominally a part was suffering to an appalling extent. They could have adjusted their commission, either by relating it to volume or by reducing the percentage when prices were abnormally high, but they did not. They could have agreed to sell only to *bona fide* spinners, whether in Britain or on the continent, but they did not. They could have used their near-monopoly power to relieve the spinners, while enriching themselves only slightly less, but they did not.

To the credit of some brokers, they were generous contributors to the Mayor of Liverpool's Distress Fund. Fourteen brokerages gave £4,000 between them, a quarter of the published total.[31] But that generosity perhaps belonged in a box marked 'charity', whereas business was business. Unlike the manufacturers, who encountered their employees on a daily basis and witnessed their privations at first hand, the brokers existed in an affluent bubble, insulated against an emotional connection with the wider industry. Amongst the cornucopia of brokers' comments during the civil war, many of them reproduced here, few have been found that even mention the cotton famine, let alone suggest concern for what was happening on Liverpool's own doorstep. As one broker put it, "the American war, with all its sad concomitants, has not been without its benefits."[32] The famine, and the straits of the manufacturing trade, barely appeared on the brokers' horizon. There was an obdurate determination, at all times, to keep prices as high as possible. So it is hard to feel much sympathy for those brokers who were bankrupted by the war, or who suffered severe trading losses.

The shots fired on Fort Sumter on 12 April 1861 heralded the end of an era. Rather than protecting the future of slavery, as the Confederacy intended, the shots hastened its demise. They marked the eclipse of an age when Britain, despite being in denial of the fact, had used American slaves to dominate the world market for cotton goods. The termination of slave-grown cotton in America was a significant milestone in Britain's tortuous process of disengaging from its economic dependence on human bondage, and heralded a freer, more diverse global cotton community.

However, in America, the bondage remained, albeit in a different form. The growing of cotton continued to be a burden, both physically and financially, and one that was now shared between impoverished African Americans and impoverished whites. In the South, the economy remained not only dependent on cotton, but throttled by cotton, and with no escape route. It had been founded on debt before the war, and it was founded on debt after the war. For the freedmen, avoiding starvation meant work, and work meant labouring for white men in one way or another. For the planters, avoiding ruin meant coming to whatever accommodation they could with the freedmen. Neither race was satisfied. They were as divided as ever, united only in debt.

While the British cotton trade suffered heavy losses during the war that ended slavery, those losses were dwarfed by the profits which slavery had enabled before the war, and which America's failure to exploit its dominant status as a producer continued to enable after the war.

* * *

No one involved in British cotton during the American Civil War could have failed to recall it as one of the most memorable eras of their lives, whether for good or for ill. Several names have weaved their way through this narrative, many of them brought blinking into the limelight for only a brief moment of time. Their memory of the war years must have stayed with them to the end of their days. Here is a brief account of what happened to some of them after the war.

Thomas Ellison continued his dual career of cotton broker and historian until his death in 1904 at the age of 72. However dense the veil he drew over the excesses of his trade, he remains a significant cotton historian. According to Farnie's biography, his death "caused considerable grief on the exchange, where the flag was hoisted at half-mast. ... Ellison's work has retained its value, unimpaired by the passage of time and unsullied by criticism" (except perhaps here). Having been apprenticed to Maurice Williams, "Ellison declined the offer of a partnership because he disliked the speculation to which ... Williams had become addicted. He established his own firm, and resolved to confine his operations to brokerage."[33]

Williams, having made and lost a fortune, left the world of cotton in 1875 and became an estate agent. He died in 1879. "As a performer on his own trumpet," wrote the *Porcupine*, "Mr Maurice Williams emits no uncertain sound, and whether the subject is cotton or politics, he [lets] us know that he is ... 'great pumpkins'." Among the many people with whom he had spats were the Neill brothers. Ellison's estate on his death amounted to £16,278, while Williams left under £200.[34]

Paul Hemelryk was an immigrant from Leyden in the Netherlands. He published his slim autobiographical notes as late as 1916, but they gave a valuable insight into the cotton market during the civil war. Hemelryk was a pioneer in the establishment of stronger financial procedures for the newly formed Cotton Association and was the first Chairman of the Settlement Association. He became Vice-Chairman of the Liverpool Chamber of Commerce and Chairman of the School of Commerce. At the end of his reminiscences, he reflected on an era of "substantial risks and unexampled recklessness", with brokers "dreaming of unbounded wealth and of an El Dorado which is only within the reach of a few. ... It should be remembered," he concluded, "that human nature is not ideal."[35]

The address of William Forwood, later Sir William, to the Statistical Society of London in 1870, is a rich mine of information. Forwood was a Liverpool merchant from the cradle: his father was senior partner in the importing firm Leech, Harrison and Forwood, and his mother the daughter of an early cotton broker. He and his brother "rapidly made their fortunes, first from wartime speculation and blockade running, and then from exploiting telegraph and cotton futures". In addition to his business interests, Forwood had an energetic civic life. He served on Liverpool town council for more than 40 years. He was president of the Liverpool Chamber of Commerce, deputy Chairman of Cunard, Chairman of the Bank of Liverpool, High Sheriff of Lancashire and a pioneer of the Mersey tunnel. He died in 1928.[36]

Arthur Arnold, later Sir Arthur, had a varied and distinguished public life, whatever his shortcomings as an economist and historian. He was MP for Salford from 1880 to 1885, on the radical wing of the Liberal Party. The list of political causes that he espoused was endless, most of them unpopular at the time, many of them later becoming accepted opinion. They included church disestablishment, land law reform, state ownership of the railways, reform of metropolitan government, temperance reform, the enfranchisement of women, home rule for Ireland and reform of the married women's property laws. He died in 1902.[37]

Arnold was joined in Parliament by Hugh Mason, also as a Liberal, also from 1880 to 1885, and representing Ashton-under-Lyne. Mason was a successful mill-owner and philanthropist, dedicated to improving the welfare of his employees. According to his online biography by Farnie, "he continued to run his own mills full time throughout [the cotton famine]; only ten other millowners out of two thousand did so." He was President of the Manchester Chamber of Commerce for three terms, from 1871 to 1874, and was appointed a member of the Mersey Docks and Harbour Board, the first member ever from outside Liverpool. How he must have enjoyed that. He became a deputy lieutenant of Lancashire and President of the Society for the Promotion of Scientific Industry. It comes as no surprise to learn that Hugh Mason "preserved an abiding love of plain speech". He died in 1886.[38]

In 1882, Samuel Smith joined Arnold and Mason on the Liberal benches, having beaten William Forwood's brother in a Liverpool by-election. He was defeated in 1885, but was elected for Flintshire the following year, retaining his seat until 1905. Gladstone was a constituent, and became a friend. Smith "spoke in the House of Commons on moral, social, religious, currency, and Indian questions. He was an industrious … representative of the nonconformist conscience." The Prevention of Cruelty to Children Act embodied reforms that Smith had advocated in Liverpool. Given his multiple talents – business acumen, incisive judgment and clarity in communication – it is surprising that he never served in government, but he was said to have been "an effective back-bench politician, representing the old radical tradition of campaigning without seeking office." Smith became a Privy Councillor on his retirement from politics in 1905, and died a year later.[39]

The Neill brothers were among the casualties of the civil war. Their British firm was bankrupted in September 1865, following a failed investment in a cotton ginning factory in Turkey. The American firm continued. The Neills travelled extensively through the Southern States in late 1865, reporting back to Britain on the ravages of the war and the prospects for the future. William Neill remained in England and diversified his business interests beyond cotton. He died in 1913. Henry Neill stayed in New Orleans until the end of his life and was a founder member of both the New York and the New Orleans Cotton Exchanges. Apart from trading cotton, he specialised in forecasting the size of the cotton crop, putting himself permanently at odds with the producers, who always predicted a small crop in the hope of raising the price. Jamie Pietruska has written: "A recognized authority in Britain by the 1860s, Neill achieved 'cotton prophet' status on both sides of the Atlantic in the 1890s on the basis of his uncannily accurate predictions of the three largest yields in history." When he died in 1906, the cotton exchanges in Houston and Austin, Texas, closed early as a mark of respect, and obituaries appeared in newspapers throughout the USA. The *New York Times* said that he was reputed to be "the greatest cotton crop estimate expert in the world".[40]

Appendix
Notes on Statistical Sources

This book relies on trade statistics to tell the story of Britain's cotton supply during the extended period of the American civil war. In view of the importance of these figures to the arguments presented, it is essential to state which sources have been used, and how, and to assess the degree to which they may be relied upon.

All significant raw cotton data were collected under the auspices of the LCBA by a rota of its brokers, on a weekly basis. At the end of each year, most brokers wrote an annual report for their clients, summarising the data for the year that had ended. No better, and indeed no other, information exists for many of the key indicators. As one would expect, there were negligible differences between the figures quoted by different brokers. George Holt is the broker whose reports are used here. He included detailed historical data in each annual report so that, simply by looking at one year's report, most of the information for the years under study is instantly available. Holt's data were reproduced by Thomas Ellison in Table 1 of *The Cotton Trade of Great Britain*, which provides reassurance that Ellison trusted Holt's statistics. The last Holt circular discovered was for 1866, so his data for two subsequent years have been taken directly from Ellison. Holt's figures are the basis for all the annual raw cotton data presented for the period 1853–68.

The weekly data upon which Holt's summaries were based were published verbatim by Ezekiel Donnell in his *Chronological and Statistical History of Cotton*. The one significant difference is that Donnell reported imports only into Liverpool, whereas Holt reported them for the whole country. The difference between the two totals is small, but there is a difference. Donnell's figures have therefore been amended here. The method has been to take each week within each year, to express that week as a percentage of Donnell's total for the year, and then to apply those percentages to Holt's total. The weekly figures in this book therefore agree with the annual figures. Donnell's figures, adjusted to Holt's totals, are the basis for all the weekly raw cotton data presented for the period 1858–67. Most numbers, for both annual and weekly statistics, have been rounded to tens of thousands of pounds weight.

The difficulty with both Holt and Donnell as sources is that Holt (mainly) and Donnell (entirely) presented figures in bales. As described in Chapter 4, bale weights varied from one producing country to another and between years. It is essential to convert all bale figures to weights before the information can be used. Holt presents some data in weights as well as bales: total annual imports, sales to speculators, sales to spinners, re-exports and end-of-year stocks. These figures have all been used. Again, and where relevant, Donnell's weekly figures have been amended to agree with the annual figures, in the manner described above.

The outstanding omission is for imports by country of origin. Holt gives these figures in bales alone, with no average bale weight per country provided. The missing information is given in John Pender's *Statistics of Trade*. This handbook provides details of raw cotton imports by weight from all sources for the relevant years. The totals are not identical to Holt's, but they are similar. Again, to provide consistency across all data, Pender's figures have been converted into percentages and applied to Holt's totals. It is especially helpful that Pender includes separate columns for the import of cotton from the Bahamas and Bermuda, and also from Mexico. (This was not done in the Board of Trade figures for imports by weight, reproduced in Ellison, *Cotton Trade*, Table 3, which is why those figures are not used here.) During the civil war, most of this cotton originated in America. These totals have therefore been added to the American total. One effect is to reduce, and to make more accurate, the amount of cotton shown as coming from the West Indies, overstated in many other statistics.

Some data are taken from a broader period in the nineteenth century. Table 3, showing cotton imports by source at 20-year intervals, uses information from the Parliamentary Papers, Statistical Abstracts for the United Kingdom. Other long-term data are taken from Mitchell and Deane's *Abstract of British Historical Statistics* (*ABHS*). Figures for the production and export of cotton goods, and for the stocks of those goods, as well as for levels of wastage in spinning, have been taken from Ellison & Haywood's cotton circulars. Export volumes (Figure 7) are also taken from Ellison's circulars. Tables 9 and 10, detailing shipments of raw cotton into Liverpool Docks, use information from the B Lists of the Liverpool Bills of Entry. The statistical information on American cotton in Chapter 8 is taken from the US Department of Agriculture.

Two issues arising from this methodology must be mentioned. The first is that the three main sources (Holt, Donnell and *ABHS*) are inconsistent in their reports of prices. None of them is likely to be wholly accurate. Different prices would have been quoted for the same description of cotton on the same day, let alone in the same week. All prices are approximate. As a generalisation, the *ABHS* prices are the highest, and Holt's the lowest. Both Donnell (American and Indian) and Holt (American, Indian and Brazilian) quoted prices for more than one description, and in their cases an average price has been created using the relative weights of import during the relevant time period. In every case, the source used for price or values is the same source as for the rest of the information in that table or figure, which means that this information, unlike the rest, is not consistent throughout the book. This, however, seems preferable to making an arbitrary choice of which prices to use.

The second issue of methodology is more significant. There are two means of assessing how much cotton was bought by spinners each year. The first ('reported sales') is to take the consumption column provided verbatim by Holt and Donnell. The second ('calculated sales') is to take the Holt/Donnell total import figure, deduct re-exports and make an adjustment for port stock movement. The two methods should produce identical results, but they do not. The reason can now be explained.

There is a column that purports to state the stocks of cotton held by spinners at their mills at the end of each year. It transpires that, in order to balance the books, the LCBA hid the discrepancy between reported and calculated sales within the mill stock column. An examination of Ellison's data from 1811 through to 1874 reveals that – with a reasonable tolerance for rounding – the difference in the mill stock figure from one year to the next is almost invariably accounted for by the discrepancy between the two consumption figures. Moreover, the purpose of this sleight of hand was to make the figures agree with the reported consumption column. It is therefore impossible to make them retrospectively agree with the calculated consumption column. Common sense would suggest that the calculated figure is likely to be the more accurate, since it relies on verified end-of-year stock counts rather than on the brokers making consistently correct judgments during the year on whether cotton had been bought for consumption or for speculation, which, as explained in the text, would affect whether it continued to be counted as stock. The calculated figure has therefore been used throughout for the annual figures and has then been extended through into Donnell's weekly figures.

The mill stock figures are bogus and should be ignored altogether. It seems significant that Ellison, who knew the statistics as well as anyone and was mostly meticulous in his use of them, also ignored mill stock movement in his calculations of spinning output, although this did not stop him from including the erroneous data in his book, without comment.

Finally, one should ask how accurate are the resulting tables and figures in this book, and what reliance can be placed upon them. If the interpretation of any issue depended on a few percentage points in the data, it would be unwise to make that interpretation. Had accurate figures for mill stocks existed, they would have affected to a small extent the usage data for individual years but would have made little difference to the period as a whole. Within the parameters of a complex industry – albeit one that was assiduously recorded – and the lapse of a century and a half, it is submitted that the statistics are generally reliable, and will support the broad conclusions drawn from them in this book.

Notes to Chapters

These are composite notes for each relevant paragraph, except where clarity dictates otherwise. Full references are given in the Bibliography.

Notes to Introduction

[1] Rose, *Lancashire Cotton*; Buck, *Anglo-American*; Woodman, *King Cotton*; Ellison, *Cotton Trade*.
[2] Hall, 'Cotton Importers'; Hall, 'Business Interests'; Hall, 'Brokers'; Hall, 'Emergence'; Hall, 'Governance'; Hall, 'Re-exports'; Hall, 'Civil War'.
[3] Farnie, *English Cotton*, pp. 135–70.
[4] CSA, Annual Reports, JRL, OTEA, GB 133 OLD/6/17/1-11; I. Watts, *Cotton Supply Association*.
[5] LCBA, Minute Books, LRO, 380 COT/1/2/2–4.
[6] Custom Bills of Entry, Liverpool B Bills, Merseyside Maritime Museum, C/BE/Liverpool.
[7] LRO, 380 COT/1/11/62, /64 and /66–71; the reports of the Neill Brothers' circulars have been taken from a variety of newspapers, referenced individually and taken from the British Newspaper Archive (BNA) <www.britishnewspaperarchive.co.uk/>.
[8] Ellison, *Cotton Trade*, p. 211; Norgate, *ODNB*, 'Smith'; *Mansions of Wallasey* website; Orchard, *Liverpool's Legion*, pp. 638–44; Smith, *Trade of India*.
[9] Mann, *Cotton Trade*, p. 53; J. Powell, *The Neills* web article; *War of the Rebellion* website, Series 2, vols 2 and 4 (Lowber) and Series 1, vol. 1 (Schultz).
[10] Arnold, *History*; J. Watts *Facts*.
[11] Hewitt, *ODNB*, 'Watts'; J. Watts, *Facts*, p. iii; Farnie, *English Cotton*, p. 169.
[12] Ellison, *Gleanings*.
[13] Ellison (published anonymously), 'Cotton Merchants', *Liverpool Post*.
[14] Farnie, 'Structure', p. 50.
[15] Farnie, *English Cotton*, p. 144.
[16] Silver, *Manchester Men*; Beckert, *Empire*.

Notes to Chapter 1

1. Farnie, 'Structure', p. 47; Farnie, *English Cotton*, pp. 24, 86; Howe, *Cotton Masters*, p. 48; Levi, 'Cotton Trade', pp. 32–33; Ellison, *Cotton Trade*, p. 66.
2. Schoen, *Fragile Fabric*, p. 259.
3. Parthasarathi, *Why Europe*; Riello, *Cotton: The Fabric*.
4. Beckert, *Empire*, pp. xi, xvi.
5. CSA, Annual Reports, JRL, OTEA, 1859, pp. 11–12, 19–28.
6. Beckert, *Empire*, pp. 65, 68, 142.
7. Olmstead and Rhode, 'Cotton, Slavery', p. 2.
8. Beckert, *Empire*, p. 85; Parthasarathi, *Why Europe*, p. 9; Riello, *Cotton: The Fabric*, p. 149.
9. W. Ashworth, *Industrial Revolution*.
10. W. Ashworth, *Industrial Revolution*, pp. 9, 53, 101, 166–67; Parthasarathi, *Why Europe*, pp. 95, 125–26; Riello, *Cotton: The Fabric*, pp. 26–27, 86, 123.
11. Riello, *Cotton: The Fabric*, pp. 134, 227; Parthasarathi, *Why Europe*, pp. 98–109.
12. Riello, *Cotton: The Fabric*, pp. 134, 147–54, 227; Parthasarathi, *Why Europe*, pp. 21–50, 98–113, 258; Redford, *Manchester Merchants*, vol. 1, p. 110; Beckert, *Empire*, pp. 171–72.
13. Beckert, *Empire*, p. 85; Deane, *Industrial Revolution*, p. 64; Ellison, *Cotton Trade*, p. 16.
14. Riello, *Cotton: The Fabric*, pp. 141, 204; Farnie, *English Cotton*, p. 82; Phalen, *Consequences*, pp. 26–29; Ellison and Haywood, annual cotton circular (CC) for 1866, LRO, 380 COT/1/11/71.
15. Ellison and Haywood, annual CC for 1866, LRO, 380 COT/1/11/71; Farnie, 'Cotton, 1850–1896', p. 405.
16. Chapman, *Cotton and Commerce*, p. 2. Although the demand for American cotton was growing constantly, there were no fewer than seven individual years in the two decades before the civil war when America's total cotton exports were 10 per cent or more lower than in the previous year (Pender & Co., *Statistics*, Table 1).
17. H. Ashworth, *A Tour*, p. 86; Cunningham and Hinshaw, annual CC for 1865, LRO, 380 COT/1/11/70.
18. Beckert, *Empire*, pp. 105, 115–20; Phalen, *Consequences*, p. 64; Riello, *Cotton: The Fabric*, p. 198.
19. Olmstead and Rhode, 'Cotton, Slavery', p. 5.
20. Shaw (attrib.), 'Cotton Crisis', p. 429; Danson, 'Connection', pp. 1–21; *New York Herald*, 6 Dec. 1856; CSA, Annual Reports, JRL, OTEA, 1859, p. 22. See also H. Ashworth, 'Cotton', p. 261.
21. Phalen, *Consequences*, p. 6; Ransom and Sutch, *One Kind*, p. 2; Longmate, *Hungry Mills*, pp. 22–23; Mann, *Cotton Trade*, pp. 53–56; Phalen, *Consequences*, pp. 67–74.
22. Wright, *Political Economy*, pp. 129, 144–54; *Charleston Mercury*, 11 Oct. 1860, quoted in Wright, *Political Economy*, p. 149.
23. Huzzey, *Freedom Burning*, pp. 98–106, 110–11, 126, 183.
24. Huzzey, 'Moral Geography', pp. 128–34; Dattel, *Cotton: Mississippi* web article, p. 4.

25. H. Ashworth, *A Tour*, p. 45.
26. J. Watts, *Facts*, p. 116.
27. Boyson, *Ashworth*, p. 233.
28. George Holt & Co., annual CC for 1860, LRO, 380 COT/1/11/64; Ellison, *Cotton Trade*, p. 175.
29. Francis Hollins, Wm. Clare & Sons, annual CCs for 1860, LRO, 380 COT/1/11/64.
30. Olusoga, *Black and British*, p. 345. Farnie referred to 'the ever-present clash of interests' between Liverpool and Manchester (Farnie, 'Cotton, 1850–1896', p. 458); Samuel Smith acknowledged that 'there was commercial jealousy between these two cities' (Smith, *My Life-Work*, p. 156).
31. Ellison, *Gleanings*, pp. 243–44.
32. Ellison, *Gleanings*, pp. 244, 294; *Porcupine*, 29 July 1865.
33. Levi, 'Cotton Trade', p. 39. Levi, a Liverpool merchant and political economist, was responsible for refounding the Liverpool Chamber of Commerce in 1850 (Bennett, *Local Business*, pp. 262–63).

Notes to Chapter 2

1. L. Bailey, *The Gilbert and Sullivan Book*, p. 393.
2. I. Watts, *Cotton Supply Association*, pp. 10–11; Huzzey, *Freedom Burning*, pp. 128–29; Farnie, *English Cotton*, pp. 15–16, 138.
3. CSA, Annual Reports, JRL, OTEA, 1860, p. 36.
4. Farnie, *English Cotton*, p. 151; Smith, *Trade of India*, pp. 4–7.
5. Silver, *Manchester Men*; Harnetty, *Imperialism*. See also J. Watts, *Facts*, pp. 420–36.
6. CSA, Annual Reports, JRL, OTEA; I. Watts, *Cotton Supply Association*; Smith, *Trade of India*.
7. I. Watts, *Cotton Supply Association*, p. 15; Shaw (attrib.), 'The Cotton Crisis', p. 418; *Manchester Examiner & Times*, quoted in Silver, *Manchester Men*, p. 44; Arnold, *History*, p. 327.
8. Hansard, 3rd Series, 1850, cxii, 40.
9. Farnie, *English Cotton*, pp. 39–40; Redford, *Manchester Merchants*, vol. 1, p. 234; Silver, *Manchester Men*, pp. 15–22, 100; Redford, *Manchester*, pp. 244–45; Howe, *Cotton Masters*, pp. 199–202.
10. Silver, *Manchester Men*, pp. 57, 97, 112.
11. CSA, Annual Reports, JRL, OTEA, 1862, p. 5.
12. CSA, Annual Reports, JRL, OTEA, 1858, pp. 10–11.
13. *Manchester Courier*, 25 Apr. 1857; Arnold, *History*, p. 36; CSA, Annual Reports, JRL, OTEA, 1858, pp. 12–13; 1862, p. 26; 1859, p. 38.
14. Baynes, *Cotton Trade*, pp. 92–93; CSA, Annual Reports, JRL, OTEA, 1858, pp. 6–8; 1859, p. 11. See also Mann, *Cotton Trade*, pp. 59–92 (a book dedicated to the CSA).
15. CSA, Annual Reports, JRL, OTEA, 1862, pp. 22–23; 1861, pp. 12–19; 1859, p. 24 (address of Thomas Bazley MP to the AGM) and p. 27 (address of Edmund Ashworth to the AGM); 1860, pp. 15–16 (quoting Captain Richard Sprye); J. B. Smith MP reported in the *Liverpool Daily Post*, 12 Mar. 1857; I. Watts, *Cotton Supply Association*, pp. 53, 100; letter to *Liverpool Mercury*, 5 May 1860;

Levi, 'Cotton Trade', pp. 44–45; Thomas Bazley MP cited in Sandford, *Cotton Supply*, p. 72; Wray, 'Culture', p. 85.
16. CSA, Annual Reports, JRL, OTEA, 1861, p. 7.
17. Shaw (attrib.), 'Cotton Crisis', p. 438; Silver, *Manchester Men*, p. 80; CSA, Annual Reports, JRL, OTEA, 1861, pp. 8–11.
18. I. Watts, *Cotton Supply Association*, pp. 19–22.
19. Wray, 'Culture', p. 85; CSA, Annual Reports, JRL, OTEA, 1859, p. 30.
20. Silver, *Manchester Men*, pp. 8, 78.
21. Mackay, quoted in Shaw (attrib.), 'Cotton Crisis', p. 440.
22. *Liverpool Mercury*, 22 Jan. 1861; Lord Canning, quoted in Silver, *Manchester Men*, p. 154 (Parliamentary Papers 1863 XLIV [132] and [132-I]). Earl Russell was Sir John Russell until July 1861; in this book, he is referred to as Earl Russell throughout.
23. CSA, Annual Reports, JRL, OTEA, 1859, p. 16; *The Times*, 14 Aug. 1862.
24. CSA, Annual Reports, JRL, OTEA, 1859, p. 29; 1862, p. 7; *The Times*, 7 July 1862.
25. Smith, *Trade of India*, pp. 2, 6, 7, 18, 58–59.
26. Smith, *Trade of India*, pp. 12–14, 27–31, 37, 53–57; Beckert, *Empire*, p. 111; article in *Friend of India*, quoted in CSA, Annual Reports, JRL, OTEA, 1862, p. 14; Ellison, *Cotton Trade*, p. 143; Farnie, *English Cotton*, p. 151.
27. Silver, *Manchester Men*, p. 213; *Manchester Guardian*, 24 Sept. 1862; Sir Charles Wood to Lord Canning, 26 Nov. 1861 (Halifax Collection, I.O., Letter Books, IX, p. 125), quoted in Harnetty, *Imperialism*, p. 42.
28. Quoted in Sandford, *Cotton Supply*, p. 8.
29. Hobhouse's speech in Hansard, 3rd Series, 1850, cxii, 40; Ashworth, quoted in CSA, Annual Reports, JRL, OTEA, 1859, p. 31; *The Times*, quoted in *Liverpool Mercury*, 2 Aug. 1862.
30. I. Watts, *Cotton Supply Association*, p. 117; Williams, *Seven Years' History*, 1862, pp. v, ix; Forwood, 'Influence', p. 368; Earle, 'Egyptian Cotton', p. 528; Farnie, *English Cotton*, p. 150; *Liverpool Mercury*, 3 Sept. 1861; Cunningham & Hinshaw, annual CC for 1861, LRO, 380 COT/1/11/66.
31. Hemelryk, *Reminiscences*, pp. 8–11.
32. Smith, *My Life-Work*, pp. 60–61.
33. CSA, Annual Report, JRL, OTEA, 1862, p. 5.
34. Earle, 'Egyptian Cotton', p. 521; Forwood, 'Influence', p. 368; Beckert, *Empire*, p. 256; Silver, *Manchester Men*, p. 75.
35. Ellison and Haywood, annual CC for 1863, LRO, 380 COT/1/11/68.
36. Smith, *Trade of India*, p. 13.
37. Hansard, 3rd Series, 1863, clxxii, 226; Baynes, *Cotton Trade*, p. 108.
38. *Liverpool Mercury*, 19 Feb. 1861; Proceedings of the Manchester Chamber of Commerce, 8 July 1862, quoted in Redford, *Manchester*, pp. 251–52.
39. Beckert, *Empire*, p. 250.
40. Beckert, *Empire*, pp. 251–56; Harnetty, *Imperialism*, pp. 7, 35; J. Watts, *Facts*, p. 430; *Manchester Examiner & Times*, 20 July 1864.
41. Beckert, 'Emancipation', pp. 1406, 1411; Beckert, *Empire*, p. 273.
42. Harnetty, *Imperialism*, pp. 123–26; W. Ashworth, *Industrial Revolution*, pp. 191, 234, 240–41; Parthasarathi, *Why Europe*, pp. 111–13; J. Watts, *Facts*, pp. 420–36; Silver, *Manchester Men*, p. 171; Olmstead and Rhode, 'Cotton, Slavery', p. 6.

43 Hansard, 3rd Series, 1862, clxviii, 1022–23.
44 I. Watts, *Cotton Supply Association*, p. 62; Smith, *My Life-Work*, p. 45.
45 Sexton, *Debtor*, pp. 137–38; Jones, *Blue and Gray*, p. 208; Beckert, *Empire*, p. 258.
46 Ellison, *Cotton Trade*, p. 142. See also Forwood, 'Influence', p. 369: China was prepared to pay a higher price than Britain for raw cotton.
47 *Manchester Guardian*, 26 Jan. 1864, quoted in Olmstead and Rhode, 'Cotton, Slavery', p. 6; CSA, Annual Reports, JRL, OTEA, 1862, p. 9.
48 CSA, Annual Reports, JRL, OTEA, 1861, pp. 5–6; I. Watts, *Cotton Supply Association*, p. 12; Ellison, *Cotton Trade*, p. 142.
49 Henderson, *Famine*, p. 8; Farnie, *English Cotton*, p. 168; Cobden, quoted in Howe, *Cotton Masters*, p. 246.
50 CSA, Annual Reports, JRL, OTEA, 1859, p. 35.
51 Beckert, *Empire*, p. 336.

Notes to Chapter 3

1 Chase, 'Secession', pp. 94–95; Samuel Smith, annual CC for 1860, LRO, 380 COT/1/11/64; John Wrigley & Sons, annual CC for 1861, LRO, 380 COT/1/11/66
2 Williams, *Seven Years' History*; Hall, 'Civil War'.
3 Machin, 'History, Part 1', p. 278.
4 Campbell, *Public Opinion*, p. 102; Owsley, *King Cotton*, p. 558; E. Adams, *Great Britain*, pp. 266–67; Beloff, 'Great Britain', p. 46; the *Liverpool Mercury* published this assertion, *inter alia*, on 8 Jan., 30 Apr., 7 May, 2 Aug., 22 Nov. 1861; 24 Mar., 19 May, 30 Aug., 30 Dec. 1862; 28 Apr., 6 Aug., 10 Dec., 31 Dec. 1863; 29 Mar., 21 June, 20 July, 1 Aug., 5 Sept. 1864.
5 The *Liverpool Mercury* predicted the imminent end of the war, on the basis of Confederate success, on 30 Apr., 19 July, 28 July, 8 Aug., 10 Oct. 1862; 6 Feb., 10 July 1863; 24 Aug., 22 Sept. 1864.
6 Owsley, *King Cotton*, p. 140; *Liverpool Mercury*, 18 Dec. 1862.
7 M. Ellison, *Support*; P. Foner, *British Labor*; Blackett, *Divided Hearts*.
8 E. Adams, *Great Britain*; Sexton, *Debtor*; Jones, *Blue and Gray*; Owsley, *King Cotton*.
9 Campbell, *Public Opinion*.
10 *Liverpool Mercury*, 6 Nov., 26 Dec. 1860 (Iverson); *De Bow's Review*, 4.3 (Nov. 1847), p. 340.
11 Varina Davis, quoted in Owsley, *King Cotton*, p. 19; Russell, *My Diary*, p. 118; *Charleston Mercury*, 4 June 1861, quoted in E. Adams, *Great Britain*, p. 224; Schultz, quoted in *London Standard*, 20 July 1861.
12 Marler, 'Merchant Capitalist', pp. 247–76; H. Ashworth, 'Cotton', p. 262; Russell, *My Diary*, p. 118; Sexton, *Debtor*, pp. 138–39.
13 J. Watts, *Facts*, p. 104.
14 *Porcupine*, 9 Nov. 1861.
15 Complacency of spinners in Redford, *Manchester*, p. 247; *The Economist*, 18 May 1861; Samuel Smith, annual CC for 1861, LRO, 380 COT/1/11/66; Smith, *My Life-Work*, p. 34.

16. Anon., 'American Cotton Crops', pp. 595–97. According to Donnell, it was more than double this amount – about 36 million lb (Donnell, *Chronological*, p. 507).
17. Quoted in the Neill Bros circular of 21 Aug. 1861 (*Glasgow Daily Herald*, 23 Aug. 1861).
18. Neill Bros circular of 21 Aug. 1861 (*Glasgow Daily Herald*, 23 Aug. 1861).
19. Marler, 'Merchant Capitalist', pp. 248, 264–67; Owsley, *King Cotton*, pp. 29–30; Marler, *Merchants' Capital*, p. 138; Dattel, 'Cotton, the Oil', p. 62.
20. Neill Bros circular of unknown date (*Daily Alta California*, 9 Sept. 1861).
21. Neill Bros circular of 26 Oct. 1861 (*Liverpool Morning Post*, 9 Nov. 1861).
22. Neill Bros circular of 19 Dec. 1861 (*Liverpool Morning Post*, 4 Jan. 1862).
23. Russell Papers, Russell to Lyons (first letter), Public Record Office, 30/22/96, 10 Jan. 1861, quoted in Sebrell, *Civil War* web article, p. 1; Lyons Papers, Russell to Lyons (second letter), Jan. 22 1861, quoted in E. Adams, *Great Britain*, p. 36; *London Gazette*, 14 May 1861.
24. Garibaldi, quoted in Doyle, *Cause*, p. 24; Palen, 'Conspiracy', pp. 33–47; Blackett, *Divided Hearts*, p. 21; Sexton, *Debtor*, p. 92; *Liverpool Mercury*, 28 June 1861; Campbell, *Public Opinion*, pp. 17–18, 104; Huzzey, *Freedom Burning*, pp. 22–24.
25. *Liverpool Mercury*, 25 Nov. 1863.
26. Huzzey, *Freedom Burning*, pp. 21–24, 29; Boyson, *Ashworth*, p. 235; Sexton, *Debtor*, pp. 95–104.
27. *Liverpool Mercury*, 31 Mar. 1863, reporting a speech by Palmerston in Glasgow on 30 March.
28. Corsan, *Two Months*, p. 196.
29. Russell, quoted in *Leeds Mercury*, 14 Mar. 1862; Neill Bros circular of 23 May 1862 (*Manchester Courier*, 24 May 1862).
30. Neill Bros circular of 11 Feb. 1862 (*The Times*, 17 Feb. 1862).
31. The coverage of *The Times* was dismal throughout the war: wrong on almost every count. Such was the anger at the newspaper's coverage that a full-length diatribe against it was published (Stephen, *The Times*).
32. James Howell & Sons, Marriott & Co., Newall & Clayton, Robson & Eskrigge, annual CCs for 1862, LRO, 380 COT/1/11/67; Cowie, Smith & Co., Mayall & Andersson, James Howell & Sons, annual CCs for 1863, LRO, 380 COT/1/11/68; Farnie, *English Cotton*, p. 162.
33. Williams, *Seven Years' History*, 1862, p. 30.
34. Neill Bros circular of 15 July 1862 (*Liverpool Morning Post*, 18 July 1862).
35. H. Adams, *Education*, p. 154; Jones, *Blue and Gray*, p. 170; Campbell, *Public Opinion*, pp. 163–79.
36. Sebrell, *Persuading*, p. 88; M. Ellison, *Support*, p. 126; *Liverpool Mercury*, 25 Apr., 9 Oct. 1862; Jones, *Blue and Gray*, pp. 253–84; Campbell, *Public Opinion*, pp. 104, 177; Jones, 'Union'.
37. Sebrell, *Civil War* web article, p. 9; Jones, *Union in Peril*, p. 135; Campbell, *Public Opinion*, pp. 240–41; Beloff, 'Great Britain', p. 41.
38. K. Marx, Address to the First International, London 1864, cited in P. Foner, *British Labor*, p. 13.
39. Campbell, *Public Opinion*, pp. 2–8.

40 M. Ellison, *Support*, p. 191; *The Economist*, 4 July 1863, pp. 732–33, quoted in Campbell, *Public Opinion*, p. 172.
41 Russell, quoted in *Liverpool Mercury*, 28 Sept. 1863.
42 *Liverpool Mercury*, 7, 8 Oct. 1862.
43 *Liverpool Mercury*, 18 Nov. 1862.
44 The *Liverpool Mercury* reported the likelihood of war or of recognition of the Confederacy or of some form of intervention, by either Britain or France or both, on 30 Apr. 1861; 17 Feb., 30 Apr., 17 May, 13 June, 4 Sept., 13 Oct., 15 Nov., 19 Dec. 1862; 30 Jan., 1 May, 30 June 1863; 24 Feb. 1864; 20 Jan., 17 Feb. 1865.
45 Williams, *Seven Years' History*, p. v (Appendix), 19 Nov. 1862.
46 Edmund Jardine, Cruttenden & Oulton, Kearsley & Cunningham, annual CCs for 1862, LRO, 380 COT/1/11/67.
47 J. Watts, *Facts*, pp. 227–28; Beckert, 'Emancipation', p. 1410; Rathbones, quoted in *Liverpool Mercury*, 2 Aug. 1862.
48 Daniel C. Buchanan & Co., Cowie, Smith & Co., Cruttenden & Oulton, Ellison & Haywood, Smith, Edwards & Co., annual CCs for 1863, LRO, 380 COT/1/11/68; Stead Brothers, annual CC for 1862, LRO, 380 COT/1/11/67; *Liverpool Mercury*, 19 May 1862; Neill Bros circular of 19 Dec. 1861 (*Liverpool Morning Post*, 4 Jan. 1862).
49 Owsley, *King Cotton*, pp. 43–50; Jones, *Union in Peril*, p. 131; Roark, *Masters*, pp. 39–41; Johnson, 'Northern Profit', pp. 101–15; Roberts, 'Federal Government', pp. 262–75.
50 Neill Bros circular of 1 Dec. 1863 (*Glasgow Daily Herald*, 3 Dec. 1863). See also the circular of the brokers Cowie, Smith & Co. (annual CC for 1863, LRO, 380 COT/1/11/68), who gave a similar warning.
51 *Liverpool Mercury*, 4 Dec. 1863.
52 Dumbell, 'Origin', p. 261; Robson & Eskrigge, annual CC for 1864, LRO, 380 COT/1/11/69; *Liverpool Mercury*, 15 Aug. 1864.
53 Williams, *Seven Years' History*, 1864, p. 69; Robson & Eskrigge, annual CC for 1864, LRO, 380 COT/1/11/69. Smith, Ellison and Williams were among many brokers to blame *The Times* for the crash (LRO, 380 COT/1/11/69), as did the Neill brothers (Neill Bros circular of 1 Jan. 1865 [*Leeds Mercury*, 6 Jan. 1865]).
54 Hemelryk, *Reminiscences*, pp. 10–11.
55 Smith, Edwards & Co., annual CC for 1864, LRO, 380 COT/1/11/69; *Liverpool Mercury*, 2 Feb. 1865; Neill Bros circular of 1 Apr. 1865 (*Manchester Courier*, 5 Apr. 1865).
56 Pender & Co., *Statistics*, p. 90.
57 Cunningham & Hinshaw, annual CC for 1864, LRO, 380 COT/1/11/69.
58 Helm, 'Cotton Trade', p. 429; Neill Bros circular of 1 Mar. 1865 (*Manchester Courier*, 3 Mar. 1865); Smith, Edwards & Co., annual CC for 1864, LRO, 380 COT/1/11/69.

Notes to Chapter 4

1 In chronological order: Arnold, *History*, p. 80; Donnell, *Chronological*, p. 465; Ellison, *Cotton Trade*, p. 77; Henderson, *Famine*, p. 11; Beloff, 'Great Britain', p. 45; Owsley, *King Cotton*, p. 135; Brady, 'Reconsideration', p. 156; Silver,

Manchester Men, p. 158; Longmate, *Hungry Mills*, p. 68; Farnie, *English Cotton*, p. 150; Sexton, *Debtor*, pp. 137–38; Hall, 'Civil War', p. 149; Jones, *Blue and Gray*, p. 226; Marler, *Merchants' Capital*, p. 140; Beckert, *Empire*, p. 247; Olusoga, *Black and British*, p. 350.

2 Brady, 'Reconsideration', p. 156; Farnie, *English Cotton*, p. 150.
3 Arnold, *History*, p. 80.
4 Ellison & Haywood, annual CC for 1863, LRO, 380 COT/1/11/68; Arnold, *History*, p. 80.
5 Ellison & Haywood, annual CCs for 1863, 1865, LRO, 380 COT/1/11/68, /70; Ellison, *Cotton Trade*, p. 77.
6 Donnell, *Chronological*; George Holt & Co., annual CC for 1866, LRO, 380 COT/1/11/71; Ellison, *Cotton Trade*, Table 1; Ellison & Haywood, annual CCs for 1864 and 1865, LRO, 380 COT/1/11/69–70; Pender & Co., *Statistics*.
7 Harnetty, *Imperialism*, p. 57; Farnie, *English Cotton*, p. 141; Hall, 'Civil War', p. 153; Machin, 'History, Part 1', pp. 107–304.
8 Hall, 'Re-exports', p. 266; Hollinshead, Tetley & Co., annual CC for 1862, LRO, 380 COT/1/11/67.
9 Farnie, *English Cotton*, pp. 17, 149; Brady, 'Reconsideration', p. 161.
10 Hall, 'Re-exports', p. 267.
11 Williams, *Seven Years' History*, 1862, p. 22; 1864, pp. 61–62; Neill Bros circular of 1 June 1864 (*Liverpool Mercury*, 4 June 1864); Hall, 'Re-exports', pp. 264–65.
12 *The Economist*, 11 Jan. 1862.
13 Farnie, *English Cotton*, p. 14.
14 Ellison & Haywood, annual CC for 1865, LRO, 380 COT/1/11/70. Indian cotton had set the world standard for centuries, the one that Britain had needed to emulate. It is worth asking why the quality of Indian cotton at mid-nineteenth century was so poor. Perhaps the worst cotton went for export. But it may be that the standard was set by the cloth, that the cotton was always inferior, and that the skill of the artisans was able to overcome the deficiency in a way that machines were not.
15 CSA, Annual Reports, JRL, OTEA, 1862, pp. 9–10; Arnold, *Cotton Famine*, p. 166. Ellison, quoted from a speech by John Bright in Birmingham in 1862: 'When [the minister] prayed for [a supply of] cotton some man with a keen sense of what he had suffered ... exclaimed "Oh, Lord, but not Surats"' (Ellison, *Gleanings*, p. 331).
16 John Wrigley & Sons, Francis Hollins, annual CCs for 1859, LRO, 380 COT/1/11/62; Baynes, *Cotton Trade*, pp. 98–99.
17 Baynes, *Cotton Trade*, pp. 98–99; Smith, *Trade of India*, p. 29; *The Times*, 9 Feb. 1863; Thornely & Pownall, annual CC for 1862, LRO, 380 COT/1/11/67.
18 Arnold, *History*, pp. 167–69; Forwood, 'Influence', p. 375; Levi, 'Cotton Trade', p. 43; Williams, *Seven Years' History*, p. iv, 19 Nov. 1862.
19 Ellison & Haywood, annual CC for 1865, LRO, 380 COT/1/11/70; Forwood, 'Influence', p. 382; Williams, *Seven Years' History*, 1862, p. 26.
20 Brady, 'Reconsideration', p. 157.
21 J. Watts, *Facts*, pp. 227–28; Owsley, *King Cotton*, p. 144.
22 Arnold, *Cotton Famine*, p. 81.

23. *Liverpool Mercury*, 8 Nov. 1865.
24. Smith, Edwards & Co., annual CC for 1864, LRO, 380 COT/1/11/69.
25. Ellison, *Cotton Trade*, p. 96.
26. Brady, 'Reconsideration', p. 156.
27. Williams, *Seven Years' History*, 1863, p. 38; Colin Campbell & Son, annual CCs for 1860 and 1863, LRO, 380 COT/1/11/64 and /68.
28. Williams, *Seven Years' History*, 1864, p. 79.
29. Brady, 'Reconsideration', p. 162.
30. CSA, Annual Reports, JRL, OTEA, 1860, p. 28.
31. *The Economist*, 1 Nov. 1862.
32. *Edinburgh Review*, Jan. 1863, p. 280.
33. *The Economist*, 31 Jan. 1863.
34. Henderson, *Famine*, p. 11 n.; J. Watts, *Facts*, p. 356.
35. *The Economist*, 31 Jan. 1863; Arnold, *Cotton Famine*, p. 81.
36. Arnold, *Cotton Famine*, p. 81; Henderson, *Famine*, p. 19.
37. Jones, *Union and Confederate* web article, p. 2; Wright, *Old South*, p. 56; Surdam, 'King Cotton', pp. 113–32.
38. Farnie, *English Cotton*, pp. 138–53.
39. Farnie, *English Cotton*, p. 149.
40. Forwood, 'Influence', p. 373.
41. Neill Bros circular of 1 Feb. 1865 (*Glasgow Daily Herald*, 4 Feb. 1865).
42. *The Economist*, 31 Jan. 1863. And this despite 'the failure of the Rice crops, and the famine which was desolating large tracts of the country' (Cunningham & Hinshaw, annual CC for 1861, LRO, 380 COT/1/11/66).
43. Harnetty, *Imperialism*, p. 23, Table. The debate about over-supply to India also needs to take account of the fact that the surge in exports in 1859 was accompanied by a near doubling of the import tariff (Harnetty, *Imperialism*, pp. 7–35).
44. Ellison & Haywood, annual CC for 1866, LRO, 380 COT/1/11/71; Williams, *Seven Years' History*, 1862, p. 27.
45. Henderson, *Famine*, p. 1; Farnie, 'Cotton, 1780–1914', pp. 746–47.
46. Hollinshead, Tetley & Co., T. & H. Littledale & Co., Maurice Williams, J. C. Ollerenshaw, Isaac Cooke & Sons, Hall & Mellor, annual CCs for 1859, LRO, 380 COT/1/11/62.
47. Robson & Eskrigge, John Wrigley & Sons, Thornely & Pownall, Hollinshead, Tetley & Co., Cunningham & Hinshaw, Samuel Smith, annual CCs for 1860, LRO, 380 COT/1/11/62.
48. Isaac Cooke & Sons, annual CC for 1861, LRO, 380 COT/1/11/66.
49. Owsley, *King Cotton*, pp. 139–40; Helm, 'Cotton Trade', p. 432.
50. Redford, *Manchester Merchants*, vol. 1, p. 265; Williams, *Seven Years' History*, 1868, pp. 11, 15; Forwood, 'Influence', p. 375. The reports of H.M. Inspectors of Factories showed a 13 per cent increase in factory spindles between 1861 and 1867 (*ABHS*, p. 185). See also Helm, 'Cotton Trade', p. 434; Farnie, *English Cotton*, p. 73.
51. Cunningham & Hinshaw, annual CC for 1861, LRO, 380 COT/1/11/66.
52. James Howell, annual CC for 1862, LRO, 380 COT/1/11/67.
53. Newall & Clayton, annual CC for 1862, LRO, 380 COT/1/11/67.

54 Robson & Eskrigge, annual CC for 1862, LRO, 380 COT/1/11/67.
55 *ABHS*, p. 179.
56 Farnie, 'Structure', p. 45.

Notes to Chapter 5

1. Olusoga, *Black and British*, p. 356; Beckert, *Empire*, p. 260; M. Ellison, *Support*, p. 167; Sexton, *Debtor*, p. 181; Milton, *Lincoln's Spymaster*, p. 19; Jones, *Blue and Gray*, p. 192.
2. Beckert listed all the things that Liverpool did for the Confederacy, with footnotes running to 41 references. There is no mention of any support for the Union (Beckert, *Empire*, p. 260).
3. Orchard, *Portraits*, p. 5; Ellison, *Gleanings*, pp. 315–19.
4. Both topics are dealt with comprehensively in Thorp, *Mersey Built*. The most thorough account of blockade-running from an American perspective is in Wise, *Lifeline*.
5. Milne, *Trade and Traders*; Sexton, *Debtor*; Ashcroft, 'British Maritime'; Hughes, 'Liverpool'.
6. Sebrell, *Civil War* web article, p. 11; *Liverpool Mercury*, 17 Oct. 1863; Ellison, *Gleanings*, pp. 180–83; *Liverpool Mercury*, 8 Feb., 2 Aug. 1862.
7. *Liverpool Mercury*, 17 Feb. 1863; Milton, *Lincoln's Spymaster*, p. 75.
8. *Liverpool Mercury*, 7 Aug., 6 Oct. 1862; 28 Apr. 1863; 31 Dec. 1863; 21 June, 5 Sept. 1864.
9. Brown, *A Hundred Years*, pp. 104–06; *Liverpool Mercury*, 11 Feb., 9 Oct. 1862.
10. N. Collins, *Politics*, p. 83; *Derby Mercury*, 1 Jan. 1879, quoted in *Legacies* web article, 'Thomas Berry Horsfall'; *The Times*, 24 Dec. 1878; *Legacies* web article, 'Joseph Christopher Ewart'; *Liverpool Mercury*, 16 Dec. 1868; Ellison, *Cotton Trade*, p. 190.
11. *Legacies* web articles, person views 946224849, 44892; McClelland, *Legacies*, Appendix 4; Sebrell, *Civil War* web article, p. 11; *Liverpool Mercury*, 4 Feb. 1862; 17 May 1864.
12. M. Ellison, *Support*, pp. 155–72.
13. Ashcroft, 'British Maritime', pp. 19, 77; Forwood, *Recollections*, pp. 53–54.
14. Hughes, 'Liverpool', p. 92; *The Times*, 6 Aug. 1862; National Archives (NA), Interference with Trade between New York and the Bahamas, May 1862–July 1863, FO 881/1162.
15. US Department of Agriculture, 'Cotton Crop', Circular 32, Table 1; M. Ellison, *Support*, p. 172; Pender & Co., *Statistics*, pp. 8–9; Ashcroft, 'British Maritime', p. 171; Mersey Docks and Harbour Board collection, Merseyside Maritime Museum, Liverpool.
16. Ashcroft, 'British Maritime', p. 169.
17. N. Collins, *Politics*, p. 68; Farnie, *English Cotton*, p. 60; Deane, *Industrial Revolution*, p. 219.
18. Mersey Docks and Harbour Board collection, Merseyside Maritime Museum, Liverpool. The author is indebted to Dr Graeme Milne, who provided these data from his own unpublished research. They provide the source for all the figures in this paragraph and the next.

19. *Liverpool Mercury*, 23 Oct. 1863.
20. Farnie, *English Cotton*, p. 103.
21. Schmidt, *Wheat and Cotton*, pp. 32–34; Parliamentary Papers, Statistical Abstract for the United Kingdom in Each of the Last Fifteen Years, 1866; *Liverpool Mercury*, 27 Dec. 1861; Crook, *The North*, pp. 268–72; Sexton, *Debtor*, pp. 9, 12.
22. *Liverpool Mercury*, 31 Oct. 1862, quoting *The Times*; M. Ellison, *Support*, p. 132.
23. Ashcroft, 'British Maritime', pp. 99, 124; Hall, 'Cotton Importers', pp. 89–91; Machin, 'History, Part 1', p. 283; Williams, 'Liverpool Merchants', pp. 192–96; Milne, *Trade and Traders*, p. 103; Buck, *Anglo-American*, pp. 8–12.
24. Ashcroft, 'British Maritime', pp. 58–59; *Liverpool Mercury*, 8 Jan. 1862, quoting the *Morning Post*.
25. Milne, *Trade and Traders*, p. 10; M. Ellison, *Support*, pp. 35, 87; Blackett, *Divided Hearts*, pp. 64–65.
26. Spencer, *Confederate Navy*, pp. 6, 211; Milton, *Lincoln's Spymaster*, pp. 27–28, 34, 53, 72–73; M. Ellison, *Support*, p. 132.
27. M. Ellison, *Support*, pp. 150–51; Marler, *Merchants' Capital*, p. 142.
28. *Liverpool Mercury*, 29 Nov. 1861.
29. Pelzer, 'Liverpool', p. 51; *Liverpool Mercury*, 3, 10 Nov. 1862, 24 July 1863; Milne, *Trade and Traders*, p. 133; Pender & Co., *Statistics*, p. 119.
30. Dudley's list is reproduced in full in Hughes, 'Liverpool', Appendix D, pp. 341–55; Custom Bills of Entry, Liverpool B Bills, 1860; Sebrell, *Civil War* web article, p. 4; Pelzer, 'Liverpool', p. 52; Brown, *A Hundred Years*, p. 96.
31. *Liverpool Mercury*, 12 Aug., 10 Nov. 1862; M. Ellison, *Support*, p. 129; Blackett, *Divided Hearts*, p. 64.
32. Parliamentary Papers, Memorial from Certain Shipowners of Liverpool Suggesting an Alteration in the Foreign Enlistment Act, 1863, lxxii, 3200; *Liverpool Mercury*, 10 Apr., 3 Aug. 1863.
33. M. Ellison, *Support*, pp. 104–05.
34. Anon., *Brief Sketch*, pp. 3, 13, 14; Tuffnell, 'Expatriate', pp. 5, 15–16; Henderson, 'American Chamber of Commerce', p. 57; Custom Bills of Entry, Liverpool B Bills; *American Chamber* website.
35. Smith, Edwards & Co., Robson & Eskrigge, annual CCs for 1863, LRO, 380 COT/1/11/68; Williams, *Seven Years' History*, 1863, p. 40.
36. Owsley, *King Cotton*, pp. 553–54; *The Scotsman*, quoted in *Liverpool Mercury*, 10 Apr. 1863; Sexton, *Debtor*, p. 106.
37. Russell, quoted in *Liverpool Mercury*, 17 Mar. 1863; Hansard, 3rd Series, 1863, clxx, 68–72 (Laird's speech).
38. *Liverpool Mercury*, 31 Mar. 1863; Sexton, *Debtor*, pp. 105–06; Milne, *Trade and Traders*, p. 174. See also Tuffnell, 'Expatriate', pp. 11–12.
39. Sexton, *Debtor*, pp. 142, 145; Drysdale, 'Blockade-Running', p. 334; Boaz, *Guns for Cotton*, p. 68.
40. Thorp, *Mersey Built*, pp. 53–82, 115–26; Jones, *Blue and Gray*, pp. 193–99, 201; Sexton, *Debtor*, pp. 106–08.
41. Hansard, 3rd Series, 1864, clxxiii, 975; Howe and Morgan, *Cobden*, vol. 4, p. 487; Sexton, *Debtor*, pp. 111–12; *Liverpool Mercury*, 18 Feb. 1864; *List of Vessels*

website; NA, Letter, Iron-Clad Vessels Launched at Liverpool (Mr Laird), 1863, FO 881/1174; Letter, To Treasury, Detention of Iron-Clad Vessels at Liverpool, 1863, FO 881/1175.
42. Sexton, *Debtor*, pp. 108–10; Milton, *Lincoln's Spymaster*, pp. 83–84; Grady, *Forbes and Aspinwall* web article.
43. Hansard, 3rd Series, 1863, clxx, 68–72.
44. Grady, *Forbes and Aspinwall* web article.
45. *Liverpool Mercury*, 27 July 1863.
46. *Liverpool Mercury*, 27 July 1863.
47. Laird was a member of the Southern Independence Association (Blackett, *Divided Hearts*, p. 68).
48. *Liverpool Mercury*, 24 Aug. 1863.
49. Milton, *Lincoln's Spymaster*, p. 79.
50. *Liverpool Mercury*, 10, 17 Apr. 1863.
51. *Liverpool Mercury*, 13 Oct. 1862.
52. *War of the Rebellion* website, Series 2, vol. 2, p. 586; *Preston Guardian*, 18 June 1862. The ship on which Neill was sailing, the SS *Cumbria*, was scheduled for New Orleans, but the Union captured that city at exactly the time the *Cumbria* left Liverpool, without her crew being aware of the fact. In Nassau, the ship was diverted to Charleston. Nine other blockade-runners were in Nassau at the time, an unusually high number. This is entirely speculative, but it is possible that the entire flotilla was originally destined for New Orleans, to rearm its poor defences and to take off the large quantities of cotton that were still in the port, despite the embargo. Commander James Bulloch had returned from Richmond, Virginia at the end of February 1862 and immediately arranged the purchase of the *Cumbria* from the Silloth Bay Steam Navigation Company and its urgent refitting. The captain of the *Cumbria* was reported to be receiving £10,000 for a successful run – an astronomical sum and said to be double the going rate at the time. This suggests that he may have been hired for more than the command of a solitary blockade-runner. Such speculation is irrelevant to this book but is mentioned because it may be of interest to civil war historians. For more detail, see J. Powell, *The Neills* web article.
53. *Porcupine*, 29 July 1865.

Notes to Chapter 6

1. Hemelryk, *Reminiscences*, p. 7; *Liverpool Mercury*, 1 Jan. 1864.
2. A Lazy-Un (E. Braddyll), *Lays*, pp. 3–4.
3. Buck, *Anglo-American*; Woodman, *King Cotton*.
4. LCBA, Minute Books, LRO, 380 COT/1/2/2–4.
5. Woodman, *King Cotton*, pp. xi–xii, 14, 47–48, 69; Stirling, *Letters*, pp. 181–82; Boodry, *August Belmont* web article, p. 16; Stone, 'Cotton Factorage', pp. 559, 562; Phalen, *Consequences*, pp. 97–101; Buck, *Anglo-American*, p. 82; Hall, 'Brokers', long abstract p. 7; Killick, 'Cotton Operations', p. 171.
6. Woodman, *King Cotton*, pp. xi–xii, 17–18; Buck, *Anglo-American*, pp. 15, 42, 84, 87, 97; Hidy, 'Anglo-American', pp. 53–66; Hall, 'Cotton Importers', p. 87.

NOTES TO CHAPTERS

Cotton was also traded in up-country stores; Lehman Brothers began life as a store trading cotton in Montgomery, Alabama (Woodman, *King Cotton*, p. 81).

7. Woodman, *King Cotton*, pp. 34–35; Buck, *Anglo-American*, pp 43, 55–56, 71; Mitchell Jones, *Middlemen*, p. 22; Schoen, *Fragile Fabric*, p. 50.
8. Hyde, Parkinson and Marriner, 'Cotton Broker', p. 77. See also Hall, 'Emergence', p. 79; Buck, *Anglo-American*, pp. 44, 55–56; D. Williams, 'Liverpool Merchants', p. 197; Hall, 'Business Interests', pp. 343–44; Hall, 'Brokers', p. 193.
9. Schoen, *Fragile Fabric*, pp. 148–60; Sexton, *Debtor*, p. 134; Phalen, *Consequences*, pp. 173–74; Woodman, *King Cotton*, p. 130; *New York Times*, Secession, p. 16.
10. Killick, 'Cotton Operations', pp. 169–74; Boodry, *August Belmont* web article, p. 14; Killick, 'Risk', pp. 4–6; Boodry, 'The Common Thread', pp. 121–22, 212; Marler, 'Merchant Capitalist', p. 253.
11. Corsan, *Two Months*, p. 240; Marler, *Merchants' Capital*, pp. 126, 143; Woodman, *King Cotton*, pp. 203, 206; *Liverpool Mercury*, 24 Jan. 1862.
12. *Hunt's Merchants' Magazine*, 1841, vol. 4, p. 224; Woodman, *King Cotton*, p. 169; Cowie, Smith & Co., annual CC for 1860, LRO, 380 COT/1/11/64; Neill Bros circular of unknown date (*The Times*, 21 Nov. 1860). See also Marler, *Merchants' Capital*, p. 127.
13. Another way in which some British merchants may have attempted to recoup pre-war advances for cotton that never arrived was through the mechanism of the Confederate Loan. The evidence for this is uncertain and oblique. Pre-war, the London bankers J. K. Gilliat & Co. were among the largest importers of American cotton. In 1863, the firm was gifted £250,000 in Erlanger bonds 'for repayment of a Confederate debt' (Owsley, *King Cotton*, p. 382).
14. *ABHS*, pp. 180–81, 491.
15. Ellison, *Gleanings*, pp. 138–39.
16. Ellison (anon.), 'Cotton Merchants', *Liverpool Post*, 5 Apr. 1882.
17. Ellison, *Gleanings*, pp. 322–23.
18. Dumbell, 'Origin', pp. 259–67; Ellison, *Cotton Trade*, pp. 272–87; Hall, 'Brokers', pp. 123, 138; Ellison & Haywood, Smith, Edwards & Co., annual CCs for 1863, LRO, 380 COT/1/11/68.
19. Daniel C. Buchanan & Co., Cowie, Smith & Co., W. Arthur Gorst, Edgar Musgrove & Co., Stead Brothers, annual CCs for 1863, LRO, 380 COT/1/11/68.
20. Smith, Edwards & Co., annual CC for 1863, LRO, 380 COT/1/11/68.
21. Quoted in Ellison, *Gleanings*, p. 333.
22. Ellison, *Gleanings*, p. 323; Edgar Musgrove, annual CC for 1863, LRO, 380 COT/1/11/68.
23. Ellison, *Gleanings*, pp. 243–44; A Cotton Spinner, *Anomalies*, pp. 10–11; *Liverpool Mercury*, 1 Feb. 1865; LCBA, Minute Book, LRO, 380 COT/1/2/4.
24. Slack, *Remarks*, p. 19; Ellison, *Cotton Trade*, pp. 237–38; Ellison, *Gleanings*, pp. 334, 328; Bank of Liverpool Reference Book no. 6, p. 121 (1858) and Reference Book no. 1, p. 32 (1860), both cited in Hall, 'Brokers', pp. 222–23; Anon., *Alphabet*, p. 4.
25. Ellison, *Gleanings*, pp. 319–20 (Ellison had served his apprenticeship with Maurice Williams [Ellison, *Cotton Trade*, p. 256]); Orchard, *Liverpool's Legion*, p. 640; Smith, *My Life-Work*, p. 35; Ellison, *Cotton Trade*, p. 211; Orchard, *Portraits*, pp. 63–64.

[26] Neill Bros circular of 1 Dec. 1863 (*Glasgow Daily Herald*, 3 Dec. 1863); Ellison & Haywood, annual CC for 1863, LRO, 380 COT/1/11/68.
[27] Ellison, *Gleanings*, p. 302; Ellison, *Cotton Trade*, p. 214; Hemelryk, *Reminiscences*, p. 10; Forwood, *Recollections*, p. 60.
[28] Buck, *Anglo-American*, p. 65; Francis Hollins, annual CC for 1860, LRO, 380 COT/1/11/64; Cruttenden & Oulton, Robson & Eskrigge, annual CCs for 1862, LRO, 380 COT/1/11/67; Farnie, *English Cotton*, p. 159; Daniel C. Buchanan & Co., annual CC for 1863, LRO, 380 COT/1/11/68.
[29] Neill Bros circular of 1 Feb. 1865 (*Glasgow Daily Herald*, 4 Feb. 1865), responding to *The Times*, 10 Dec. 1864.
[30] Hemelryk, *Reminiscences*, pp. 13–14.
[31] Hemelryk, *Reminiscences*, pp. 6–7, 12, 15–16, 28.
[32] Smith, *My Life-Work*, p. 34.
[33] Ellison, *Gleanings*, p. 323.
[34] A Lazy-Un, *Lays*, pp. 8–9.
[35] Smith, *My Life-Work*, p. 35; Francis Hollins, Edgar Musgrove, annual CCs for 1862, LRO, 380 COT/1/11/67.
[36] *Porcupine*, 21 May 1870.
[37] Machin, 'History, Part 1', p. 290.
[38] Lalor, *Money*, pp. 83, 86; Searle, *Morality*, pp. 6, 81.
[39] Weld & Co., *Cotton Futures*, p. 7.
[40] *The Times*, 12 Nov. 1863.
[41] Ellison & Haywood, annual CC for 1863, LRO, 380 COT/1/11/68.
[42] *The Times*, 24 Aug. 1857, quoted in Milne, *Trade and Traders*, p. 4.
[43] *Liverpool Mercury*, 21 Dec. 1863.
[44] A Lazy-Un, *Lays*, p. 6.
[45] Ellison, *Gleanings*, pp. 243–44.
[46] Ellison (anon.), 'Cotton Merchants', *Liverpool Post*, 5 Apr. 1882.
[47] *Manchester Courier*, 20 July 1864.
[48] 'The meeting was not numerously attended. ... Out of 1,190 persons or firms in the trade, only 283 had joined the Association' (*Manchester Examiner & Times*, 20 July 1864). A list of the committee was included in the cutting in the LCBA minute book.
[49] Ellison (anon.), 'Cotton Merchants', Liverpool Post, 20, 27 Apr. 1882.
[50] LCBA, Minute Books, LRO, 380 COT/1/2/2–4.
[51] The handwritten note says that the cutting was taken from the *Manchester Examiner & Times* of 21 Jan. 1865. It has not been possible to discover the original in either the BNA online archive or Manchester Central Library.
[52] *The Times*, 12, 13 Dec. 1867.
[53] *Manchester Examiner & Times*, 25 Oct. 1866.

Notes to Chapter 7

[1] Ellison, *Cotton Trade*, pp. 272–73.

NOTES TO CHAPTERS

2. Hall, 'Business Interests', pp. 339–55; Hall, 'Emergence', pp. 65–81; Hall, 'Brokers'; Hall, 'Civil War', pp. 149–69; Hall, 'Governance', pp. 98–115.
3. Ellison, *Cotton Trade*, pp. 272–73.
4. Milne, 'Reputation', p. 31; Ellison & Haywood, annual CC for 1866, LRO, 380 COT/1/11/71; Perkins, *Financing Trade*, p. 101.
5. LCBA, Minute Book, LRO, 380 COT/1/2/4.
6. LCBA, Minute Book, LRO, 380 COT/1/2/3.
7. *Manchester Courier*, 20 July 1864; Farnie, *English Cotton*, p. 77; Ellison, *Gleanings*, p. 302; Hall, 'Brokers', p. 255; Bennett, *Local Business*, pp. 17, 307, 830.
8. Anon., *List of Merchants*.
9. Ellison, *Cotton Trade*, pp. 182, 352–55; Membership Lists of the LCBA, 1866–81, LRO, 380 COT/1/7/1; LCBA Minute Book, LRO, 380 COT/1/2/2.
10. *Gore's Directory* (1864); Ellison, *Cotton Trade*, pp. 187–271.
11. C. Hall, Draper, McClelland et al., *Legacies*, p. 90. Among the examples are Belcher, Bower, Buchanan, Comer, Cooke, Eason, Ewart, Gladstone, Holt, Littledale, Musgrove, Myers, Reyner, Salisbury, Shakespeare, Swainson and Waterhouse (*Legacies* website).
12. Ellison, *Cotton Trade*, pp. 187–271.
13. Ellison, *Cotton Trade*, p. 184; Hall, 'Governance', p. 99; Ellison (anon.), 'Cotton Merchants', *Liverpool Post*, 5 Apr. 1882.
14. Ellison, *Cotton Trade*, p. 182; *Gore's Directory* (1860; 1864); Ellison, *Gleanings*, pp. 322, 329.
15. Ellison, *Gleanings*, pp. 118–19; Ellison, *Cotton Trade*, p. 176; *Gore's Directory* (1841; 1860; 1862; 1864; 1865; 1867–71); *British Surnames* website; *Liverpool Mercury*, 1860–65; Orchard, *Liverpool's Legion*; N. Collins, *Politics*, p. 60; Howe, *Cotton Masters*, pp. 61, 105.
16. *Porcupine*, 21 May 1870.
17. Ellison, *Gleanings*, p. 123.
18. Custom Bills of Entry, Liverpool B Bills.
19. McCulloch, *Dictionary*, p. 30. The relevant text is: '*Bill of Entry to be delivered.–* The person entering any goods inwards (whether for payment of duty, or to be warehoused upon the first perfect entry thereof ...) shall deliver to the collector or comptroller a bill of the entry of such goods ... expressing ... the name of the person in whose name the goods are to be entered, and the quantity and description of the goods. *Unauthorized Persons not permitted to make Entries.–* Proviso.– Every person who shall make or cause to be made any such entry inwards of any goods, not being duly authorized thereto by the proprietor or consignee of such goods, shall for every such offence forfeit the sum of 100l.'
20. Milne, *Trade and Traders*, pp. 114–16; D. Williams, 'Liverpool Merchants', p. 186; Ashcroft, 'British Maritime', pp. 112–15; Hall, 'Cotton Importers', p. 83.
21. Quoted in Milne, *Trade and Traders*, p. 114.
22. The full data are available at www.jim-powell.net/academic/. The two files (for 1860 and 1864) include the raw data transcribed from the Bills of Entry, the

conversion of bales to pounds weight, and a detailed analysis by source of import and recipient.

23 The presumed speculators were: Joseph Armstrong (Armstrong & Berey), James Bell (Bell, Nott & Co.), Walter Wignall (Buchanan, Wignall & Co.), Joseph Barnes (Bushby & Co.), James Cunningham (Cunningham & Hinshaw), Edwin Haigh (T. Haigh & Co.), Arthur Ryley (Hodgson & Ryley), Henry Thomas Jefferson and J. R. Taylor (Jefferson & Taylor), Thomas Powell (Mellor, Cunningham & Powell), J. J. Myers (Molyneux, Taylor & Co.), James Buckley, H. A. Grey and John Hayward Turner (Salisbury, Turner & Grey), John Bouch, Thomas Bouch, John D. Waterhouse and Rogers Waterhouse (N. Waterhouse & Sons), E. Habershon, John Penson Whitaker and Walter Horrocks Whitehead (Whitaker, Whitehead & Co.) and James H. Macrae (John Wrigley & Son).

24 Ellison, *Cotton Trade*, p. 355.

25 Among many examples of the overlap of names are Belcher, Bell, Cowie, Duckworth, Eccles, Harrison, Hodgson, Hornby, Houghton, Mason, Mellor, Percival, Tetley, Thomson, Waterhouse, Whitaker, Whitehead and Wignall. These names all appear on the LCBA membership list for 1864, and also on the list of recipients of raw cotton from Liverpool docks in 1864, but under a different corporate entity in each case.

26 Hemelryk, *Reminiscences*, p. 4; Hall, 'Business Interests', pp. 343–44; Ellison, *Gleanings*, p. 245.

27 Perkins, *Financing Trade*, pp. 8–9; Machin, 'History, Part 1', p. 265; Milne, *Trade and Traders*, p. 154.

28 T. & H. Littledale & Co., annual CC for 1864, LRO, 380 COT/1/11/69.

29 Williams, *Seven Years' History*, 1867, p. 19.

30 Crick and Wadsworth, *Hundred Years*, p. 143; M. Collins, *Banks*, pp. 22–32; M. Collins and Hudson, 'Provincial', pp. 69–79; Ellison, *Cotton Trade*, p. 202.

31 M. Collins, *Banks*, p. 25; M. Collins & Hudson, 'Provincial', pp. 72, 75–76.

32 Hemelryk, *Reminiscences*, pp. 4–6.

33 *Ancestry* website; Ellison, *Gleanings*, p. 362.

34 Ellison, *Gleanings*, p. 325.

35 Smith, *My Life-Work*, p. 35.

36 Forwood, *Recollections*, p. 5.

37 Crick and Wadsworth, *Hundred Years*, pp. 155–56.

38 Pressnell and Orbell, *Guide*, p. 94; *Liverpool Daily Post*, 23 Oct. 1867; 5 May 1868; *Liverpool Mercury*, 14 Feb. 1862.

39 BNA, Liverpool, 1864–72; Pressnell and Orbell, *Guide*, p. 85; Mills, 'Post-Panic', p. 94.

40 *Liverpool Mercury*, 27 Dec. 1865; 7 July 1866, 14 Oct. 1864; 25 Mar. 1868.

41 Full references for the bankruptcies can be found in Appendix 3 of the thesis on which this book is based (Powell, 'Cotton, Liverpool').

42 *Liverpool Mail*, 19 Oct. 1867; Ellison, *Gleanings*, pp. 188–89, 319–20; Hemelryk, *Reminiscences*, p. 12; *Mansions of Wallasey* website.

43 *Liverpool Mercury*, 27 May, 4 June 1868; Milton, *Lincoln's Spymaster*, pp. 37, 120–21 (there are inaccuracies in some of the details given in this source, which have been corrected here); *Liverpool Daily Post*, 18 Dec. 1866; *Liverpool Mail*, 16 May 1868.

44 Membership Lists of the LCBA, 1866–81, LRO, 380 COT/1/7/1; Ellison, *Cotton Trade*, p. 355.
45 Ellison (anon.), 'The LCBA', *Liverpool Post*.

Notes to Chapter 8

1 Goschen, *Essays*, p. 93.
2 LCBA, Minute Books, LRO, 380 COT/1/2/2–3.
3 Ellison, *Cotton Trade*, p. 274; Constitution, Laws, 380/COT/1/1/1. The 1871 and 1879 Laws are bound into the same volume.
4 Ellison, *Cotton Trade*, p. 275.
5 Ellison, *Cotton Trade*, pp. 275–80.
6 Membership Lists of the LCBA, 1866–81, LRO, 380 COT/1/7/1.
7 Ellison, *Cotton Trade*, p. 276.
8 Ellison (anon.), 'Cotton Merchants', *Liverpool Post*, 28 Mar., 5, 20 Apr. 1882.
9 Ellison (anon.), 'Cotton Merchants', *Liverpool Post*, 20 Apr. 1882.
10 Ellison (anon.), 'Cotton Merchants', *Liverpool Post*, 20 Apr. 1882.
11 Wright, *Political Economy*, p. 35; Fitzgerald, *Splendid Failure*, p. 58; Roark, *Masters*, p. 173; Ransom & Sutch, *One Kind*, pp. 51, 81–82; E. Foner, *Reconstruction*, pp. 124–29, 204, 372–79, 536–37; Lerner, 'Southern Output', p. 117; Woodman, *New South*, pp. 6–8; Woodman, *King Cotton*, pp. 245, 345–59.
12 Roark, *Masters*, pp. 48–49, 77; L. Powell, *New Masters*, pp. xii, 55.
13 L. Powell, *New Masters*, pp. 42, 145–50; Fitzgerald, *Splendid Failure*, p. 58.
14 E. Foner, *Reconstruction*, pp. 80–81, 158; Davis, *Good and Faithful*, pp. 73–83; letter from William Neill to his wife Susan, 17 Oct. 1865; Litwack, *Been in the Storm*, pp. 401–04; Fitzgerald, *Splendid Failure*, pp. 55–56.
15 Litwack, *Been in the Storm*, pp. 374–79, 392–99, 411–25; Aiken, *Cotton Plantation*, p. 19; Davis, *Good and Faithful*, pp. 89–115; Ransom and Sutch, *One Kind*, pp. 56–61, 64–65; Woodman, *New South*, p. 68; Roark, *Masters*, pp. 142–43; E. Foner, *Reconstruction*, p. 404; Beckert, *Empire*, pp. 284–88.
16 Roark, *Masters*, pp. 41–44, 137; Woodman, *King Cotton*, pp. 204–41; Ransom and Sutch, *One Kind*, pp. 108–09; Woodman, *New South*, pp. 5–27, 28–66.
17 Woodman, *New South*, pp. 10, 23–24, 32–33; Davis, *Good and Faithful*, pp. 133–35.
18 USBC, *American Cotton Supply*; Beckert, *Empire*, pp. 287–90; E. Foner, *Reconstruction*, pp. 140–42, 393, 404–09; Ransom and Sutch, *One Kind*, pp. 104–05; L. Powell, *New Masters*, p. 37; Wright, *Political Economy*, pp. 164–76; Woodman, *King Cotton*, p. 322.
19 Ransom and Sutch, *One Kind*, pp. 13, 123, 128–31, 149–51, 181–86; E. Foner, *Reconstruction*, p. 394.
20 *Atlanta Constitution*, 8 Mar. 1903, quoted in Pietruska, 'Cotton Guessers', p. 54.
21 *Birmingham Age Herald*, 5 Sept. 1899; *Raleigh News and Observer*, 15 Oct. 1899; *Atlanta Constitution*, 11 Mar. 1899, 2 Nov. 1899, 7 Nov. 1899, all quoted in Pietruska, 'Cotton Guessers'; *Natchez Democrat*, 24 Aug. 1899.
22 E. Foner, *Reconstruction*, pp. 309–408; L. Powell, *New Masters*, p. 108; Ransom and Sutch, *One Kind*, pp. 6–7, 45 (Figure 3.1), 233 (Table C.1); Davis, *Good and Faithful*, pp. 152–65; Wright, *Political Economy*, pp. 94–95.

[23] Smith, *Trade of India*, p. 14; USBC, *American Cotton Supply*, p. 29.
[24] Ransom and Sutch, *One Kind*, p. 191.
[25] *ABHS*, pp. 180, 491.
[26] Ellison, *Cotton Trade*, p. 286.
[27] LCBA, Minute Book, LRO, 380 COT/1/2/4.
[28] Ellison (anon.), 'Cotton Merchants', *Liverpool Post*, 5 Apr. 1882.
[29] Anon., 'Consumption', p. 332; Donnell, *Chronological*, pp. 508–09, 528–29.
[30] Ellison (anon.), 'Cotton Merchants', *Liverpool Post*, 5 Apr. 1882.
[31] *Liverpool Mercury*, 2 Aug. 1862.
[32] Francis Hollins, annual CC for 1863, LRO, 380 COT/1/11/68.
[33] Farnie, *ODNB*, 'Ellison'.
[34] Ellison, *Gleanings*, p. 320; *Liverpool Mercury*, 16 June 1879; *Porcupine*, 6 May 1865; Williams, *Seven Years' History*, 1865, pp. 8–9; Farnie, *ODNB*, 'Ellison'.
[35] Ellison, *Cotton Trade*, p. 295; *Catholic Who's Who* website; Hemelryk, *Reminiscences*, p. 28.
[36] *Liverpool Mercury*, 11 Nov. 1861; Killick, *ODNB*, 'Forwood'.
[37] Woods, *ODNB*, 'Arnold'.
[38] Farnie, *ODNB*, 'Mason'.
[39] Norgate, *ODNB*, 'Smith'.
[40] *Burnley Free Press*, 2 Oct. 1864; *London Gazette*, 15 Sept. 1865; *Levant Herald*, 19 Apr. 1865; letters of William Neill; Pietruska, 'Cotton Guessers', p. 50; J. Powell, *The Neills* web article; *New York Times*, 13 Sept. 1906.

Bibliography

Primary Sources

Archives

American Chamber of Commerce, Liverpool, resolution of meeting, reproduced at <https://history.state.gov/historicaldocuments/frus1865p4/d446> [accessed 12 August 2016].

Constitution, Laws and Usages of the Liverpool Cotton Brokers Association, 1871 (Liverpool: Joseph A. D. Watts & Sons, 1871), Liverpool Record Office, 380/COT/1/1/1.

Cotton Supply Association, Annual Reports, John Rylands Library, Archive of the Oldham Textile Employers' Association, GB 133 OLD/6/17/111.

Custom Bills of Entry, Liverpool B Bills, Merseyside Maritime Museum, C/BE/Liverpool [selected data reproduced at www.jim-powell.net/academic/].

Letters of William Neill (held by the author).

Liverpool Cotton Brokers' Association Records, Liverpool Record Office, 380 COT/1/11/62, /64, /66–71: cotton circulars for 1859–66, issued by Colin Campbell & Son, Cowie, Smith & Co., Cruttenden & Oulton, Cunningham & Hinshaw, Daniel C. Buchanan & Co., Edgar Musgrove, Edmund Jardine, Ellison & Haywood, Francis Hollins, George Holt & Co., Hall & Mellor, Hodgson & Ryley, Hollinshead, Tetley & Co., Isaac Cooke & Sons, J. C. Ollerenshaw, James Howell, John Wrigley & Sons, Kearsley & Cunningham, Marriott & Co., Maurice Williams, Mayall & Andersson, Newall & Clayton, Robson & Eskrigge, Rogers & Calder, Samuel Kearsley & Co., Samuel Smith, Smith, Edwards & Co., Stead Brothers, T. & H. Littledale & Co., Thornely & Pownall, William Peers & Son and Wm. Clare & Sons.

Membership Lists of the LCBA, 1866–81, Liverpool Record Office, 380 COT/1/7/1.

Mersey Docks and Harbour Board collection, Merseyside Maritime Museum, Liverpool.

Minute Books of the LCBA, 1864–70, Liverpool Record Office, 380 COT/1/2/2–4.

National Archives: Interference with Trade between New York and the Bahamas, May 1862–July 1863 (FO 881/1162); Letter, Iron-Clad Vessels launched at Liverpool (Mr Laird), 1863 (FO 881/1174); Letter, to Treasury, Detention of Iron-Clad Vessels at Liverpool, 1863 (FO 881/1175).

The War of the Rebellion: A Compilation of the Official Records of the Union and Confederate Armies <https://catalog.hathitrust.org/Record/004388999>, Series 1, vol. 1; Series 2, vols 2 and 4.

Government publications

Hansard, 3rd Series: 1850, cxii, 40; 1862, clxviii, 1022–23; 1863, clxx, 68–72; 1863, clxxii, 226; 1864, clxxiii, 975.

Parliamentary Papers, Memorial from Certain Shipowners of Liverpool Suggesting an Alteration in the Foreign Enlistment Act, 1863, lxxii, 3200.

Parliamentary Papers, Statistical Abstract for the United Kingdom in Each of the Last Fifteen Years: 1st No. 1840–53 (1854), 11th No. 1849–63 (1864), 13th No. 1851–65 (1866), 17th No. 1855–69 (1870), 36th No. 1874–88 (1889), 58th No. 1896–1910 (1911).

US Bureau of the Census, *American Cotton Supply and Its Distribution* (Washington, DC: US Government Printing Office, 1915).

US Department of Agriculture, 'Cotton Crop of the United States, 1790–1911' (Washington, DC: US Government Printing Office, 1912), Circular 32.

Books, memoirs and pamphlets

Adams, H., *The Education of Henry Adams* (Boston: Houghton Mifflin, 1918).

Anon., *List of Merchants & Shipowners Entitled to Vote for Members of the Committee of the Liverpool Docks, 1st July 1846* (Liverpool: J. Mawdsley, 1846) (Athenaeum Club Library, Liverpool).

Anon., *The Liverpool Cotton Brokers' Alphabet* (Liverpool: *Leader* office, 1873).

Arnold, R., *The History of the Cotton Famine, from the Fall of Sumter to the Passing of the Public Works Act* (London: Saunders, Otley, & Co., 1864).

Ashworth, H., *A Tour in the United States* (London: A. W. Bennett, 1861).

Baynes, J., *The Cotton Trade: Two Lectures on the Above Subject* (Blackburn: John N. Haworth, 1857).

Chapman, J., *The Cotton and Commerce of India Considered in Relation to the Interests of Great Britain* (London: John Chapman, 1851).

Corsan, W. ('An English Merchant'), *Two Months in the Confederate States* (London: Richard Bentley, 1863).

'A Cotton Spinner', *The Anomalies of the Cotton Trade: The Liverpool Brokerage System* (Manchester: Simms and Dinham, 1841).

Donnell, E., *Chronological and Statistical History of Cotton* (New York: James Sutton & Co., 1872).

Ellison, T., *The Cotton Trade of Great Britain* (London: Effingham Wilson, Royal Exchange, 1886).

—— *Gleanings and Reminiscences* (Liverpool: Henry Young & Sons, 1905).

Forwood, W., *Recollections of a Busy Life* (Liverpool: Henry Young & Sons, 1910).
Goschen, Viscount, *Essays and Addresses on Economic Questions (1865–1893)* (London: Edward Arnold, 1905).
Hemelryk, P., *Forty Years' Reminiscences of the Cotton Market* (Liverpool: Rockcliff Bros, 1916).
Howe, A. and S. Morgan (eds), *The Letters of Richard Cobden*, vol. 4 (Oxford: Oxford University Press, 2015).
Lalor, J., *Money and Morals: A Book for the Times* (London: John Chapman, 1852).
'A Lazy-Un' (E. Braddyll), *The Lays of Cotton Broking* (Liverpool: Harris & Co., 1865).
McCulloch, J., *A Dictionary, Practical, Theoretical, and Historical of Commerce and Commercial Navigation* (London: Longman, Brown, Green and Longmans, 1844).
Mann, J., *The Cotton Trade of Great Britain: Its Rise, Progress, and Present Extent* (London: Simpkin, Marshall, & Co., 1860).
New York Times, *The Effect of Secession upon the Commercial Relations between the North and South* (New York: Office of *The New York Times*, 1861).
Orchard, B., *Liverpool's Legion of Honour* (Birkenhead: self-published, 1893).
—— *Twenty Literary Portraits of Business Men* (Liverpool: Matthews Brothers, 1884).
Pender, J. & Co., *Statistics of Trade* (Manchester: A. Ireland & Co., 1869).
Russell, W., *My Diary North and South* (Boston: Burnham, 1863).
Sandford, W. (ed.), *Cotton Supply from the Ottoman Empire* (London: J. E. Taylor, 1862).
Slack, J., *Remarks on Cotton* (Liverpool: J. Lang, 1817).
Smith, Samuel, *The Cotton Trade of India* (London: Effingham Wilson, 1863).
—— *My Life-Work* (London: Hodder & Stoughton, 1902).
Stephen, L., *The Times on the American War* (London: William Ridgway, 1865).
Stirling, J., *Letters from the Slave States* (London: J. W. Parker & Son, 1857).
Watts, I., *The Cotton Supply Association: Its Origin and Progress* (Manchester: Tubbs & Brook, 1871).
Watts, J., *The Facts of the Cotton Famine* (London: Simpkin, Marshall, & Co., 1866).
Weld & Co., *Cotton Futures: Their Use and Method of Working* (Liverpool: self-published, 1905).
Williams, M., *Seven Years' History of the Cotton Trade of Europe* (Liverpool: William Potter, 1868).

Journal articles

Anon., 'American Cotton Crops and Prices, 1857–61', *Journal of the Statistical Society of London*, 24.4 (December 1861), pp. 595–97.
Anon., 'The Consumption of Raw Cotton and the Price of Raw and Manufactured Cotton, 1860–64', *Journal of the Statistical Society of London*, 28.2 (June 1865), pp. 229–32.
Ashworth, H., 'Cotton: Its Cultivation, Manufacture and Use', *Journal of the Society of Arts*, 6.277 (March 1858), pp. 256–64.

Chase, W., 'The Secession of the Cotton States', *De Bow's Review*, 30, art. 8 (January 1861), pp. 98–101.
Danson, J., 'On the Existing Connection between American Slavery and the British Cotton Manufacture', *Journal of the Statistical Society of London*, 20.1 (March 1857), pp. 1–21.
De Bow's Review, 4.3 (November 1847), p. 340.
Edinburgh Review (Edinburgh: A. & C. Black, 1863), vol. 117 (January 1863), 'Public Affairs', pp. 269–305.
Ellison, T. (published anonymously), 'Cotton Merchants, Brokers, and Spinners', *Liverpool Post*, pts 1–4 (28 March; 5, 20, 27 April 1882).
—— (published anonymously), 'The Liverpool Cotton Brokers' Association', *Liverpool Post*, pts 1–11 (2, 12, 27, December 1881; 11 January, 23 February, 7, 22 March, 1, 22 June, 5, 12 July 1882).
Forwood, W., 'The Influence of Price upon the Cultivation and Consumption of Cotton during the Ten Years 1860–70', *Journal of the Statistical Society of London*, 33.3 (September 1870), pp. 366–83.
Helm, E., 'The Cotton Trade of the United Kingdom, during the Seven Years, 1862–68', *Journal of the Statistical Society of London*, 32.4 (December 1869), pp. 428–37.
Hunt's Merchants' Magazine (1841), IV, p. 224.
Levi, L., 'On the Cotton Trade and Manufacture as Affected by the Civil War in America', *Journal of the Statistical Society of London*, 26 (March 1863), pp. 26–48.
Mills, J., 'On the Post-Panic Period 1866–70', *Journal of the Manchester Statistical Society* (1871), pp. 81–104.
Shaw, A. (attributed), 'The Cotton Crisis; and How to Avert It', *British Quarterly Review*, 52 (October 1857), pp. 416–48.
Wray, L., 'The Culture and Preparation of Cotton in the United States of America', *Journal of the Society of Arts*, 7.318 (December 1858), pp. 77–92.

Newspapers

Atlanta Constitution, 11 March, 2 November, 7 November 1899; 8 March 1903.
Birmingham Age Herald, 5 September 1899.
Burnley Free Press, 2 October 1864.
Charleston Mercury, 11 October 1860; 4 January 1861.
Derby Mercury, 1 January 1879.
The Economist, 18 May 1861; 11 January, 1 November 1862; 31 January, 4 July 1863.
Leeds Mercury, 14 March 1862.
Levant Herald, 19 April 1865.
Liverpool Daily Post, 12 March 1857; 18 December 1866; 23 October 1867; 5 May 1868.
Liverpool Mail, 19 October 1867; 16 May 1868.
Liverpool Mercury, 1860–65.
London Gazette, 14 May 1861; 15 September 1865.
London Standard, 20 July 1861.

Manchester Courier, 25 April 1857; 20 July 1864.
Manchester Examiner & Times, 20 July 1864; 21 January 1865; 25 October 1866.
Manchester Guardian, 24 September 1862; 26 January 1864.
Natchez Democrat, 24 August 1899.
New York Herald, 6 December 1856.
New York Times, 13 September 1906.
Porcupine, 9 November 1861; 6 May, 29 July 1865; 21 May 1870.
Preston Guardian, 18 June 1862.
Raleigh News and Observer, 15 October 1899.
The Times, 24 August 1857; 17 February, 7 July, 6 August, 14 August 1862; 9 February, 12 November 1863; 10 December 1864; 12, 13 December 1867; 24 December 1878.
Neill Bros & Co. circulars:
  The Times, 21 November 1860 (circular of unknown date).
  Glasgow Daily Herald, 23 August 1861 (circular of 21 August 1861).
  Daily Alta, California, 9 September 1861 (circular of unknown date).
  Liverpool Morning Post, 9 November 1861 (circular of 26 October 1861).
  Liverpool Morning Post, 4 January 1862 (circular of 19 December 1861).
  The Times, 17 February 1862 (circular of 11 February 1862).
  Manchester Courier, 24 May 1862 (circular of 23 May 1862).
  Liverpool Morning Post, 18 July 1862 (circular of 15 July 1862).
  Glasgow Daily Herald, 3 December 1863 (circular of 1 December 1863).
  Liverpool Mercury, 4 June 1864 (circular of 1 June 1864).
  Leeds Mercury, 6 January 1865 (circular of 1 January 1865).
  Glasgow Daily Herald, 4 February 1865 (circular of 1 February 1865).
  Manchester Courier, 3 March 1865 (circular of 1 March 1865).
  Manchester Courier, 5 April 1865 (circular of 1 April 1865).

Directory

Gore's Directory for Liverpool and its Environs (1841; 1860; 1862; 1864; 1865; 1867–71) (Athenaeum Club Library, Liverpool).

Secondary Sources

Books

Adams, E., *Great Britain and the American Civil War* (Project Gutenberg ebook #13789) (London: Longmans, Green and Company, 1925).
Aiken, C., *The Cotton Plantation South since the Civil War* (Baltimore, MD: Johns Hopkins University Press, 1998).
Anon, *Brief Sketch of the American Chamber of Commerce in Liverpool* (Liverpool: Liverpool Printing & Stationery Co., 1908).

Ashworth, W., *The Industrial Revolution: The State, Knowledge and Global Trade* (London: Bloomsbury, 2017).
Bailey, L., *The Gilbert and Sullivan Book* (London: Cassell, 1952).
Beckert, S., *Empire of Cotton: A New History of Global Capitalism* (London: Allen Lane, 2014).
Bennett, R., *Local Business Voice: The History of Chambers of Commerce, 1760–2011* (Oxford: Oxford University Press, 2011).
Blackett, R., *Divided Hearts: Britain and the American Civil War* (Alexandria: Louisiana State University Press, 2001).
Boaz, T., *Guns for Cotton: England Arms the Confederacy* (Shippensburg, PA: Burd Street Press, 1996).
Boyson, R., *The Ashworth Cotton Enterprise: The Rise and Fall of a Family Firm, 1818–1880* (Oxford: Clarendon Press, 1970).
Brown, J., *A Hundred Years of Merchant Banking* (New York: Arno Press, 1978).
Buck, N., *The Development of the Organisation of Anglo-American Trade, 1800–1850* (New Haven, CT: Yale University Press, 1925).
Campbell, D., *English Public Opinion and the American Civil War* (Woodbridge: Royal Historical Society, 2003).
Collins, M., *Banks and Industrial Finance in Britain 1800–1939* (London: Macmillan, 1991).
Collins, N., *Politics and Elections in Nineteenth-Century Liverpool* (Aldershot: Scolar Press, 1994).
Crick, W. and J. Wadsworth, *A Hundred Years of Joint Stock Banking* (London: Hodder & Stoughton, 1936).
Crook, D., *The North, the South, and the Powers* (New York: John Wiley & Sons, 1974).
Davis, R., *Good and Faithful Labor: From Slavery to Sharecropping in the Natchez District, 1860–1890* (Westport, CT: Greenwood Press, 1982).
Deane, P., *The First Industrial Revolution* (Cambridge: Cambridge University Press, 1967).
Doyle, D., *The Cause of All Nations: An International History of the American Civil War* (New York: Basic Books, 2015).
Ellison, M., *Support for Secession: Lancashire and the American Civil War* (Chicago: University of Chicago Press, 1973).
Farnie, D., 'Cotton, 1780–1914', in D. Jenkins (ed.), *The Cambridge History of Western Textiles*, vol. 2 (Cambridge: Cambridge University Press, 2003).
—— *The English Cotton Industry and the World Market, 1815–1896* (Oxford: Clarendon Press, 1979).
—— 'The Structure of the British Cotton Industry, 1846–1914', in A. Okochi and S. Yonekawa (eds), *The Textile Industry and its Business Climate*, Proceedings of the Fuji Conference (Tokyo: Tokyo University Press, 1982).
Fitzgerald, M., *Splendid Failure: Postwar Reconstruction in the American South* (Chicago: Ivan R. Dee, 2007).
Foner, E., *Reconstruction: America's Unfinished Revolution* (New York: Harper & Row, 1988).
Foner, P., *British Labor and the American Civil War* (New York: Holmes & Meier, 1981).

Hall, C., N. Draper, K. McClelland, K. Donington and R. Lang, *Legacies of British Slave-Ownership: Colonial Slavery and the Formation of Victorian Britain* (Cambridge: Cambridge University Press, 2014).

Harnetty, P., *Imperialism and Free Trade: Lancashire and India in the Mid-Nineteenth Century* (Manchester: Manchester University Press, 1972).

Henderson, W., *The Lancashire Cotton Famine 1861–1865* (New York: Augustus M. Kelley, 1969).

Howe, A., *The Cotton Masters 1830–1860* (Oxford: Clarendon Press, 1984).

Huzzey, R., *Freedom Burning: Anti-Slavery and Empire in Victorian Britain* (Ithaca, NY: Cornell University Press, 2012).

Jones, H., *Blue and Gray Diplomacy* (Chapel Hill: University of North Carolina Press, 2010).

—— *Union in Peril: The Crisis over British Intervention in the Civil War* (Chapel Hill: University of North Carolina Press, 1992).

Litwack, L., *Been in the Storm So Long* (London: Athlone Press, 1979).

Longmate, N., *The Hungry Mills* (London: Maurice Temple Smith, 1978).

McClelland, K., 'MPs and Their Connections: An Indicative List', in C. Hall, N. Draper, K. McClelland, K. Donington and R. Lang, *Legacies of British Slave-Ownership: Colonial Slavery and the Formation of Victorian Britain* (Cambridge: Cambridge University Press, 2014), Appendix 4.

Machin, W., 'A Short History of the Liverpool Cotton Market, Part 1', in *Liverpool Raw Cotton Annual* (Liverpool: Turner Routledge & Co., 1957).

Marler, S., *The Merchants' Capital: New Orleans and the Political Economy of the Nineteenth-Century South* (Cambridge: Cambridge University Press, 2013).

Milne, G., *Trade and Traders in Mid-Victorian Liverpool* (Liverpool: Liverpool University Press, 2000).

Milton, D., *Lincoln's Spymaster: Thomas Haines Dudley and the Liverpool Network* (Mechanicsburg, PA: Stackpole Books, 2003).

Mitchell, B. with P. Deane, *Abstract of British Historical Statistics* (Cambridge: Cambridge University Press, 1962).

Mitchell Jones, F., *Middlemen in the Domestic Trade of the United States, 1800–1860* (Champaign: University of Illinois Press, 1937).

Novak, D., *The Wheel of Servitude: Black Forced Labor after Slavery* (Lexington: University Press of Kentucky, 1978).

Olusoga, D., *Black and British: A Forgotten History* (London: Pan Macmillan, 2016).

Owsley, F., *King Cotton Diplomacy: Foreign Relations of the Confederate States of America* (Chicago: University of Chicago Press, 1959 [1931]).

Palen, M.-W., *The 'Conspiracy' of Free Trade: The Anglo-American Struggle over Empire and Economic Globalisation, 1846–1896* (Cambridge: Cambridge University Press, 2016).

Parthasarathi, P., *Why Europe Grew Rich and Asia Did Not* (Cambridge: Cambridge University Press, 2011).

Perkins, E., *Financing Anglo-American Trade: The House of Brown 1800–1880* (Cambridge, MA: Harvard University Press, 1975).

Phalen, W., *The Consequences of Cotton in Antebellum America* (Jefferson, NC: McFarland & Co., 2014).

Pietruska, J. L., '"Cotton Guessers": Crop Forecasters and the Rationalizing of Uncertainty in American Cotton Markets, 1890–1905', in H. Berghoff, P. Scranton and U. Spiekermann (eds), *The Rise of Marketing and Market Research* (London: Palgrave Macmillan, 2012).

Powell, L., *New Masters: Northern Planters during the Civil War and Reconstruction* (New Haven, CT: Yale University Press, 1980).

Pressnell, L. and J. Orbell, *A Guide to the Historical Records of British Banking* (Aldershot: Gower Publishing Co., 1985).

Ransom, R. and R. Sutch, *One Kind of Freedom: The Economic Consequences of Emancipation* (Cambridge: Cambridge University Press, 2001).

Redford, A., *The History of Local Government in Manchester*, vol. 2 (London: Longmans, 1940).

—— *Manchester Merchants and Foreign Trade*, vol. 1 (Manchester: Manchester University Press, 1973).

Riello, G., *The Fabric that Made the Modern World* (Cambridge: Cambridge University Press, 2015).

Roark, J., *Masters Without Slaves: Southern Planters in the Civil War and Reconstruction* (New York, W. W. Norton, 1977).

Rose, M. (ed.), *The Lancashire Cotton Industry: A History since 1700* (Preston: Lancashire County Books, 1996).

Schmidt, B., *The Influence of Wheat and Cotton on Anglo-American Relations during the Civil War* (Iowa City: State Historical Society, 1918).

Schoen, B., *The Fragile Fabric of Union* (Baltimore, MD: Johns Hopkins University Press, 2009).

Searle, G., *Morality and the Market in Victorian Britain* (Oxford: Clarendon Press, 1998).

Sebrell, T., *Persuading John Bull: Union and Confederate Propaganda in Britain, 1860–65* (Lanham, MD: Lexington Books, 2014).

Sexton, J., *Debtor Diplomacy: Finance and American Foreign Relations in the Civil War Era 1837–1873* (Oxford: Oxford University Press, 2005).

Silver, A., *Manchester Men and Indian Cotton, 1847–1872* (Manchester: Manchester University Press, 1966).

Spencer, W., *The Confederate Navy in Europe* (Tuscaloosa: University of Alabama Press, 1983).

Thorp, R., *Mersey Built: The Role of Merseyside in the American Civil War* (Wilmington, DE: Vernon Press, 2017).

Williams, D., 'Liverpool Merchants and the Cotton Trade 1820–1850', in J. Harris (ed.), *Liverpool and Merseyside* (London: Frank Cass & Co., 1969).

Wise, S., *Lifeline of the Confederacy: Blockade Running during the Civil War* (Columbia: University of South Carolina Press, 1988).

Woodman, H., *King Cotton and his Retainers* (Washington, DC: Beard Books, 2000).

—— *New South – New Law* (Baton Rouge: Louisiana State University Press, 1995).

Wright, G., *Old South, New South: Revolutions in the Southern Economy since the Civil War* (New York: Basic Books, 1986).

—— *The Political Economy of the Cotton South: Households, Markets, and Wealth in the Nineteenth Century* (New York: W. W. Norton, 1978).

Journal articles

Beckert, S., 'Emancipation and Empire: Reconstructing the Worldwide Web of Cotton Production', *American Historical Review*, 109.5 (December 2004), pp. 1405–38.

Beloff, M., 'Great Britain and the American Civil War', *Historical Revision*, 118 (February 1952), pp. 40–48.

Brady, E., 'A Reconsideration of the Lancashire "Cotton Famine"', *Agricultural History*, 37.3 (July 1963), pp. 156–62.

Collins, M. and P. Hudson, 'Provincial Bank Lending: Yorkshire and Merseyside, 1826–60', *Bulletin of Economic Research*, 31 (1979), pp. 69–79.

Dattel, E., 'Cotton, the Oil of the Nineteenth Century', *International Economy* (Winter 2010), pp. 60–63.

Drysdale, R., 'Blockade-Running from Nassau', *History Today*, 27.5 (May 1977), pp. 332–37.

Dumbell, S., 'The Origin of Cotton Futures', *Economic History*, 1 (May 1927), pp. 259–67.

Earle, E., 'Egyptian Cotton and the American Civil War', *Political Science Quarterly*, 41.4 (December 1926), pp. 520–45.

Hall, N., 'The Business Interests of Liverpool's Cotton Brokers, c.1800–1914', *Northern History*, 41.2 (September 2004), pp. 339–55.

—— 'The Emergence of the Liverpool Raw Cotton Market, 1800–1850', *Northern History*, 38.1 (March 2001), pp. 65–81.

—— 'The Governance of the Liverpool Raw Cotton Market, c.1840–1914', *Northern History*, 53.1 (March 2016), pp. 98–115.

—— 'The Liverpool Cotton Market and the American Civil War', *Northern History*, 34.1 (March 1998), pp. 149–69.

—— 'The Liverpool Cotton Market and Cotton Re-exports, c.1815–1914', *Northern History*, 43.2 (September 2006), pp. 257–71.

—— 'Liverpool's Cotton Importers', *Northern History*, 54.1 (March 2017), pp. 79–93.

Henderson, W., 'The American Chamber of Commerce for the Port of Liverpool, 1801–1908', *Journal of the Historic Society of Lancashire & Cheshire*, 85 (1933), pp. 1–61.

Hidy, R., 'The Organization and Functions of Anglo-American Merchant Bankers, 1815–1860', *Journal of Economic History*, 1 (Supplement) (December 1941), pp. 53–66.

Huzzey, R., 'The Moral Geography of British Anti-Slavery Responsibilities', *Transactions of the Royal Historical Society*, 22 (December 2012), pp. 111–39.

Hyde, F., B. Parkinson and S. Marriner, 'The Cotton Broker and the Rise of the Liverpool Cotton Market', *Economic History Review*, 8.1 (1955), pp. 75–83.

Johnson, L., 'Northern Profit and Profiteers: The Cotton Rings of 1864–65', *Civil War History*, 12.2 (June 1966), pp. 101–15.

Killick, J., 'The Cotton Operations of Alexander Brown and Sons in the Deep South, 1820–1860', *Journal of Southern History*, 43.2 (May 1977), pp. 169–94.

—— 'Risk, Specialization and Profit in the Mercantile Sector of the Nineteenth-Century Cotton Trade: Alexander Brown and Sons, 1820–80', *Business History*, 16.1 (1974), pp. 1–16.

Lerner, E., 'Southern Output and Agricultural Income, 1860–1880', *Agricultural History*, 33.3 (July 1959), pp. 117–25.
Marler, S., 'The Merchant Capitalist Community of New Orleans, 1860–1862', *Civil War History*, 54.3 (September 2008), pp. 247–76.
Milne, G., 'Reputation, Information and Ethics' (unpublished working paper, Mercantile Liverpool Project, University of Liverpool).
Olmstead, A. and P. Rhode, 'Cotton, Slavery, and the New History of Capitalism', *Explorations in Economic History*, 67 (January 2018), pp. 1–17.
Pelzer, J., 'Liverpool and the American Civil War', *History Today* (March 1990), pp. 46–52.
Roberts, A., 'The Federal Government and Confederate Cotton', *American Historical Review*, 32.2 (January 1927), pp. 262–75.
Stone, A., 'The Cotton Factorage System of the Southern States', *American Historical Review*, 20.3 (April 1915), pp. 557–65.
Surdam, D., 'King Cotton: Monarch or Pretender? The State of the Market for Raw Cotton on the Eve of the American Civil War', *Economic History Review*, 51.1 (February 1998), pp. 113–32.
Tuffnell, S., 'Expatriate Foreign Relations: Britain's American Community and Transnational Approaches to the U.S. Civil War', *Diplomatic History*, 40.4 (September 2016), pp. 635–63.

Unpublished theses

Ashcroft, N., 'Unnatural and Unexpected Vicissitudes: British Maritime Enterprise and the American Civil War, 1856 to 1870', PhD, University of Hull, 1999.
Boodry, K., 'The Common Thread: Slavery, Cotton and Atlantic Finance from the Louisiana Purchase to Reconstruction', PhD, Harvard University, 2014.
Farnie, D., 'The English Cotton Industry, 1850–1896', MA, University of Manchester, 1953.
Hall, N., 'The Cotton Brokers and the Development of the Liverpool Cotton Market c.1800 to 1914', DPhil, University of Oxford, 1999.
Hughes, F., 'Liverpool and the Confederate States: Fraser, Trenholm and Company Operations during the American Civil War', PhD, University of Keele, 1996.
Powell, J., 'Cotton, Liverpool and the American Civil War', PhD, University of Liverpool, 2018.

Online reference works

Oxford Dictionary of National Biography (ODNB):
    Farnie, D., 'Ellison, Thomas (1833–1904)' <www.oxforddnb.com/view/article/58116> [accessed 22 December 2017].
    Farnie, D., 'Mason, Hugh (1817–1886)' <www.oxforddnb.com/view/article/47905> [accessed 22 December 2017].
    Hewitt, M., 'Watts, John (1818–1887)' <www.oxforddnb.com/view/article/28890> [accessed 20 April 2015].

Killick, J. 'Forwood, Sir William Bower (1840–1928)' <www.oxforddnb.com/view/article/47004> [accessed 22 December 2017].

Norgate, G., 'Smith, Samuel (1836–1906)', rev. H. Matthew <www.oxforddnb.com/view/article/36157> [accessed 8 December 2014].

Woods, G., 'Arnold, Sir (Robert) Arthur (1833–1902)' <www.oxforddnb.com/view/article/30454> [accessed 21 November 2014].

Web pages

Ancestry <www.ancestry.co.uk/> [accessed 29 July 2018].

Boodry, K., *August Belmont and the Atlantic Trade in Cotton 1837–1865* <www.rothschildarchive.org/materials/review_2009_2010_august_belmont_1.pdf> [accessed 7 October 2017].

British Surnames <www.britishsurnames.co.uk/> [accessed 17 November 2015].

The Catholic Who's Who <https://archive.org/stream/1908catholicwhoooburnuoft/1908catholicwhoooburnuoft_djvu.txt> [accessed 22 December 2017].

Dattel, E., *Cotton in a Global Economy: Mississippi (1800–1860)* <http://mshistorynow.mdah.state.ms.us/articles/161/cotton-in-a-global-economy-mississippi-1800–1860> [accessed 7 October 2017].

Grady, J., *Forbes and Aspinwall Go to War* <http://opinionator.blogs.nytimes.com/2013/07/26/forbes-and-aspinwall-go-to-war/?_r=0> [accessed 7 October 2016].

Jones, H., *Union and Confederate Diplomacy during the Civil War* <www.essentialcivilwarcurriculum.com/union-and-confederate-diplomacy-during-the-civil-war.html> [accessed 21 May 2015].

Legacies of British Slave Ownership:
   'Joseph Christopher Ewart' <www.ucl.ac.uk/lbs/person/view/44892> [accessed 7 October 2016].
   'Thomas Berry Horsfall' <www.ucl.ac.uk/lbs/person/view/946224849> [accessed 7 October 2016].

List of Vessels Constructed by Cammell Laird Shipbuilders <www.wirralhistory.com/lairds.html#1860> [accessed 7 October 2016].

Mansions of Wallasey <www.historyofwallasey.co.uk> [accessed 20 March 2015].

Powell, J., *The Neills & the American Civil War* <https://jimpowellblog.files.wordpress.com/2016/02/genealogy-neills-the-american-civil-war-131011.pdf> [accessed 8 October 2017].

Sebrell, T., *The American Civil War in Britain* <www.essentialcivilwarcurriculum.com/the-american-civil-war-in-britain.html> [accessed 8 October 2017].

Index

Abercromby Square 110
Adams, Charles 115
Adams, Henry 62
Agincourt, HMS 116
Alabama 174
Alabama, CSS 10, 60, 110, 111, 113, 115, 116, 118, 163
Alexandra, CSS 116
America *see* American Civil War; Confederacy; USA
American Civil War
 ending 67–68
 'impossibility' of Northern victory 53, 55, 104
 military events 57, 66, 103–04, 115
 outbreak 15, 51, 54, 124–25
Anglo-American War (1812–15) 31
Anti-Corn Law League 34
Arkansas 174
Arkwright, Sir Richard 17, 19
Arnold, Arthur 82, 84, 89, 94, 97
 alleged over-production 71–72, 86, 87–88, 179
 background 4–5, 184
 The Cotton Famine 4
 EIC 33
Ashcroft, Neil 102, 109
Ashworth, Henry 41–42, 54–55
 duration of war 68
 Indian cotton 37, 48
 slave-grown cotton 22, 24–25
Ashworth, William 18, 46
Aspinwall, William 116–17

Atlanta Constitution 175–76
Atwool, David 163–64

Bahamas 188
Bank of England discount rate 67, 68
Bank of Liverpool 130, 159, 184
 lending policies 160
Baring, Thomas 115
Barings Bros 115, 116, 124, 152, 155
Barned's Bank 163
Barnsley, Godfrey 167
Baynes, John 44, 77–78
Bazley, Thomas 23, 33, 48
Beckert, Sven 12, 20, 40, 48
 Empire of Cotton 16–18, 32, 45
 slavery 22
Beecher, Henry Ward 103
Beloff, Max 62
Berar 37
Bermuda 106, 188
Bertois, Jules 129
Bibby family 161
Blackburn, Schofield & Co. 165
Blackburn, Thomas B. 165
Blackburne, J. 36
Blackett, R. J. M. 64, 110
 Liverpool 113
blockade *see* USA
blockade-running 105–07
 arrest of Neill, Henry 119
 insignificance of trade 10, 106–07
 ship-building 107
 see also USA

221

Bombay 3, 37, 40
Braddyll, Edward 121, 133, 137–38
Brady, Eugene 88, 89, 179
    alleged over-production 9, 71, 84, 85, 90
    re-exports 75
    stock levels 80–81
Brancker family 161
Bright, John 34, 44, 59, 198n15
    Indian cotton 33, 38
British Government
    neutrality and intervention 61–63, 112
    outbreak of war 58
    relations with Manchester 32, 36–37, 38, 40–41, 44–46
    wheat imports 109
British public opinion
    American perspective 59–60
    antagonised by Union 58–59
    historical interpretations 63–65
    neutrality and non-intervention 64–65
Brown, John Crosby 112
Brown, Shipley & Co. 104, 112, 114, 115, 144
Brown & Co 124
Buchanan, Daniel C. & Co. 132
Bulloch, Commander James 110, 117–18, 202n52
Burn, Richard 39
Bushby, John 111

Campbell, Charles 163
Campbell, Colin & Son 84–85, 163
Campbell, Duncan 62
    Public Opinion 63–64
Canning, Lord 38
Cartwright, Edmund 17
Chapman, John 21
Charleston, SC 54, 57, 106, 110, 117, 119, 124, 202n52
Charleston Mercury 23, 54
Chase, Colonel 51
Chase, Salmon P. 116
Cheetham, John 34, 39

China 36, 46–47, 53, 95, 97
Christie, R., Jr 169
Christy, David 54
Clare, William & Sons 27, 163
Clegg, Mr 41
Cobden, Richard
    American shipping 112
    effects of cotton scarcity 49
    reasons for secession 59
    sourcing of Union warships 117
Confederacy
    British intervention 58, 61–63, 64–65, 104, 112, 197n44
    commercial weakness 54–55, 124
    Confederate Loan 133–34, 203n13
    debts at outbreak of war 124
    embargo 9, 51, 56–57, 89, 90, 111
    King Cotton strategy 8, 54–55, 57, 66, 88–89
    relations with Liverpool 10, 101–02, 110–11, 112
    secession 15, 23–24, 54–55, 58
    slavery and slave trade 23, 54, 59
    sourcing of arms 107, 115
Conservative Party 63, 105, 115
Cooke, Isaac & Sons 94, 95, 163
cotton, American 192n16
    alleged over-supply 88–89
    credit merchants 174–75
    crop of 1860–61 56, 90 97–98, 179
    during the war 56, 106
    exporting ports 110
    factors 56–57, 122–23, 140
    financial system 122–25
    imports from UK 75
    planters 122
    pre-war dominance 7, 20, 31–32
    price 37–38, 50, 174, 176
    Reconstruction period 172–75, 176–77, 183
    Sea Island 172
    see also USA
cotton, Brazilian 24, 35, 46–47, 125, 189
cotton, Egyptian 35, 50, 125, 175

INDEX

quality problems 78
suppression of agriculture 44
wartime supply 46–47
cotton, Indian 22, 68, 161, 189, 199n43
  Bright, John 33, 38
  CSA and Manchester 35, 36–38
  distrust of British market 44
  effect of war 42–43, 48
  EIC 33
  fabrics 18–19
  import tariffs 19, 45
  local manufacture 37, 48
  price 37–38, 66
  quality problems 40, 77–78, 198n14
  as replacement for American 7, 12, 32–33, 36, 50
  ryots 37, 40, 44, 82, 175
  size of crop 37, 39–40
  Smith, Samuel 39–40
  Surat 77, 78, 198n15
  transportation 37
  wartime supply 41–44, 46–49, 61, 65, 129, 154
  see also India
cotton, manufactured
  adulteration of goods 82
  alleged over-production 8–9, 71–74, 86–96, 98, 179
  investment in new mills 96–97, 199n50
  prices 12, 90, 181–82
  short-time working 9, 60, 90, 93, 97, 179
  speculation by spinners 10, 132–33, 142
  stocks of finished goods 8–9, 90–91, 93–95
  stocks of raw cotton 76, 189–90
  wartime production 9, 81–84, 91–93
  wastage 77–78
  see also cotton trade, British; Lancashire cotton famine
cotton, raw
  alternative sources 35–36
  bale weights 74

  deterioration in quality 77
  financing the trade 122–25, 158–60
  futures market 128–29, 132–33, 135, 168, 171, 178
  post-war period 11, 168, 177–78
  pre-war history 31–32
  price 9, 12, 37–38, 48, 52, 61, 67, 90, 97, 177, 178, 181–82, 188–89
  re-exports 74–76
  shipments to Liverpool 155–57
  staple lengths 78
  statistics 3, 73–74, 187–90
  stocks 76, 80–81
  supply to Britain 15, 20–22, 24, 25, 31–32, 34, 38–39, 46–49, 50, 56, 68–69, 71–85, 98–100, 177, 178–79
  unit of measurement 74
  value of market 10, 125–28
  wartime sources 7, 46–49
  withdrawal of stocks 80, 144
  see also cotton trade, British
cotton, speculation 61, 66
  definition 134–35
  effect on prices 131, 181–82
  involvement of brokers 127–28, 130–31, 135–37, 155, 180–81, 206n23
  involvement of spinners 10, 132–33, 142
  wartime practices 27–28, 127–31, 133, 135–37, 161, 180–81
  see also cotton brokers; LCBA
cotton, Turkish 46, 185
Cotton Association 6, 74, 134, 138, 145, 168, 178, 184
cotton brokers
  bankruptcies 134, 157–58, 161–65
  cotton circulars 3, 53, 84, 94–96, 114
  cotton dealers 150–51, 162
  as dock electors 145, 157
  dubious practices 6, 130–31, 133, 139–41, 180–81, 182
  financial role 123–24, 158–61
  non-LCBA brokers 148, 150, 181

probate values 161
as recipients of cotton 11, 155–57
role within Liverpool 10–11, 145, 147–48, 182
see also cotton, speculation; LCBA
Cotton Brokers' Bank 178
cotton circulars 3, 4, 52, 53, 55–56, 72, 74, 84, 94–96, 114, 122, 144, 187, 188
cotton dealers *see* cotton brokers
Cotton Exchange 6, 168
cotton famine *see* Lancashire cotton famine
cotton futures *see* cotton, raw
cotton merchants *see* Liverpool
Cotton Spinners' Association
  dispute with LCBA 3, 10, 122, 138–42
  formation 138
cotton stocks *see* cotton, manufactured; cotton, raw
cotton supply *see* cotton, raw
Cotton Supply Association 3, 31, 32, 77, 142
  activities 35–38
  delusions 37, 48–49
  formation 33–34
  glutting of markets 86
  Indian cotton 35, 36–38, 39
  issue of price 12, 37–38
  lack of trade support 34
  potential sources of supply 16, 43–44
  reasons for failure 49
  revenue 35
cotton trade, British
  complacency at start of war 51, 55–56, 58, 60
  conflicts of interest 7, 27–28, 130–31, 144, 181
  export trade 20, 42, 91–93
  exports to India and China 93
  glutting of markets 8–9, 71, 86–87, 93–96
  importance to Britain 1, 15
  pre-war history 7, 8–9, 16–20

shipping time lag 40, 42, 53, 65, 97
temporary wartime market 12, 51, 53, 61, 68–69, 91, 179
terminology 12–13
wartime anxieties 11, 68–70, 176
see also cotton, manufactured; cotton, raw
cotton trade, global
  financing transatlantic trade 122–25
  global supply 31–32, 42, 49–50
  history 17–18
  paralysis of demand 9, 60, 90, 97, 179
  price elasticity 69
  stock pipeline 9, 61, 68–69, 90–91, 97, 179
Cowie, Charles 111
Cowie, Smith & Co. 125
Crick, W. F. & Wadsworth, J. E. 159, 161
Crompton, Samuel 17, 19
Cruttenden & Oulton 65
Cuba 24
Cumbria, SS 202n52
Cunningham & Hinshaw 42, 68–69, 95
Custom Bills of Entry *see* Liverpool

Dattel, Eugene 24
Davis, Jefferson 4, 54, 57
Davis, Varina 54
Donnell, Ezekiel 3, 9, 74, 122, 187–89
Douglass, Frederick 4
Drake, Kleinwort 155
Duckworth family 161
Dudley, Thomas 112, 118

East India Company 34, 36
  cotton cultivation 33
  Manchester 32
  neglect of Indian interests 17
The Economist
  alleged over-production 86–87

cotton manufacture 91
'impossibility' of Northern victory 55
recognition of Confederacy 63
re-exports 76
Edinburgh Review 86
Ellison, Mary
  blockade-running 105–06
  Liverpool 109, 110, 111, 113
  Support for Secession 63
Ellison, Thomas 1, 4, 102, 130, 131, 135–36, 150, 155, 157, 158, 164, 181
  alleged over-production 72–73, 86, 94, 179
  anonymous articles for *Liverpool Post* 6
  background 183
  bankruptcies 161
  brokerage system 10, 26, 28–29, 143–44, 170–71 (anon.)
  cotton brokers 130, 131, 182 (anon.)
  cotton statistics 3, 74, 187–89
  Cotton Trade of Great Britain 2, 6, 164, 165, 187, 188
  failure of CSA 49
  falsification of record 164–65
  formation of LCBA 151
  LCBA and speculators 180–81 (anon.)
  LCBA membership 146–50, 148 (anon.) 170
  mill-owners 84
  post-war period 167–68, 178
  selling futures 127 (anon.)
  size of Indian crop 40
  Smith, Samuel 3
  speculation 127–28, 133
  spinners 138, 138 (anon.)
  Titherington, William 165 (anon.)
  wartime imports 48
  wastage 78
  Williams, Maurice 131, 163, 183
  withdrawal of stocks 144
Ellison & Haywood 44, 49
  alleged over-production 72
  statistics 74, 188

Emancipation Proclamation 64–65, 103
embargo *see* Confederacy
Europe 48, 68, 80, 108, 110, 115, 125
  growth of cotton industry 16–18
  re-exports 74–76
Ewart, Joseph 105
Ewart, Myers & Co. 105

Farnie, Douglas 2, 8, 20, 33, 74, 100, 108, 145
  alleged over-production 9, 71, 89–90, 178
  books on the famine 5
  Ellison, Thomas 183
  Mason, Hugh 184
  re-exports 75
  size of Indian crop 40
  speculation 132
Fernie, William 111
Fiji 16, 36
Fingal, SS 115
Finlay, James & Co. 3, 131
Finlay & Lance 130
Fitzgerald, Maurice 138, 140
Florida, CSS 10, 110, 111, 115–16
Foner, Philip 63
Forbes, John 116–17
Forbes Watson, Dr John 39
Foreign Enlistment Act 105, 113, 114, 116
Foreign Office 102, 106, 116
Fort Sumter 55, 89, 182
Forwood, William 111, 161, 185
  background 184
  blockade-running 106
  Confederate sympathies 110
  dock extension 107
  investment in new mills 96
  Liverpool in the war 131
  wastage 78
France 51, 88
  intervention 54, 68
Fraser, John & Co. 106
Fraser, Trenholm & Co. 106, 110
free labour 11, 22, 69, 176–77

Free Trade 5, 18, 24, 89, 111
    Confederacy 59
    Manchester 33, 44–46
Friend of India 40

Garibaldi, Giuseppe 58–59
Garrison, William Lloyd 4
Gaskell, Sam 130
Gath, Samuel, Jr 163, 167
George Griswold 103
Georgia 174, 175
Giannacopulo, Mr 167, 169
Gill family 161
Gilliat, J. K. & Co. 155, 203n13
Gladstone, William
    recognition of Confederacy 62, 104
    Smith, Samuel 185
Gore's Directory 10, 146, 147, 149–50, 162
Goschen, George 167
Government of India 32
Grant, General Ulysses 104
Granville, Lord 62
Guion, S. B. 114
Guion & Co. 114
Gulf of Mexico 57, 106

Habeas Corpus 59
Hall, Nigel 2, 52, 74, 143
    LCBA membership 148
    re-exports 75
Hall & Mellor 94–95
Hamilton, Francis 104
Hargreaves, James 17, 19
Harnetty, Peter 45, 74
Haywood, G. R. 49
Hemelryk, Paul
    background 184
    bank credit 160
    collapse in price 43
    dubious practices 133
    Joynson, Peter, Jr 163
    Liverpool in the war 121, 131
    market collapse 67
Henderson, Otto
    alleged over-production 87

Arnold, Arthur 88
    glutting of markets 93
Hime, Mr 169
Hobhouse, Sir John 33, 41
Holland, Charles 44
Hollins, Francis 27, 77, 134
Hollinshead & Tetley 94, 95
Holt, George 3, 6, 74, 122, 187–89
Hornby & Robinson 157
Horsfall, Thomas 105, 116
Howard, Mr 118
Howell, James 98
Hughes, Francis 102
Huse, Caleb 115
Hutchison, Robert 161–62
Hutchison family 161
Huth, F. & Co. 155
Huzzey, Richard 24

India 17, 58, 82, 95, 107, 125, 175, 181, 185
    Britain 19
    EIC 17
    import tariffs 19, 45, 199n43
    Rebellion 34, 40, 45
    shipping time lag 53, 97
    see also cotton, Indian
Iverson, Alfred 54

Japan 46–47
Jardine, Edmund 65
Jee, Matthew 157
Jones, Howard 48, 62, 88
Joynson, Peter, Jr 163

Kay, John 17
Kearsley & Cunningham 65
King Cotton strategy *see* Confederacy

Laird, John
    approach to build Union warships 117–18, 119
    missing files in National Archives 116
    Union arms shipments 115

INDEX

Laird Brothers 10
  CSS *Alabama* 116
  'rams' 110
Lalor, John 135
Lancashire cotton famine 104
  causes 179
  historical consensus 4, 8, 26
  statistics 65, 81
Lea & Walthew 167
Leech, Harrison and Forwood 184
Levi, Leone 29, 193n33
Lincoln, Abraham 68
  abolition of slavery 23–24, 59, 64, 103
  blockade 56
  civil war 61
  election 8, 51, 114, 125
  Liverpool Mercury 103
Littledale, T. & H. & Co 94, 111, 130, 159, 162
Littledale family 161
Liverpool
  arms shipments 114–15
  banking system 159–60, 161
  building of warships 10, 115–18
  Confederate links 9–10, 101–02, 110–11, 112
  Custom Bills of Entry 3, 11, 143, 155–57, 180, 188, 205n19, 205–06n22
  divergence from Manchester 6, 27–28, 34–35, 75, 85, 104, 122, 129–30, 137, 181, 193n30
  dock revenues 107
  during the war 6, 9–10, 103–19, 121, 131, 179
  financial laxity 136
  memorials to Government 106, 113
  merchant attitudes to war 111–14, 119, 179
  merchant community 147–48, 151–55, 157–58, 169–71, 181
  MPs during the war 105
  public opinion 103, 110, 119
  relations with America 102, 107–09, 112, 119
  role in cotton trade 1, 13
  ship-owners and agents 109
  slave trade 101–02, 105, 147, 205n11
Liverpool Chamber of Commerce 44, 78, 105, 184
  American Chamber 113–14
  ceremony for *George Griswold* 103
  LCBA 145
  protests about CSS *Alabama* 111, 113
  wartime sympathies 112–13
Liverpool Commercial Banking Co. 163
Liverpool Cotton Brokers' Association
  bankruptcies 162–63
  brokerage system 26–29, 127–28, 130, 143–44
  clearing house 168, 171, 178
  commissions 27, 136–37, 140–42, 144, 182
  contract of sale 135
  dispute with spinners 3, 10, 122, 139–42, 145, 179
  falsification of record 164–65
  formation 145, 149, 151, 170–71
  laws 141, 167–68
  membership 145–47, 148–51, 156–57, 164–65, 167–71
  post-war period 167–72
  see also cotton brokers; cotton speculation
Liverpool Distress Fund 65, 182
Liverpool Mercury 4, 53, 66, 82, 102, 105, 109, 113, 118, 121, 119, 130
  Emancipation Proclamation 64
  'impossibility' of Northern victory 104
  'indignation meeting' 111
  intervention 64–65, 104
  Lancashire cotton famine 104
  outbreak of war 54
  political views 103–04
  predictions of end of war 195n5
  predictions of intervention 197n44
  reply to commercial criticism 136
  sourcing of Union warships 118

Liverpool Post
   anonymous articles by Ellison, Thomas 6, 127, 138, 148, 165, 170–71, 180–81, 182
Liverpool Record Office 3
Liverpool Union Bank 160
Livingstone, Dr David 35
London 31, 102, 107, 115, 123, 130, 136, 152, 171, 184
Longrigg, Thomas 111
Louisiana 57, 119, 175
Lowber, Daniel C. 4
Lyons, Lord 58

Machin, W. F. 52–53
MacIver, C. & D. 114
Mackay, Alexander 38
McMonnies, James 162
Macrae, James 141, 161
Manchester 19, 37, 67, 107
   divergence from Liverpool 6, 10, 27–28, 34–35, 75, 85, 104, 122, 129–30, 137, 181, 193n30
   economic self-interest 18–19, 33, 44–46
   EIC 33, 36
   relations with Government 36–37, 38, 40–41, 44–46
   role in cotton trade 13
Manchester Chamber of Commerce 22, 40, 45, 48, 139, 184
   British Government 38
   radicalism 33
   Smith, Samuel 3, 32, 39
Manchester Commercial Association 33
Manchester Cotton Company 49
Manchester Examiner & Times 204n51
   EIC 33
   Lancashire cotton famine 104
Marler, Scott 111
   embargo 57
   King Cotton strategy 54, 57
Martin, Studley 140, 165
Marx, Karl 63, 87

Mason, Hugh 55, 145
   background 184–85
   cotton brokers 180
   impeachment of Wood, Sir Charles 40
   spinners' dispute with LCBA 138–42, 144, 145, 179
   withdrawal of stocks 144
Maxwell, W. 114
Mayall & Andersson 167
Mellor & Co. 167
Melluish, Charles 114
Melly, Forget & Co. 114
Melly, George 114
Mersey Docks and Harbour Board 184–85
Mexico 106, 188
Mill, John Stuart 59
Millbrook Mills 3
Miller, William C. & Sons 115–16
Mills, John 162
Milne, Graeme 102, 110, 158–59
Mississippi 172, 175
Mississippi river 35, 66, 172, 173
Mobile, AL 4, 57, 110, 124
Molyneux, Taylor & Co. 162
Molyneux family 161
Morning Post 110
Morrill Tariff 59, 89, 111
Mozley, Albert Charles 163–64
Mozley, Charles 163–64
Musgrove, Edgar 134, 141

Nassau, Bahamas 63, 106, 115, 202n52
National Bank of Liverpool 163
Neill, Henry 54
   arrest 119, 202n52
   background 4, 185
   post-war period 173, 175
Neill, William
   background 4, 185
   post-war period 173
   warning of scarcity 58
Neill Brothers 3, 66, 125
   awakening to the crisis 61
   bankruptcy 185

blockade and embargo 57
cotton circulars 4, 53
duration of war 57–58, 60, 68
effect of speculation on prices 131
speculation by spinners 132
stock pipeline 91
warning of financial crash 66
Williams, Maurice 184
New Orleans, LA 4, 35, 57, 66, 110, 172, 175, 202n52
  embargo 56–57
  financial centre 124
New Orleans Cotton Exchange 185
New York 4, 24, 58, 59, 103, 104, 115, 116
  cotton shipments 110
  financial centre 123–24
New York Chamber of Commerce 113
New York Cotton Exchange 185
New York Herald 23
New York Times 124, 185
Newall, John 130
Newall & Clayton 98, 167
Norbury, Mr 167
North-Western Bank 164

Ollerenshaw, J. C. 94
Olmstead, Alan 17
Olusoga, David 28
Orchard, B. Guinness 102
Ottoman Empire 20
Overend, Gurney & Co. 162
Owsley, Frank 66

Palmer, Sir Roundell 116
Palmerston, Viscount 8, 41
  Laird 'rams' 116
  neutrality vs. intervention 59, 62
Parkinson, Hamilton & Ingleby 162
Parthasarathi, Prasannan 16–19
Pender, John 3, 74, 188
Phalen, William 20
Pietruska, Jamie 185
Platt, John 55
Porcupine 29, 55, 119, 134, 151, 183–84
Price Edwards, Samuel 163–64

Prioleau, Charles K. 110, 111
Proclamation of Neutrality 58, 114
Protectionism 18–19
  Manchester 44–46
public opinion *see* British public opinion

Queen Victoria 50, 58, 114, 145

Ralli, Mr 169
Ranger, Morris 144
Rathbone, William, Jr 65
Rathbone, William, Sr 65
Rathbone Bros & Co. 114
Reconstruction *see* cotton, American; USA
Reede, John 130
Reeve, Henry 86
Rhode, Paul 17
Richardson, Spence & Co. 114
Riello, Giorgio 16–19, 22
Robson & Eskrigge 66–67, 95, 98, 114
Royal Bank of Liverpool 161
Russell, Earl
  arms purchases by Union 115
  CSS *Alabama* 116
  duration of war 60
  Liverpool ship-owners 106, 111, 113
  mediation in war 62
  outbreak of war 38, 58
  public opinion 64
Russell, William Henry 54, 55
Ryley, Mr 35

Savannah, GA 57, 110, 124
Schilizzi, Mr 169
Schleswig-Holstein 68
Schmidt, B. 108–09
Schoen, Brian 15
Schroder, J. H. & Co. 155
Schultz, Alexander 4, 54
Schuyler, George 115
Searle, Geoffrey 135
Sedgewick, Charles 118

Seward, William 4, 54, 59
Sexton, Jay 48, 55, 102
   arms purchases by Union 115
Shand family 161
Shaw, Alexander Nisbet 36
Shipley, Joseph 112
Silver, Arthur 12
Slack, John 130
slavery
   abolition 23–24, 58–59, 64, 103
   association with Liverpool 101–02, 105, 147, 205n11
   British attitudes 22, 24–25, 177
   British dependence 16–17, 22–23, 182–83
   British slave trade 19, 20
   Confederacy 23, 54, 58–59
   economic importance to South 23–24
   Emancipation Proclamation 64, 103
   freedmen after the war 11, 172–74
   see also Confederacy
Smith, Edwards & Co 3
Smith, J. B. 33, 46, 48
Smith, Samuel 37, 95, 114
   adulteration of goods 82–84
   background 3–4, 185
   bankruptcies 161
   cotton circulars 3
   duration of war 56, 67–68
   election as MP 105
   Indian cotton 3, 32, 39–40, 43, 44, 48, 77–78
   speculation 129, 131, 133, 134, 161
   trade prospects 51, 55
South Carolina 172, 175
Southern Club 110
Speltz, Louis 162
Spence, James 110, 111, 112–13, 169
spinners *see* Cotton Spinners' Association; cotton, manufactured
'Stay' laws 124
Stitt, Mr 169
Stolterfoht, Thomas 114
Stone, Alfred 122

Stowe, Harriet Beecher 59
Sumner, Charles 117
Surat cotton *see* cotton, Indian
Surdam, David 88–89
Swainson, Anthony & Sons 163

Taylor family 161
Texas 172, 175, 185
Thompson, Charles 162
Thomson, Finlay & Co 164
Thorburn, James 130
Thornely & Pownall 78, 95
The Times 39, 42, 54, 78, 103, 106, 109, 132, 135, 142, 196n31
   commercial morality in Liverpool 136
   false peace rumours 67
   'indignation meeting' 111
   Neill Brothers 60
   sourcing of Union warships 116
The Times of India 39
Titherington, William 163–65
Titherington & Gill 163–64
Tomlinson family 161
Topp & Coupland 167
transatlantic cable 28, 102, 128, 143, 168, 171, 178
Trent, SS 59, 63, 68, 95, 111

Uncle Tom's Cabin 59
United States of America
   merchant marine 112
   national debt 109
   post-war land tenure 173–74
   Reconstruction period 11, 172–78
   Union blockade 9, 45, 51, 54, 56, 63, 90, 105–07, 111
   Union relations with Britain 58–59, 61, 115
   Union relations with Liverpool 107–09, 112, 119
   Union sourcing of arms 114–15, 116–18
   wheat exports 108–09
   see also Confederacy; Cotton, American

Vicksburg, MS 66

Washington, DC 58, 118
Watts, Isaac
   Cotton Supply Association 3, 32
   delusions about CSA 46, 49
   EIC 33
   Indian cotton 36–37, 42
Watts, John
   alleged over-production 87
   background 5
   Facts of the Cotton Famine 5
   likelihood of war 55
   slavery 25
Welles, Gideon 116, 117–18
West Indies 20, 24, 48, 147, 188
wheat imports 108
Whitney, Eli 20, 22
Williams, Maurice 94, 163
   background 183–84
   bank confidence 159, 160

civil war 114
cotton circulars 52, 84
investment in new mills 96
market collapse 67
shipping time lag 65
speculation 119, 131
Surat cotton 78
wastage 78
Wilmington, NC 106
Wood, Sir Charles
   free trade 46
   Manchester 37, 40
Wood, T. 162
Woodman, Harold 123, 124
World War I 62, 127, 128
Wray, Leonard 37, 39
Wright, Gavin 23, 88, 179
Wright, Henry C. 4
Wrigley, John & Sons 77, 95

Zwilchenbart family 161